T0319939

Understanding and Conducting Information Systems Auditing

Founded in 1807, John Wiley & Sons is the oldest independent publishing company in the United States. With offices in North America, Europe, Asia, and Australia, Wiley is globally committed to developing and marketing print and electronic products and services for our customers' professional and personal knowledge and understanding.

The Wiley Corporate F&A series provides information, tools, and insights to corporate professionals responsible for issues affecting the profitability of their company, from accounting and finance to internal controls and performance management.

Understanding and Conducting Information Systems Auditing

VEENA HINGARH
ARIF AHMED

WILEY

John Wiley & Sons Singapore Pte. Ltd.

Cover Image: © Olena Timashova/iStockphoto
Cover Design: John Wiley & Sons, Inc.

Other Wiley Editorial Offices

John Wiley & Sons, 111 River Street, Hoboken, NJ 07030, USA
John Wiley & Sons, The Atrium, Southern Gate, Chichester, West Sussex, P019 8SQ, United Kingdom
John Wiley & Sons (Canada) Ltd., 5353 Dundas Street West, Suite 400, Toronto, Ontario, M9B 6HB, Canada
John Wiley & Sons Australia Ltd., 42 McDougall Street, Milton, Queensland 4064, Australia
Wiley-VCH, Boschstrasse 12, D-69469 Weinheim, Germany

Library of Congress Cataloging-in-Publication Data

ISBN 978-1-118-34374-6 (Hardcover)
ISBN 978-1-118-34375-3 (ePDF)
ISBN 978-1-118-34376-0 (Mobi)
ISBN 978-1-118-34377-7 (ePub)

Typeset in 10/13pt. Photina Regular by MPS Limited, Chennai, India.

10 9 8 7 6 5 4 3 2 1

Families that bind the world

Contents

Preface

THIS BOOK FOCUSES ON an information systems audit as a management control and not a technology-driven subject. Complete with resources to understand the subject, definitions of technical terms, ready checklists to conduct an information systems audit, and multiple-choice questions to review the level of understanding, the book is designed to be an indispensable resource for the information systems practitioner and aspirant alike. Readers will find enough resources for their audit needs, examination needs, and even continuing professional education requirements.

Increased dependence on information systems assets for performing critical functions of an organization has strengthened the need for using information systems audits as a control to ensure confidentiality, integrity, and availability of information systems resources. Major problems that an information systems auditor faces include apparent technology bias of the subject, lack of a standardized audit approach, and lack of availability of standardized checklists. In this book, we have attempted to address these problems by approaching the subject from the viewpoint of management control, providing readers with requisite knowledge resources, and making available an audit tool in the form of checklists.

Our approach to an information systems audit is essentially nontechnical in nature. We firmly believe that an information systems audit is a managerial control tool and use of technology is subordinate to it. We hold that attempts to consider an information systems audit as a technical control would make it an esoteric subject and be counterproductive in the long run. Technical tools are most useful for specific applications within the domains of an information systems audit, but may not be the primary focus. The primary focus should be to establish a framework of management control, and technology could be used wherever necessary to implement the control. An information systems auditor is free to seek the help of a technology specialist to examine specific controls, whenever such a need arises. The scope of the audit will determine the extent of use of technology-driven tools. For example, an audit of network security or website penetration testing definitely requires technical competence and appropriate tools. It must be clarified that we are not underestimating the importance and convenience of technology; we are merely assigning a specific role for it within the domain of an information systems audit.

The book is divided over two parts—Part One focuses on the knowledge that all information systems auditors must have to be able to effectively conduct an information systems audit. This part will act as reference material for the aspiring information systems auditors who are preparing for a certifying examination. There are 10 chapters in this part, progressively building up the competence of conducting a real-life information systems audit. The chapters in Part One are the following:

Chapter 1: "Overview of Systems Audit": This chapter will make readers aware of the challenges they are likely to face while conducting an information systems audit. The importance of such an audit is established in this chapter.

Chapter 2: "Hardware Security Issues": This chapter identifies the security aspects of hardware and network assets that should be taken care of.

Chapter 3: "Software Security Issues": This chapter sensitizes the reader about the critical aspect of software security.

Chapter 4: "Information Systems Audit Requirements": This chapter develops understanding about the general scope of information systems audit, types of evidences, and areas of focus of an information systems auditor.

Chapter 5: "Conducting an Information Systems Audit": This chapter discusses the process of conducting an information systems audit and provides an overview of an audit program, plan, and procedure, compliance and substantive testing, testing tools, and the process of reporting.

Chapter 6: "Risk-Based Systems Audit": This chapter deals with the approach that an information systems auditor needs to adopt in situations where the auditee is exposed to various risks of different magnitude and also under situations of resource constraints.

Chapter 7: "Business Continuity and Disaster Recovery Plan": This chapter provides the knowledge resource to understand and audit business continuity and disaster recovery systems of the auditee. A large number of useful forms have been provided in this chapter.

Chapter 8: "Auditing in the E-Commerce Environment": This chapter identifies areas for additional focus required for auditing an e-commerce environment. The knowledge resource provided is equally applicable for auditing an e-banking environment.

Chapter 9: "Security Testing": The aspect of security testing is often a technology-driven exercise. This chapter introduces the readers to the critical concept of cyberattacks and vulnerability testing.

Chapter 10: "Case Study: Conducting an Information Systems Audit": This chapter demonstrates how the knowledge acquired in previous chapters is put to use in real life. An example of conducting an information systems audit in a bank branch has been provided to take the readers on a step-by-step journey through the entire auditing process.

The second part contains checklists under ISecGrade methodology—a proprietary open source information systems audit methodology developed by the South Asian

Management Technologies Foundation. During development of this methodology and checklists, in addition to internal resources, resources from various public domains have been used. Various checklists, regulatory guidelines, best practice standards, and others have been consulted to develop these checklists. The authors have added their own personal experiences in conducting information systems audits while designing the methodology. The reader will find reference to the checklists during discussions in various chapters. These references allow the reader to refer to the relevant checklist and appreciate its implications. Part Two comprises the following two chapters:

> Chapter 11: "ISecGrade Auditing Framework": This chapter explains the process involved in conducting an ISecGrade audit for awarding a security grade to an auditee. A detailed process of the audit, selecting checklists, and drafting the audit report are described.
>
> Chapter 12: "ISecGrade Checklists": This chapter provides one of the most comprehensive information systems audit checklists for the use of the practitioner. There are 40 domain-specific checklists covering numerous control points that an information systems auditor must examine during an audit process.

Discussions in each chapter have generally avoided the temptation of becoming technical and verbose. Instead, we have provided action points against each body of knowledge. This will enable readers to remember the key issues introduced in the chapter. In order to bridge any prior technical requirement we have defined in each chapter technical terms whenever they are cited.

> Chapter 13: "Session Quiz": Readers will find this chapter useful to verify the level of understanding they have achieved. Answers to session questions are provided in the companion website (www.wiley.com/go/understandingisauditing). The website also contains other useful learning material.

We sincerely hope that readers will find that the book addresses their need for a quality single-point reference for knowledge resources on information systems audits. We will be grateful for comments from our readers on what they liked and what they did not like. We will consider our efforts justified if this book contributes to making information technology installation across the world a little more secure.

Acknowledgments

NO BOOK CAN BE published unless supported by various people who take upon themselves various roles. Some encourage, some command, some endure, some smile, some are seen, some are unseen, and yet they all lend their support. We must thank John DeRemigis of John Wiley & Sons for the afternoon we met, overlooking the Indian Ocean in Mumbai (Bombay), and discussed this book with him. Nick Melchior, thank you for clearing all hurdles and getting us to write the book. Gemma Rosey and Kimberly Monroe-Hill must have had difficulties through the process of scheduling and rescheduling target dates—thank you for bearing with us. There must be a host of others whom we have not met but we recognize that without their help this manuscript would not have turned into a book.

Professor Amitava Sarkar, thank you for being a part of the journey through Kathmandu, where the idea of the book was finalized, and for your continuous support ever after. Thank you, Subrata Kar, for convincing us that knowledge is a journey and not a goal. Santosh Maheswari, you deserve a special mention for having the courage to print our first book on this subject. We thank all our students, workshop participants, and clients, who have been instrumental in our mustering up the courage to write books. Let us tell our teachers that whatever we know, we owe it all to you.

What an author owes to his or her family is beyond acknowledgment of any kind, and we make no effort in futility. They were all with us no matter where they may be. Arif Ahmed wishes to mention Bapi and Mamoni for their continuing efforts; Alfa and Bita for standing by during those efforts; Mama, for sharing the joy of living; and Neha, Arman, Arnaaz, and Hiya, for believing that writing a book must be something important! Veena Hingarh wishes to assure Papa and Mummy that no one could have done any better, and to thank Priti, Neera, and Seema for all their encouragement and belief, and Sonal and Saejal for all the assistance they provided.

PART ONE

Conducting an Information Systems Audit

CHAPTER ONE

Overview of Systems Audit

I N THIS CHAPTER WE discuss why an information systems audit would be conducted. The chapter also identifies the challenges that an auditor will face while auditing a computerized system. Critical differences between computerized and noncomputerized systems have also been identified. Upon completion of this chapter, the reader will have an understanding of the salient features of a computerized system that an information systems auditor must keep in mind.

INFORMATION SYSTEMS AUDIT

An information systems audit is an examination of various controls within an information systems infrastructure. It is the process involving collection and evaluation of evidence of the design and functions of controls designed and implemented in information systems, practices, and operations. The auditor, subsequent to evaluation of the evidence, forms an opinion on whether the information systems safeguard assets, maintain data integrity, and operate effectively and efficiently in order to achieve the agreed-upon goals and objectives of the entity. An information systems audit can be performed independently of or along with an audit of financial statements. More often than not, it remains an independent function used during testing of controls.

 ## INFORMATION SYSTEMS AUDITOR

Under the existing practices in various countries, any person having a recognized qualification in information systems audit can conduct an information systems audit. To be a recognized qualification, it must be awarded by an institution that is acknowledged by the laws of the country. These institutions can be academic or professional bodies. The qualification can also be designated by membership of an association or body of person on the basis of their internal norms of qualification for such membership. Usually such membership is renewable annually by paying a membership fee. Qualifications from academic institutions usually do not involve any recurring membership cost. It is important to note whether the regulatory authorities recognize the qualification of an information systems auditor for conducting an information systems audit in a specific country. Industries are free to recognize qualifications awarded by institutions other than those mentioned earlier.

It may be noted that, unless specified by the auditee or regulatory authorities, there is no requirement of any additional qualification other than that of an information systems auditor, in order to conduct an information systems audit.

 ## LEGAL REQUIREMENTS OF AN INFORMATION SYSTEMS AUDIT

More often than not, an information systems audit is a best practice or an ethical exercise rather than a legal requirement. However, the audit may be legally required in some countries, such as under the Sarbanes-Oxley Act of 2002 in the United States.

Major requirements of the Sarbanes-Oxley Act with relation to information systems audit are provided in the following sections.

The Sarbanes-Oxley Act of 2002

The Sarbanes-Oxley Act came into force in 2002 to ensure better regulation of financial practices and corporate governance and requires a number of compliances. The act is named after Senator Paul Sarbanes and Representative Michael Oxley, who were its main architects.

Form 10-K

Form 10-K is the name of the form that every domestic issuer in the United States has to submit to the Securities and Exchange Commission. The form provides a comprehensive overview of the business of the filer, along with the business's financial condition and audited statements.

Securities and Exchange Commission

Better known by its acronym, SEC, the Securities and Exchange Commission is the apex regulator responsible for enforcing all of the laws and regulations of the securities industry in the United States.

1. Section 302 assigns corporate responsibility for accuracy of financial statements and operational activities to the chief executive officer (CEO) and chief finance officer (CFO). The signing officers certify that they have reviewed the reports and that they are free of untrue statements, material omissions, or misleading statements. This can be assured only if an information systems audit has reviewed the operation of the software and systems involved in producing the financial statements.
2. Section 404(b) calls for certification from auditor on management assessment of internal control. The assessment seeks to ensure that adequate controls are established and maintained for financial reporting. Naturally an information systems audit is useful for such an assessment.
3. Section 409 requires immediate disclosure of changes in financial position and operations in real time. An information systems audit can assess the readiness of an organization in this regard.
4. Section 802 requires retention of electronic records that have an impact on assets or performance of a company. An information systems auditor reviews the preparedness of any organization to prevent willful or accidental destruction of such records.

Following is a sample certification from the 10-K filing of Kraft Foods Inc. with the Securities and Exchange Commission.

CERTIFICATION

I, Irene B. Rosenfeld, certify that:

1. I have reviewed this annual report on Form 10-K of Kraft Foods Inc.;
2. Based on my knowledge, this report does not contain any untrue statement of a material fact or omit to state a material fact necessary to make the statements made, in light of the circumstances under which such statements were made, not misleading with respect to the period covered by this report;

(Continued)

3. Based on my knowledge, the financial statements, and other financial information included in this report, fairly present in all material respects the financial condition, results of operations and cash flows of the registrant as of, and for, the periods presented in this report;

4. The registrant's other certifying officer(s) and I are responsible for establishing and maintaining disclosure controls and procedures (as defined in Exchange Act Rules 13a–15(e) and 15d–15(e)) and internal control over financial reporting (as defined in Exchange Act Rules 13a–15(f) and 15d–15(f)) for the registrant and have:

Designed such disclosure controls and procedures, or caused such disclosure controls and procedures to be designed under our supervision, to ensure that material information relating to the registrant, including its consolidated subsidiaries, is made known to us by others within those entities, particularly during the period in which this report is being prepared;

Designed such internal control over financial reporting, or caused such internal control over financial reporting to be designed under our supervision, to provide reasonable assurance regarding the reliability of financial reporting and the preparation of financial statements for external purposes in accordance with generally accepted accounting principles;

Evaluated the effectiveness of the registrant's disclosure controls and procedures and presented in this report our conclusions about the effectiveness of the disclosure controls and procedures, as of the end of the period covered by this report based on such evaluation; and

Disclosed in this report any change in the registrant's internal control over financial reporting that occurred during the registrant's most recent fiscal quarter (the registrant's fourth fiscal quarter in the case of an annual report) that has materially affected, or is reasonably likely to materially affect, the registrant's internal control over financial reporting; and

5. The registrant's other certifying officer(s) and I have disclosed, based on our most recent evaluation of internal control over financial reporting, to the registrant's auditors and the audit committee of the registrant's board of directors (or persons performing the equivalent functions):

All significant deficiencies and material weaknesses in the design or operation of internal control over financial reporting which are reasonably likely to adversely affect the registrant's ability to record, process, summarize and report financial information; and

Any fraud, whether or not material, that involves management or other employees who have a significant role in the registrant's internal control over financial reporting.

Date: February 28, 2011
/s/ IRENE B. ROSENFELD
Irene B. Rosenfeld
Chairman and Chief Executive Officer

The audit under Statement on Auditing Standards (SAS) No. 70, developed by the American Institute of Certified Public Accountants (AICPA), is another example of statutory and quasi-statutory needs to perform information systems audits.

Statement on Auditing Standards

Usually referred to as SAS, these standards narrate generally accepted auditing practices that an auditor should follow while conducting an audit and issuing the audit report. These are issued by the Auditing Standards Board of the American Institute of Certified Public Accountants in the United States. Most countries have their independent accounting and auditing body, which issues such standards.

The standard identifies the factors that an independent financial auditor of an organization should consider when auditing the financial statements of an entity that uses a service organization to process certain transactions. Since the evaluation is based essentially on examination of the controls employed by the service organization, an information systems audit will be found extremely useful.

Though there may not be any specific legal requirement of an information systems audit, more often than not a statutory financial audit requires testing of adequacy and efficiency of internal control before expressing an audit opinion. With most of the auditees having a computerized environment as one of their major logistics, and using integrated enterprise resources management software, it is imperative that an information systems audit is conducted to form an opinion on the adequacy of internal control.

SYSTEMS ENVIRONMENT AND INFORMATION SYSTEMS AUDIT

Computerization is a tool that gives organizations the capability to provide better customer service, to conduct better housekeeping, and so on, to enable optimization of the use of resources. To ensure that computerization takes care of existing and emerging needs of the organization, the following nine issues must be considered:

1. Standardization of hardware, operating systems, system software, and applications: Failure to ensure such standardization creates complex technology management issues, which often manifests through involvement of multiple systems in a single process instead of an integrated process ensuring nonduplication of functions.
2. Use of software to facilitate interconnectivity of systems intensifies the need for a systems audit to ensure that information flow is smooth and not compromised.
3. The need for high levels of security not only calls for technical competence but also requires continuous testing of efficiency and searching for new, emerging vulnerabilities as well.

4. Communication and networking involving the use of networks facilitate establishing a centralized database and distributed processing on one hand, but on the other hand expose the entity to the risk of security breach from multiple sources. Consequently the scope of a systems audit enlarges and involves more complex testing.

5. A technology infrastructure with periodic up grades often leads to migration from one system to another. The information systems audit is required to keep pace with not only the technology but also the maturity of the organization. A more matured organization entrusts more critical resources to the information system and at the same time becomes more susceptible to a systems breach.

6. The need for business process reengineering is a consequence of the evolution of business complexity, which necessarily calls for an enlarged role of the information systems. Such reengineering brings about serious challenges to smooth migration and maintenance of data integrity.

7. Issues of human relations in a computerized environment are perhaps one of the greatest challenges for an information systems audit. Unpredictable and indispensable as they are, human resources define the fine line differentiating the success or failure of an information technology project. The information systems auditor finds the task of assessing adequacy and efficiency of such controls extremely difficult and often subjective.

8. Sharing of technology experiences between organizations and between various levels of an organization enriches the quality of performance as it ensures that the same mistake is not repeated twice. The comfort level of an information systems auditor is greater in an organization that enables a system of internal learning.

9. An information systems audit assumes greater importance in the face of the increased use of credit and debit cards and e-commerce interface in the regular functioning of an entity. These are activities that require closer monitoring as well as the assurance that the access and security aspects of these systems are well laid out.

An information systems audit ensures that the computerization activity of an entity follows the best practices and abides by all statutory and quasi-statutory requirements in its quest to achieve the objective of computerization.

The scope of an information systems audit extends over all information systems assets and processes that are owned or used by an entity or its representatives. An information systems audit seeks to ensure that the confidentiality, integrity, and availability of all information systems assets and processes are not compromised. In order to achieve this, an information systems audit focuses on the existence, adequacy, and efficiency of relevant controls.

INFORMATION SYSTEMS ASSETS

Information systems assets may be segregated into various kinds, such as:

- ▪ **Information assets:** These include databases, data files, system documentation, operating manuals, training guides and materials, operational and support guidelines, continuity plans, backup guidelines, archived information, and so on. More often than not, values of these assets are utilitarian and rules of physical valuation are not applicable on them.

- **Software assets:** These include operating systems, application software, system software, development tools, implementation and monitoring utilities, and so on. Essentially these are tools that enable data processing, information generation, and reporting.
- **Physical assets:** These include, among others, the following devices:
  - Computer equipment: processors, monitors, laptops
  - Communications equipment: routers, fax machines, answering machines, IP phones
  - Storage media: magnetic storages, pen drives
  - Other technical equipment: power supplies, including power backup, temperature and humidity control devices, furniture, accommodation, and so forth
- **Services:** These include computing services, interoffice and intraoffice communications services, and general utilities, for example, heating, lighting, power, and temperature control. The increased popularity of cloud computing is redefining various software and physical assets as cloud services wherein the software, processing power, and storage are all provided by a cloud computing service provider.

Cloud Computing

Cloud computing is a shared service that provides computing power inclusive of processor, software, storage space, and so on for hire. The user connects to the service through a network, usually based on the Internet. This converts computing from a product-based solution to a service and allows the user to save on procurement cost and have anywhere access.

CLASSIFICATION OF CONTROLS

Controls are central to the idea of an information systems audit. They define a point of action in a work process wherein a decision to select the subsequent action arises. Controls without an alternative are fictitious controls that exist only on paper without any impact potential.

Controls can be classified in different ways. Three basic categories are general controls, application controls, and objective-based control classification, which are discussed in the following sections.

General Controls

General controls are basic hygiene issues that any system should observe. These are applicable across all systems though the extent of application along with segmental importance may vary. General control features in most systems can be classified into the following six categories:

1. **Organization and operation controls**, which include:
   a. Segregation of functions between the information technology department and users
   b. Provision for general authorization over the execution of transactions, for example, prohibiting a person from initiating and authorizing transactions
   c. Segregation of functions within the information technology department
2. **Systems development and documentation controls**, which include:
   a. Process of review, testing, and approval of new systems as well as modified systems
   b. Control over program and parameter changes
   c. Documentation procedures
3. **Hardware and system software controls**, which include:
   a. Automatic error detection features
   b. Periodic preventive maintenance
   c. Formal procedures to recover from hardware errors
   d. Adequate authorization and control over implementation of, and changes to, operating systems software
4. **Access controls**, which are designed:
   a. To prevent and alert unauthorized access to any information system asset
   b. To prevent deliberate or accidental errors that may be caused by improper alteration of data files or by unauthorized or incorrect use of computer resources, including software
   c. To establish a robust layered authentication scheme for third-party resources being hosted by the organization, more specifically, in cases of cloud computing
5. **Data and procedural controls**, which include:
   a. A control or balancing function
   b. Written manuals in support of systems and procedures
   c. Capability to restore or replace lost, damaged, or incorrect data files
6. **Business continuity controls**, which include:
   a. A control to detect, alert, and act on identification of threats to business continuity
   b. An established plan to ensure earliest resumption of most critical functions of information technology department

Application Controls

The detailed structure of application controls will depend on the nature of the application. Broadly there are three types of application controls appropriate to any application. These are:

1. **Input controls**, which include control over:
   a. Transaction entry
   b. File maintenance transactions

    c. Inquiry transactions

    d. Error correction transactions

    e. System-induced transactions

2. **Processing controls**, which are usually included in application programs and designed to prevent or detect errors of the following nature:

    a. Failure to process all input transactions, or erroneous processing

    b. Duplicate processing or updating wrong file or files

    c. Processing inputs that are either illogical or unreasonable

    d. Loss, unintentional modification, or distortion of data during processing

3. **Output controls,** which are used to assure the accuracy of processing results, and to ensure that only authorized personnel receive the output. The basic output controls are:

    a. Balancing

    b. Visual scanning or verification

    c. Distribution

    d. Storage, retrieval, and distribution

Objective-Based Control Classification

The classification of controls on the basis of action or objectives would lead to the following five categories:

1. **Directive controls:** These controls comprise management actions, procedures, directives, or guidelines that facilitate the occurrence of a preferred event. Such controls influence the entire system or operation and address areas of usage, maintenance, audit, control, and security attributes of a system and software with the object of ensuring integrity, reliability, and availability of systems resources.

2. **Preventive controls:** These controls aim to establish a reliable system and are based on standards, methods, practices, tools, and techniques. These controls could be automated or manual depending on whether human intervention is required to trigger the same. Preventive controls also act as a deterrent that minimizes the possibility of the occurrence of undesirable events, including computer-related fraud, theft, embezzlement, possible errors, omissions, and irregularities. These controls address various issues, including maintenance, security, usage, and control features of the system.

3. **Detective controls:** These controls are designed to detect variation outside control limits. They assess whether various controls (for example, directive or preventive) have achieved their objectives. These controls primarily focus on detection of errors, omissions, and irregularities. In addition, they also highlight system quality, controls, and security issues that need management intervention.

4. **Corrective controls:** These controls continue from the detections made by detective controls by making available information, procedures, and instructions for correcting identified errors, omissions, and noncompliances. Corrective control tools and techniques can be manual and automated. These controls highlight the usability of the system along with the availability of audit trails to conduct subsequent audits.

5. **Recovery controls:** These controls assume criticality in face of exposure to events that threaten a disruption in services. These controls describe and provide tools, techniques, and procedures of backup, restoration, recovery, and restart of an information resource. These controls define a formal structure to ensure availability of all required resources necessary to ensure an early recovery from disaster. These controls may be designed for a specific activity, an entire operation, or an entire organization. Recovery controls include timely backup and rotation of data and program files, checkpoints, restart/rerun procedures, record and file retention, and so forth. Depending on the organization structure and technology implemented, the grouping of recovery controls with corrective controls may facilitate better implementation.

THE IMPACT OF COMPUTERS ON INFORMATION

Not all controls that are useful in a noncomputerized system may be as useful or even necessary in a computerized system. Arguably the functional attributes of all such controls will be necessary, but technology interface may allow a combination of different functions within one control. In order to make a better assessment of controls that need to be replicated in a computerized system, it is important to understand the impact of computers on information as well as on information systems. The fact that changes in a processing system often obscure the need for implementing a control underscores the need to review the following subprocesses to recognize the transformation of a process. The following checklist of 13 items will also serve for reviewing a system that has migrated from one platform to another.

1. **Transaction initiation:** In a computerized system, many transactions may be initiated by the system itself. Thus all transactions may not have a supporting initiation document. A common example is execution of a standing instruction in banking software.
2. **Inputs:** Information may be committed directly into the system, without any hard-copy evidence. This is common in enterprise-wide integrated software wherein one input creates a chain of inputs in various subsystems, often after partial processing by a subsystem before onward processing. For example, computation of the cost of a product is influenced by a material receipt, as it changes the average issue price, which is a component of the standard cost of a product. Though no entry is directly being made in the costing module, entry in the inventory module has an impact on the costing module.
3. **Authorization:** Unlike a manual system, in which a supervisor reviews a transaction and then authorizes it, in a computerized system the authorization limits may be set within the system itself. Thus manual supervision may not be required. A common example is found in the operation of credit cards, where predetermined limits are set.

4. **Movement of documents:** In computerized systems, documents move electronically, including on e-mail or group documentation management systems. Cloud computing even takes physical custody of the documents out of the physical perimeter of the organization. Collaborative applications allow multiple users to access the same file and work on documents simultaneously. Exclusive custody of the document is no longer necessary, which creates a need to design specific controls to manage access and usage.

5. **Transaction processing:** In computerized application systems, processing is done electronically within the computer by programs that follow predetermined rules and consequently do not leave behind any physical audit trail. Thus there must be controls to test the processing, preferably before implementation of the software. Such controls need to be redesigned to assess processing efficiency post-implementation.

6. **Complexity of processing:** By using the high processing capabilities of computers, complex processing functions can be performed that are not possible in a manual system. Consequently, no controls were designed for such processes. In fact, the entire process has to be initiated specifically for the computerized system.

7. **Information storage:** Information may be categorized into two forms—permanent and temporary. Permanent information needs to be maintained for longer periods of time. Various backup facilities and storage media are available in computer systems, which raises a question of careful selection in light of the rapid progress in technology. Third-party storage services add to the list of alternatives available for storage. One of the critical issues involving choice of storage is the ability of future hardware to access the same. Often the storage media may remain uncompromised but the hardware required to retrieve data becomes obsolete. Floppy drives and cartridges are examples of such developments.

8. **Outputs:** Unless required legally or warranted by the workflow, printed output from system is actively discouraged. In many cases the output is in the form of visual displays, including e-mail and screen displays, which make evidence collection a specialized activity. The increased use of personal handheld devices has promoted ideas about generating output as text messages or e-mailing them as an attached document. These have since emerged as common output options.

9. **Filing of documents:** In a manual system, data and information stored in files can be manually retrieved whenever required. In a computerized system, data retrieval from the database requires either running the report generation again or using alternative techniques available for storage of reports. Use of data warehousing makes preprocessed or semiprocessed data available for faster retrieval. This effectively promotes the concept of separation of data and reports, enabling organizations to prevent data access whenever reports are required.

10. **Audit trails:** When the auditor traces a transaction from initiation to the final output, the flow of events is reconstructed. This function is aided by an audit trail. In a computerized system, the auditor needs to be familiarized with the processing rules because the processing path may not be externally observable, especially when processing is complex.

11. **Procedure manual:** Procedure manuals in a manual system help an auditor to know the steps required to process any transaction. In computerized systems, help menus and program documentation have to be looked into. The major problem faced in this regard is in updating the documentation, whenever the system is modified. Often there is a gap in this area, leading to a modified feature of the software being undocumented. This is a common weakness for customized solutions.

12. **Monitoring and supervision:** In a computerized system, a large part of the monitoring and supervision is done automatically and online by the system. Controls involving data editing, validation routines, and checks and balancing are often performed by the system itself. Consequently these checks need to be analyzed at the program level rather than at the operational level, where there may not be adequate evidence available. This becomes imperative when the processing is outsourced to locations that are not under the direct supervision of the information owner.

13. **Segregation of duties:** Segregation of duties tends to be compromised in a computerized system. Unless specifically designed, it is often possible for an individual to enter, change, and delete a transaction. This requires the introduction of compensating controls, including a supervisory review to ensure that concerned individuals discharge their responsibilities within the defined scope.

THE IMPACT OF COMPUTERS ON AUDITING

Much as computers have changed the way information is handled and stored, their use has also affected the process of auditing a company. Entities produce standardized information on a real-time, online basis. The scope of a financial audit has also migrated from essentially a "backward-looking" activity to an assurance service by which the subscribers seek to form an opinion about the sustainability of an entity.

Thus, in order to ensure the accuracy and relevance of financial figures being commented upon, one needs to understand the process of generation of the same. This involves the function of an information systems auditor. The areas where the financial auditor would concentrate depend greatly on the work of the information systems auditor, and may even require continued assistance, such as in the following activities:

1. **Computerized audit trail:** Paper-based trails as a mode of evidence collection is giving place to screen-based outputs and inputs. Audit trails are now design-dependent and not function-dependent.

2. **Interwoven complex systems:** In an integrated system consisting of a number of interacting subsystems, errors or irregularity in a subsystem can quickly propagate to another subsystem and cause material losses. The auditor needs to understand the referred loss potential of a control failure.

3. **Transaction walkthroughs:** An auditor would need to follow a transaction from its initiation to its end to get an understanding of the process flow. This will be useful to identify the system's strengths and weakness and plan subsequent audit tests.

4. **Entropy in complex systems:** Entropy is the tendency of systems toward internal disorder and eventual collapse. A computerized system is exposed to this threat because of various reasons, including changed business conditions, which can make existing information redundant, or multiply the volume of computations, or increase the difficulties in maintenance.

5. **Outsourced and distributed information systems:** A large number of activities are either outsourced or take place in geographically distributed facilities. Since physical presence at all facilities may not be possible to gather audit evidence, the auditor needs to understand the process flow and may be required to design audit routines to collect evidence and identify areas where errors and irregularities are likely to happen.

INFORMATION SYSTEMS AUDIT COVERAGE

As described earlier, an information systems audit would cover all information system assets and processes. In order to develop a comprehensive opinion about the occurrence or possibility of compromise of confidentiality, integrity, and availability of information system assets and processes, the auditor should be knowledgeable about the following nine aspects:

1. Hardware security issues
2. Software security issues
3. Information systems audit requirements
4. Conducting an information systems audit
5. Risk-based information systems audit
6. Auditing disaster recovery plans
7. Auditing in the e-commerce environment
8. Security testing
9. Information security grading, such as ISecGrade framework

These topics are discussed in detail in the chapters of this book. We have also included a case study on conducting an information systems audit at a bank branch. ISecGrade checklists have been provided.

CHAPTER TWO

Hardware Security Issues

I N THIS CHAPTER WE identify the issues that are critical for implementing hardware security. After completing the chapter, we will be able to identify the aspects of hardware security and corresponding controls that are critical for ensuring the confidentiality, integrity, and availability of the systems resource. We will furthermore be in a position to recognize the areas of hardware and network security that we need to include in our audit plan.

 HARDWARE SECURITY OBJECTIVE

The primary objective of hardware security is to prevent loss, damage, and any other compromise of information system assets, to ensure there are no interruptions of business services and activities. Hardware assets may require physical protection from various security threats. It may be necessary to ensure that hardware assets do not create or are not exposed to any environmental hazards. These controls additionally reduce the risk of unauthorized data access, unauthorized equipment removal, and disposal. The scope of control may extend to protection and safeguarding of supporting facilities such as power, communication, and so on.

The information systems auditor during the audit would focus on the following four objectives:

1. Effective and efficient use of assets
2. Safeguarding of assets
3. Availability of assets to those permitted to use them
4. Maintenance of integrity of hardware

Hardware

Hardware commonly refers to information systems assets that have a physical dimension, like computers, printers, and so forth.

Network

A network commonly refers to a group of information system assets that are interconnected to promote sharing of information processing and storage capability. The span of the network may range from an office room to global locations. The Internet is the most common example of a globally spread network.

Asset Classification and Control

In order to develop an understanding of the various information system assets used by an organization, an auditor may look into the fixed asset register to determine what assets belong to the organization and their current location.

A hardware inventory register commonly called the IT fixed assets register lists all assets associated with each information system. This register contains details such as the hard-disk number, motherboard number, and the location of the asset so that the computer equipment is specifically identifiable. Each asset should have an owner assigned to it. The auditee organization should have an information asset classification guideline in place. The classification assists the organization to lay down specific procedures for handling and protecting various information system assets. The labeling and handling of assets and information should be in accordance with the approved classification scheme of the organization.

The hardware is then categorized based on its criticality to the operations and priority to the business. It must be recognized that the financial value of the asset need not be an adequate measure of the criticality. The way to find criticality is essentially to review what functions would suffer if an asset is put out of service and how long it would take to restore normal operation. The critical assets are to be accorded special focus during test of controls.

Physical Equipment Placement and Protection

Placement and protection of equipment should contribute to a reduction of exposure to loss from environmental threats and hazards and should also reduce the opportunity of unauthorized access. An information systems auditor may consider the following eight key issues:

1. Equipment location should discourage access into work areas. For example, if the thermostat that controls the heat and air-conditioning is located inside the systems room, people without any need to access systems resources will need to enter the room to control the thermostat.
2. Location and layout of facilities handling sensitive data should reduce the risk of access and chances of the process results being visible to unauthorized users. A balance inquiry screen for a banking customer that unnecessarily displays the client's signature is an example of a violation.
3. Information systems assets that require special protection should be isolated so that there is no need to enhance the general level of protection required for other assets. A server room requiring special temperature and humidity controls can be isolated and special facilities created around the specific location only.
4. Adequate controls should minimize the risk of loss arising from potential threats including thefts, fire, explosives, smoke, water, dust, vibrations, chemical effluents, electrical and electromagnetic interference, and so forth.
5. Eating, drinking and smoking near information processing facilities should be prohibited and the prohibition must be diligently observed.
6. Close monitoring of environmental conditions should be ensured to provide early warning signals of possible adverse impacts of environmental changes on information systems assets.
7. The possibility of collateral damage arising out of a disaster happening in the neighborhood, such as fire in the adjacent building, water seepage from the roof, and so forth, needs to be assessed.
8. The possibility of access to facilities from the neighborhood should also be assessed. For example, there are cases of tunnels being created to access bank booths. Similarly, if the assets for network connectivity are accessible, the possibility of data interception increases significantly.

Power Supplies

There must be a system to protect equipment from damages arising from the unreliable quality of power supply. The auditor may consider the following seven areas:

1. Whether options are available to ensure continuity of power supply, which may include multiple feeds to avoid single-point failure in the power supply, provision of uninterruptible power supply, backup generator, and so forth.

2. Whether there is a contingency plan, including action required to be taken on failure of continuous power.
3. Whether the uninterruptible power supply equipment is periodically checked to ensure adequate capacity in view of an altering demand profile for power. All such equipment is to be tested in accordance with the manufacturer's recommendations.
4. Whether standby generators are regularly tested to verify their working condition. Special attention is to be given to sourcing of fuel for the same to ensure performance over a prolonged period. For example, the stock of fuel for a generator may not be regularly maintained and, in the event of a power outage, the backup system may perform suboptimally because of fuel shortage.
5. Whether emergency power switches can be easily accessed during an emergency evacuation to facilitate rapid power-down in case of emergency. One common error in designing equipment layout is failure to locate the emergency power switch in line with emergency exit route. This saves precious time during an emergency evacuation.
6. Whether the building(s) has adequate protection against lightning, especially in lightning-prone areas, with a specific focus on protection of all power and communication lines. This caution also extends to other natural disasters.
7. Whether there are plans in place for protection of power and data communication cables.

Cabling Security

The audit requires comments on whether the power and data communication cables are protected from interruption or damage. The following controls should be reviewed:

- Power and data communication lines should be adequately protected, including being laid securely and being laid safely underground.
- Protection of network cables from unauthorized physical interception or damage, including special attention to routing through public areas.
- Proper segregation of power and communication cables to prevent interference.
- Additional protection, including providing armored conduit and/or locked rooms or boxes at inspection and termination points, may be necessary. It may be prudent to lay alternative channels for sensitive and critical systems.

Physical Access and Service Disruption

Physical barriers to information systems assets are perhaps one of the least glamorous and yet most effective controls to prevent unauthorized access. A list of 10 steps that can assist in protecting information systems assets from unauthorized physical access and disruption is provided next:

1. Consider flight paths, geological fault lines, power lines, potential terrorist targets, and so on, while selecting the physical site. This is to be supplemented by observance of all building and fire codes of the local jurisdiction in the building that houses information systems assets. Manufacturers' specifications for air-conditioning, humidity, and similar environmental variables must be completely implemented. It should be noted that absence of such conformity often makes a warranty void. The organization can additionally implement stricter controls envisaging a worst-case scenario.
2. Establish security perimeters as the first-level controls against unauthorized physical access.
3. Ensure recording of physical access, which should be strictly limited to authorized personnel. The access permission should be allocated on the basis of need and not on institutional hierarchy. It must be noted that the extent of control of access depends on the sensitivity of the location and the assets being protected.
4. Maintain adequate documentation for physical inventory of information system assets and their movements.
5. Provide for clean, adequate, and uninterrupted power supply.
6. Establish an adequate fire protection system, along with providing for emergency evacuation routes and guidelines.
7. Evaluate all engineering diagrams to identify single-point-of-failure and assess ways to eliminate those failures. It may be necessary to seek expert help in this regard.
8. Observe all requirements of the insurer to keep the insurance contract enforceable along with adhering to best safety practices, including prohibiting the storage of hazardous or combustible material within the perimeter.
9. Establish an intermediate holding area for deliveries to the critical system areas where inspection can take place to assess any potential threat. As the access to the system becomes more network-based, allowing sharing of data, enforcement of this control in its physical form becomes more and more difficult.
10. Develop a practice of escorting visitors within the premises, especially in sensitive areas.

Other Concerns

Other questions and concerns to consider include the following:

■ Are hardware facilities reasonably protected against forced entry? It may be prudent to consider the definition of forced entry as provided by the insurer.
■ Are keys to the computer facilities adequately controlled to reduce the risk of unauthorized access? Special attention needs to be provided regarding duplicate keys.
■ Are portable computing devices, such as laptops and handheld devices, secured to prevent copying of data, removal of storage media, and removal of the equipment itself? Enforcing this becomes challenging in face of the availability of multipurpose computing devices such as smartphones, tablets, and so forth.

■ Are authorized equipment removal passes required before an information systems asset can be removed from its normal secure surroundings?

Information Systems Facilities

The information systems auditor will need to look into the following three information system facilities, wherever available, that must be protected:

1. Physical assets
   a. Computer room, including backup room
   b. Computing equipment, including network equipment used in distributed locations
   c. Storage media, including removable media
2. Soft assets
   a. Programming areas
   b. Programming codes
   c. Manuals and guidelines
3. Logistics
   a. Off-site backup file storage facility
   b. Communications facilities
   c. Power sources
   d. Disposal sites

■ PERIPHERAL DEVICES AND STORAGE MEDIA

Peripheral devices are external adjuncts to the main processing facility and generally include printers, screens, projection devices, and so on. Though commonly storage media were inbuilt with the system, there has been a proliferation of external storage devices that are removable and can be plugged into virtually any system. They include flash drives, micro SD cards, external hard disks, and so forth. The portability and size enhances the security risk associated with these devices. The risks are augmented by the fact that some of these devices have wireless communication ability and can be remotely linked with system devices for data transfer.

Management of Peripheral Devices

These would include devices such as printers, scanners, card readers, USB modems, flash drives, adaptors, and the like. The information systems auditor may consider the following security measures adopted by the user:

■ Peripheral devices being placed into the system on a need-to-use basis.
■ Protection of these devices from unauthorized access.
■ Modems, including USB modems, not being connected to any machine and not lying within the organizational network without prior standing or case-based

authorization. In case of a network hosting sensitive resources, it may be necessary to use a stand-alone machine for such access.

- Limited and controlled usage of flash drives with specific authorization.
- Peripheral devices that are accessed by a number of persons not being placed near the main server or other critical information asset.

Management of Removable Computer Media

This is perhaps one of the most neglected areas that can compromise the confidentiality of data. The auditor should assess the procedures for identification and subsequent removal of storage media to review adequacy of the procedure and implementation thereof. The following six guidelines may be useful in designing an appropriate checklist:

1. No media should be used without authorization.
2. Contents of any reusable media marked for removal from the organization should be erased in a manner that prevents retrieval.
3. All removal of storage media should be authorized and documented for control and for subsequent use as an audit trail. Additional control must exist for identification and removal of sensitive items.
4. All media must be stored in a safe and secure environment.
5. Backups must be maintained in an off-site, secure place.
6. Secured storage must be provided for system documents especially for sensitive systems and access to such documentation should involve authorization and be recorded.

CLIENT-SERVER ARCHITECTURE

The client-server environment comprises the following three main parts:

1. Front-end with end-user workstation.
2. Back-end hosting the application server and the main processor.
3. Data server hosting the legacy data. In some cases the application server and data server are integrated into one, leading to two-tier client-server architecture.

Client-Server

Client-server is a computing model wherein the major application runs on a centralized system, called a server, and users send in requests from remote terminals, called clients. Requests are processed by the server and the results sent back to the client. The connectivity is established by a network that may be distributed far and wide. One of the most common client-server applications now is Internet-based e-commerce portals.

These parts work in synchronization to complete a transaction request. The goal of the client-server application is to optimize four factors:

1. Location of the processing
2. Amount of network traffic
3. Location of data storage
4. Amount of data storage

A detailed client-server audit program has been included in Chapter 12. The information systems auditor should include a detailed testing of operating systems, the database management system, the network management system and components, program libraries, and change documentation and control.

AUTHENTICATION DEVICES

Common authentication devices, in addition to user IDs and passwords to sign on, that an information systems auditor would come across include the following:

- **Smart cards:** These are widely used for authenticating remote access to computer systems. Each user desiring remote access is issued a smart card that periodically displays a new password. These passwords are synchronized with the central computer to which the user desires access. When logging into the system, the user must enter the current up-to-the-minute password in order to authenticate his or her identity to the computer. This is now being replaced by a one-time password delivered directly to handheld phones registered with the system.
- **Biometrics:** These techniques use automated processes to register and compare physiological, and often behavioral, characteristics to verify identity. Physiological biometrics uses direct measurement of a part of the human body including fingerprints, facial characteristics, retina, and hands to verify identity. Behavioral biometrics focuses on data derived from an action that indirectly measures characteristics of the human body and includes voice, signature, keystroke monitoring, and so on.

HARDWARE ACQUISITION

While verifying the acquisition of hardware the auditor would typically find five distinct phases. The auditor should form his or her opinion on the existing controls, documentation, and implementation of the hardware. These five main phases are planning, acquisition, implementation, operation and maintenance, and disposal. They are briefly discussed next.

1. **Planning:** This involves identification of requirements, defining specifications that would satisfy the requirements, resources allocation for procurement, cost-benefit analysis leading to acquisition justification, and eventual issue of purchase requisition.
2. **Acquisition:** This involves requirements analysis, study of alternative technology and process, design and release of tender document, receipt and comparative analysis of proposals, vendor selection, and order placement. The requirements analysis has to be made considering the following areas:
   a. **Hardware components:** The detailed specifications of hardware to be acquired.
   b. **Criticality:** The impact on the organization in terms of performance and consequences if the hardware is not purchased, including the cost impact.
   c. **Reliability:** Equipment reliability is measured in terms of mean time between failures (MTBF) and system redundancy. It is a measurement of the time the equipment is in good operating condition.
   d. **Availability:** It addresses the requirement to increase hardware uptime and dwells on issues such as repair response time, acceptable length of system downtime, and period of maintenance.
   e. **Selection criteria:** This would depend on the product being selected. However, generally, the following are considered:
      i. Price, performance, network instructions per second, and delivery schedules
      ii. Upgradeability
      iii. Environmental requirements
      iv. Reliability statistics (mean time between failures)
      v. Multivendor hardware interface compatibility, and integration
      vi. Maintenance requirements of vendor and customer
      vii. Configuration flexibility
      viii. Industry standard data and results from similar computing environments
      ix. User documentation
      x. Repair facilities availability
      xi. Site specifications (floor space, electrical power requirements)
3. **Implementation:** This phase commences once the contract is awarded and consists of various procedures including inspection, installation, trial run, and testing, which eventually evolves into a fully operational system. Procedures for documenting vendor response time, equipment downtime, vendor performance, access to required devices, and others are to be framed by the organization during this phase.
4. **Operation and maintenance:** This phase involves processes that maintain efficiency to ensure an optimum uptime after installation is complete. The host organization must maintain proper operating procedures and maintenance schedules, and document all equipment failures, along with causes, downtime, repair details, and frequency of negative responses.

5. **Disposal:** This phase signifies the last stage of the equipment life cycle within the organization. The need for disposal may arise for reasons different from operational failure or obsolescence. Often, changes in business may prompt disposal requirements as the fall out of a procurement decision. Disposal decisions are assuming criticality in view of increased cost of e-waste management. The organization needs to have a policy to identify disposal candidates and the process of disposal. The disposal process must keep in view that the disposed equipment is cleaned of any confidential data hosted by it. Disposal need not signify lack of usability. Many organizations prefer to donate their old equipment to various educational and charitable institutions that use them for training students.

HARDWARE MAINTENANCE

The auditor focuses on both preventive and remedial maintenance of hardware. Preventive maintenance is carried out to keep hardware in good operating condition while remedial maintenance determines why equipment is malfunctioning and repairs it.

Equipment maintenance must follow the correct process and the guideline provided by the manufacturer to ensure its continued availability and integrity. The auditor may consider the following checklist of eight items:

1. Is equipment maintenance in accordance with the service intervals and specifications recommended by the supplier?
2. Are only authorized maintenance personnel allowed to carry out repairs and service equipment?
3. Are all suspected or actual faults reported and documented?
4. Are all instances of preventive and corrective maintenance recorded?
5. Are appropriate controls adopted before sending any equipment out of the premises for maintenance?
6. Is there compliance with all conditions specified in insurance policies?
7. Is response time of vendors tracked and documented to assess contractual performance?
8. Are all instances of system downtime and actions taken by the management tracked and is special attention accorded where mean time between failures is very low?

Maintenance measures may be done using two credit methodologies. Credits are allowances for system downtime and delays in response time that exceed the limits established in the vendor's contract. Response time credits are reductions in maintenance charges resulting from failure of the maintenance vendor to arrive at the organization site within the response time stated in the contract. Downtime credit charges result when system or component downtime exceeds the limits of the contract.

> ### E-Waste
>
> The proliferation of electronic equipment in daily use and rapid technology-driven obsolescence has created a major problem of disposal of these wastes, which are not biodegradable. Some of these wastes may even contain contaminants such as lead, cadmium, beryllium, and so forth. Many countries have their own legislations and guidelines governing disposal of e-waste. In fact, disposal of e-waste is becoming a major business opportunity.

Another vital decision in the area of maintenance is who should provide the maintenance. The auditor may look into the process and documentation to assess whether the decision-making process included, at the minimum, the following six criteria:

1. **Primary business of vendor:** A vendor whose primary business is maintenance would devote more resources to it. Thus a comparative study should be made between these specialized vendors and the facilities provided versus the hardware suppliers whose main business is to sell hardware. Often the hardware vendor outsources the maintenance to a third-party franchisee who operates under the brand name of the hardware vendor.
2. **Maintaining a wide range of hardware:** A third-party vendor may provide maintenance services for a wide range of information system devices used in the organization. The hardware supplier would maintain only the product(s) supplied by it. The auditee organization needs to consider the advantage of easier administration when maintenance is done by one vendor in comparison to the specialized knowledge brought in by hardware-specific vendors.
3. **Competitive prices:** The pricing that is most advantageous to the organization is to be selected. However, the warranty clause must be verified to ensure that the warranty continues irrespective of the choice of vendor.
4. **Knowledge of hardware components:** A third-party vendor may be less experienced with unusual malfunctioning and may not be competent to maintain the same. They may not have access to proprietary knowledge and diagnostic tools.
5. **Spare parts:** A third-party vendor may not have easy access to inventory of spare parts. There may also be a markup on the cost of spare parts, resulting in a higher price to the organization.
6. **Availability of diagnostic software:** In a large number of cases the original manufacturers do not make proprietary diagnostic software available to third parties. Hence the choice for maintenance becomes severely restricted.

MANAGEMENT OF OBSOLESCENCE

For determining what devices may be obsolete, the auditor needs to understand the complete equipment life-cycle planning. Equipment life-cycle planning is the management practice that identifies business, technical, or financial criteria that will

TABLE 2.1 Key Variables in Equipment Life-Cycle Planning Phase

Areas	Costs
Programming and Technical Skill Sets	Costs of manpower appropriate for the existing technology exceed the cost to replace existing technology.
Licensing Costs	License cost of the existing technology exceeds the cost to replace it with later technology.
Performance Levels	Existing equipment performs suboptimally and costs of upgrading exceed the cost of replacement.
Technical Functionality	The best performance achievable by existing technology will need additional investment and replacement will not only be cheaper than upgrading but will also have better performance than upgraded performance.
Environmental	Existing technology is not environmentally friendly and combination of potential risk and penalty outweighs the current benefit derived against costs incurred.
Maintenance Cost	Effective maintenance expense that is the product of maintenance frequency and average unit maintenance costs exceeds the cost of replacement.
Acquisition Cost	Operating expenses, including cost of consumables, justify the acquisition of more recent technology.

trigger a replacement decision for an information asset. A list of areas and associated costs that are key variables in the equipment life-cycle planning phase to determine whether a specific information systems asset is obsolete is provided in Table 2.1.

 DISPOSAL OF EQUIPMENT

This phase marks the end of the useful life of the hardware. As discussed earlier, this consists of the steps required to dispose of equipment that can no longer be beneficially used by the organization. The auditor should ensure the following two steps have been undertaken to prevent the disclosure of sensitive information:

1. All information assets containing sensitive information have been checked and data irreversibly deleted before disposal.
2. All damaged equipment has been put through a risk assessment study to determine whether it should be destroyed, repaired, or discarded. There should be a defined process of such destruction or discarding.

PROBLEM MANAGEMENT

The auditor should check whether an effective system is in place for logging, tracking, reporting, resolving, and implementing problem and change management procedures. Problems can result from operating and application system failures, computer terminal failure, telecommunication and line equipment failure, printer failure, personal computer or workstation failure, change control failure, and so on. The availability and integrity of systems depend to some extent on how efficiently problems and changes are managed.

The auditor determines the following three aspects:

1. Whether documented procedures are present that lay down a formal procedure for identifying and reporting problems to the management so that corrective action can be taken in a timely manner.
2. Whether adequate procedures are present to guide operations personnel in logging, analyzing, resolving, and escalating problems in a timely manner.
3. Whether the procedures ensure proper maintenance of problem management mechanism, including resolution of outstanding problems in a timely manner.

The information systems auditor may follow these 14 procedures:

1. Interview information systems operations personnel.
2. Understand how problems are identified, detected, and classified.
3. Inquire how frequently the problems are logged and reported to the management. Review whether the error log includes the name of the person reporting the problem, the problem code and number, time, date, and day the problem was first noticed, a clear description of the problem, and the possible reasons for the problem.
4. Review reported problems to determine whether status of the problem is indicated.
5. Review adequacy of existing procedures for satisfactory recording, evaluating, resolving, or escalating any operating or processing problems.
6. Review the performance records to determine existence of any processing problem.
7. Review the reasons behind suboptimal processing speed achieved by an application to determine whether they are reasonable in view of the technology used and processing complexity.
8. Determine that significant and recurring problems have been identified and preventive actions have been taken.
9. Assure that each problem is assigned to an individual to research and resolve along with expected number of hours, days, or cost necessary.
10. Confirm whether reports generated by the problem management system are reviewed by senior problem management personnel.
11. Review error-log entries to identify and document problems that are outstanding and review how they are to be addressed at the earliest.

12. Review procedures for escalation of unresolved problems.
13. Take a sample of problem events recorded in the error log and calculate the time elapsed from when the problems were reported to their resolution for comparison with standard resolution time targets.
14. Ascertain whether a summarized problem report is available for senior management that presents the problem type and category, the number of occurrences in each category, the percentage of resolved and unresolved problems, the actual time lapsed in resolving the problem, the number of days a problem was open, and the cost to correct each problem.

 ## CHANGE MANAGEMENT

An unauthorized change can occur for several reasons, including the following seven examples:

1. The user responsible for the application was not aware of the change.
2. Change request procedures with relevant documents are not formally established.
3. The manager did not sign the change request form approving the start of work.
4. The user did not sign the change form signifying acceptance before the change was updated.
5. The changed source code was not properly reviewed by the appropriate programming personnel.
6. The manager did not sign the change request form approving the program for release to production environment.
7. The programmer put in nefarious code for personal benefit (i.e., committing a fraud).

Production Environment

Production environment refers to the collection of information assets involved in processing, storing, and communicating live data in a live environment. No test data or test processes are permitted in this environment. In fact, when modifying such an environment, it is suggested that a parallel run is conducted till such time that users are familiar with and confident about proper functionality of the amended system. During the parallel run, the erstwhile system as well as the amended system will use live data.

Detailed review by the information systems auditor can locate weaknesses in the procedure that can potentially cause occurrence of one of the previously mentioned conditions. If the information systems auditor finds appropriate procedures in place, compliance tests should be designed to find evidence that the identified controls functioned properly during the period under review. The detailed review should further determine whether the control procedures could be intentionally circumvented, allowing an unauthorized change to go undetected. The information systems auditor may perform the following seven functions in this regard:

1. Select a sample of program changes made during the audit period and trace it back to the change request form to determine whether the changes were authorized.
2. Check that the form has appropriate approvals and compare the date on the form with the date of production update to confirm that they were in sequence.
3. Determine whether written requests are available for all changes along with expected completion time frame, expected cost, and proper authorization of the user and relevant manager.
4. Inquire whether a continuous sequence number is assigned to the change request form for the purpose of tracking and monitoring.
5. If an independent group updates the program changes in the production environment, the information systems auditor needs to determine whether procedures exist to ensure possession of the change request form before the update is implemented.
6. Source-code comparison software is an effective and easy-to-use method for tracing changes to programs. The information systems auditor should obtain and store a control copy of the source code of the program to be tested. At some future date the information systems auditor may use a source comparison program to trace differences between the control and current source. A list of additions, deletions, and changes can be printed and used by the auditor to review the relevant change authorization approval documentation, including work requests, approvals, and program testing results.
7. Ascertain whether a summary report for changes introduced is available for review of senior management. Such report should include the change type, category, and the number of successful and unsuccessful changes in each category. The report should be issued periodically.

NETWORK AND COMMUNICATION ISSUES

A network is essentially a collection of information processing and communication resources that connect different information system assets, enabling them to share, access, and transmit information and data. The auditor should determine whether the access to both internal and external network and services are controlled so that the users with access to networks and network services do not compromise the network security. The auditor needs to verify whether the following controls are present in the system:

▪ Are interfaces between the internal private network and the public networks equipped with adequate security controls?

■ Are there appropriate authentication mechanisms for the users and equipment, especially where there is equipment-based access?

■ Is access by users to the information services controlled to prevent inappropriate use?

The main areas of focus for information systems auditors are described in the following sections.

Policy on Use of Network and Network Services

Insecure connections to network services can seriously compromise the information systems of the entire organization. Direct access to network resources should be restricted to services that specific users need to use based on their functional requirement. Use of networks and network services should be governed by a policy and not entirely left up to operational discretion.

Secure Connection

More often than not, the term *secure connection* is used from a technology perspective. This refers to encryption of the data being transmitted over the network in a manner so that even if data are intercepted, they cannot be deciphered.

Encryption

Encryption is a series of iterations in which data that are visually meaningful are transformed into data that are visually incomprehensible. Once decrypted, the data are restored to the original form. This is one of the common methods of securing a network.

Adequacy of the policy can be evaluated by the information systems auditor by reviewing whether the policy includes the following nine aspects:

1. Specification of the networks and network services that are allowed to be accessed.
2. Procedures to determine eligibility to access a network and network services.
3. Specification and adequacy of management controls and procedures protecting access to network connections and network services.
4. Consistent application of access control policy across the organization.
5. Restriction on usage of network services for only business reasons.
6. System for identification, removal, or disabling of unused or unwanted network services.
7. Requirement of documentation of all procedures involving setting of critical parameters, including configuring for installation and operation of a network operating system.

8. Process of updating security-related software and internal communication on security issues.
9. Specification of the types of information whose access needs to be logged.

The communication access should be granted strictly on a need-to-use basis to protect against threats of modification, destruction, or disclosures of information through unauthorized access.

Enforced Path

It may be necessary to define a path for establishing a connection from the user terminal to the computer service, particularly for sensitive services. The auditor may verify effectiveness of this control, which is designed to restrict the route that a user terminal uses to connect to an authorized computer service. The auditor also needs to review the effectiveness of the control in reducing exposure to the threat of unauthorized access and preventing users from selecting any routes outside the permitted path.

Path

When a data item originating from one system seeks to reach another system, it searches for a path to get there. The address of the destination is specified with the data. The data item presents this address to the router that connects various network connections. The router then inquires of other routers whether any other router is connected with the specified address. This inquiry spreads out across the web of routers till a path is identified and the data item is directed through it. If no such path is found, the transfer attempt is aborted and the user informed of the failure.

Ports

Ports are physical objects that are used to establish a connection with any external equipment for the purpose of transmitting data. Examples are the printer port, network port, and so forth. Some applications also create virtual ports to allow a physical port to be used for multiple purposes.

This may be achieved by a combination of the following two alternatives:

1. Resource based
   a. Allocating dedicated lines.
   b. Directly connecting to specified ports on designated application systems or security gateways that control access to such system.

    c. Managing and monitoring all communications from source to destination using security interfaces such as firewalls, intruder detection system, and so forth.

    d. Preventing unrestricted roaming on the network, especially in terms of connection duration and access to various network services and components.

    e. Providing limited menu and submenu access to individual users matching their authorization profile.

2. Policy based

    a. Permitting inward access to external network users only through specified application systems or security gateways controlling such access.

    b. Creating respective subdomains for user groups within the organization to restrict access to entire network.

    c. Ensuring that access control policy complements requirement of an enforced path from both managerial and technical perspective.

User Authentication for External Connections

Inbound connections from external sources are one of the resources susceptible to compromise, thereby granting unauthorized access to system resources. Therefore, when analyzing network security, the auditor needs to critically review the process of authentication of remote users. Authentication may be provided in various ways, including the following three examples:

1. Using cryptography-based techniques involving recognition of encrypted responses, hardware-based identification tokens, or protocol involving response to a challenge.

2. Using dedicated private lines as a means to secure authentication or invoking a system of source validation of a network communication.

3. Enforcing procedure where the network service will call back the requesting system to establish connection instead of establishing connection as a response to a connection request. Since the call-back is based on secured protocols, this ensures that system calls with forged identity are not responded to.

Node Authentication

Connections in response to requests from remote computer systems should be established only after the originating system is authenticated. Node authentication establishes the identity of the remote computer before proceeding with responding to the request. This control is particularly useful where specific functions are served by a dedicated node and, consequently, service requests of a specific nature can arise only from specified nodes.

    The node authentication process can be used in conjunction with job description to strengthen security. For example, in an enterprise-wide accounting system, a request for a delivery may be processed only when the originating request is from a remote node in the sales or inventory department.

Segregation of Networks

Ensuring the security of large networks may require dividing the network into multiple logical network domains of smaller size. Independent and additional security controls may be established on each of these domains irrespective of whether they are internal or external to the organization. This will allow lower access control to be implemented in areas involving open access, thus reducing the overall load of security control to be implemented across the system. The network segregation is effected by allocating a set of IP addresses to each network.

IP Address

IP address refers to Internet protocol address, which is a numeric system to identify each computer in a network. The numbering comprises four groups of three numbers. A group is separated from another group by a dot. The common format is xxx.xxx.xxx.xxx wherein each number may range from 0 to 255. There are three sets of numbers reserved for use within a private network, and the computing resources using these numbers are accessible only internally. These are 10.0.0.0 to 10.255.255.255, 172.16.0.0 to 172.31.255.255, and 192.168.0.0 to 192.168.255.255. The rest of the numbers are for public use, suggesting that they can be reached by external users. This system of classification, known as IP4 system, has a limited number of addresses, leading to introduction of the IP6 system, which has eight groups of four hexadecimal digits.

Intruder Detection System (IDS)

The IDS is a system that analyzes the communication to the protected system and verifies its source and content. Wherever the IDS finds a signature matching that of a prohibited source or communication, an alert is generated.

Intruder Prevention System (IPS)

The IPS works under the same principle as IDS but in addition to raising an alert, it prevents the communication from reaching the protected system as well.

Identification Tokens

Identification tokens are used to establish identity and are used in addition to passwords. The functionality may be limited to physical contact or may also include a keyboard to enter password or screen to display a key.

The information systems auditor would look at the implemented perimeter security such as firewall or intrusion detection system on the gateway connecting two networks to oversee access and information flow between the domains. This gateway will filter all traffic between these domains and, based on access control policy, selectively allow or deny access and service requests.

Network Connection Control

The auditor overviews the network access control policy of the organization and how it has been implemented in the system. The access control policy may incorporate controls to restrict the connection capability of the users. Such controls can be enforced at the gateways by filtering traffic based on a set of predefined tables or rules. The auditor may verify the setting of the predefined rules to ensure their conformance with the access policy of the organization. These may include user restrictions on the following four items:

1. Electronic mail
2. File transfer, one-way and/or both-way
3. Interactive access
4. Network access linked to day or date

An example of such implementation is found at airports that offer wireless access with a least-authentication process to passengers along with a highly secured network for internal use by the airport authority. Physically both communications are managed through one backbone.

Network Routing Control

In the case of shared networks extending across organizational boundaries, the information systems auditor should verify the routing controls. These controls are designed to ensure that computer connections and information flows are in line with the access control policy. Routing controls should be based on verification of source and destination address. The auditor can ask for the routing table from the auditee to get an understanding of the same.

In a Microsoft Windows environment, "route" command from the command prompt will provide various options for generating a routing table. A standard screenshot of such is provided in Figure 2.1.

Security of Network Services

Organizations using network services should ensure availability of a clear description of the security design and parameters of all services. The auditor should go through the agreement with the third party providing the service and verify whether the security norms mentioned and implemented are in line with the security norms and access policies of the organizations. This becomes critical since

```
C:\Windows\system32\cmd.exe
Microsoft Windows [Version 6.0.6002]
Copyright (c) 2006 Microsoft Corporation.  All rights reserved.

C:\Users\Arif Ahmed>route print
===========================================================================
Interface List
  9 ...00 16 d3 93 09 df ...... Intel(R) PRO/100 VE Network Connection
  8 ...00 1a 73 2f 83 bb ...... Broadcom 802.11b/g WLAN
  1 ........................... Software Loopback Interface 1
 14 ...00 00 00 00 00 00 00 e0  isatap.{39520845-D4CC-4B0D-AEFC-7F0F15EA2949}
 15 ...00 00 00 00 00 00 00 e0  isatap.{F6E86107-AC6C-4BD2-9731-1FE4936CCE52}
 10 ...02 00 54 55 4e 01 ...... Teredo Tunneling Pseudo-Interface
===========================================================================

IPv4 Route Table
===========================================================================
Active Routes:
Network Destination        Netmask          Gateway       Interface  Metric
          0.0.0.0          0.0.0.0      192.168.0.1    192.168.0.101     25
        127.0.0.0        255.0.0.0         On-link         127.0.0.1    306
        127.0.0.1  255.255.255.255         On-link         127.0.0.1    306
  127.255.255.255  255.255.255.255         On-link         127.0.0.1    306
      192.168.0.0    255.255.255.0         On-link     192.168.0.101    281
    192.168.0.101  255.255.255.255         On-link     192.168.0.101    281
    192.168.0.255  255.255.255.255         On-link     192.168.0.101    281
        224.0.0.0        240.0.0.0         On-link         127.0.0.1    306
        224.0.0.0        240.0.0.0         On-link     192.168.0.101    281
  255.255.255.255  255.255.255.255         On-link         127.0.0.1    306
  255.255.255.255  255.255.255.255         On-link     192.168.0.101    281
===========================================================================
Persistent Routes:
  None

IPv6 Route Table
===========================================================================
Active Routes:
 If Metric Network Destination      Gateway
 10     18 ::/0                     On-link
  1    306 ::1/128                  On-link
 10     18 2001::/32                On-link
 10    266 2001:0:4137:9e76:400:35ce:3f57:ff9a/128
                                    On-link
  8    281 fe80::/64                On-link
 10    266 fe80::/64                On-link
 10    266 fe80::400:35ce:3f57:ff9a/128
                                    On-link
  8    281 fe80::e950:5565:57b4:4721/128
                                    On-link
  1    306 ff00::/8                 On-link
 10    266 ff00::/8                 On-link
  8    281 ff00::/8                 On-link
===========================================================================
Persistent Routes:
  None
```

FIGURE 2.1 Route Command

most organizations outsource some critical component of the network to specialized agencies.

In the event the outsourcing vendor is noncompliant with the specific requirements of the auditee, a specific exemption must be obtained. This will also call for an added audit test to ensure that no security compromise takes place at the end of the outsourcing agency.

Other Network Controls

An organization is usually required to use a wide range of controls to achieve and maintain the desired level of security in its networks. The auditors should verify whether network managers have implemented controls adequate for ensuring the security of network data and protecting against unauthorized access. For the purpose, the following three steps may be adopted by the auditee:

1. Ensure clear segregation of duty, separating operational responsibility for networks from computer operations, unless specifically exempt.
2. Define responsibilities and procedures for management of remote equipment.
3. Establish special controls to safeguard the confidentiality and integrity of data transmitted over public networks and over connected systems.

Network Integrity

The information systems auditor should determine whether the following two sets of controls are in place to prevent the capture of a session during resumption after accidental or intentional communication line drops:

1. Controls detecting a dropped communication and triggering immediate report and termination of all associated computer sessions.
2. Compulsory reauthentication during resumption after a line drop.

Session

A session is a period of time over which a data interchange takes place between a client and a server. Once logged in, a session key is generated by the system to be appended with such a request to establish identity of the user. When the user logs off, or after a specific time, the session expires and the user needs to reestablish a session with a fresh log-in. In case a session is alive even after log-off, one may be able to access the resources permitted to the user even without logging in, as the server believes that the user is still logged in.

Network Equipment

The information systems auditor may verify whether the following four steps are taken to prevent unauthorized use of the network equipment or interruption of network services:

1. Logical access controls for all network equipment.
2. Physically secured storage environment for all network equipment, especially those that do not have logical access control.
3. Physical security of network cables, including underground cabling or through conduits.
4. Maintenance and upgrading of network equipment inventory with periodic physical verification.

Change Control Procedure

The information systems auditor assesses whether the change management process discussed earlier for other hardware is also followed in the case of networks. This will limit the network changes to only those made in accordance with the established change management procedures.

Network Monitoring

The information systems auditor may verify whether the following two steps are necessary to protect against information disclosures, modifications, or destruction while using network-monitoring devices:

1. Implementation of usage and storage controls over network monitoring devices, particularly those that record information being transmitted over a network. Software capable of intercepting network traffic for analysis can often store intercepted data. Often the intercepted data contain the user name and password in plain text form and can understandably pose a serious security threat.
2. Awareness among employees that the organization may monitor their use of the information systems asset, including data transmission on the network. This acts as a preventive control against use of the network for unauthorized purposes.

In the event that these steps are deemed necessary, the auditor needs to ascertain whether they have been implemented.

Protection during Transmission

The information systems auditor verifies whether the following three steps are taken to protect sensitive and highly sensitive information from being disclosed during transmission:

1. Encryption of sensitive information during transmission.
2. Encryption of passwords during transmission while securing remote access.
3. Authentication of information origination and verification of integrity using digital signatures or other authentication protocol.

Network Availability

The information systems auditor may verify the implementation of the following two controls that help to ensure the availability of networks:

1. Continuation of the network services using uninterrupted power supplies to protect against information loss in situations of power fluctuations or outages.
2. Protection against service outage caused by destruction or modifications of information residing in the network resources. This may be achieved by establishing and enforcing periodic backup of information. These backups are to be tested periodically to ensure their recoverability.

The disaster recovery plan must encompass network services to protect against losses due to the unavailability of the network resources.

Wireless Network Considerations

The information systems auditor may verify the following six items to ensure the security of a wireless network. A detailed checklist for a wireless network audit has been provided in Chapter 12.

1. Whether access using the wireless network is logged to create an audit trail.
2. Whether guest access is disabled to ensure that no one can use the wireless network resource incognito. It may be necessary to separate the wireless network from the mother network and add a layer of security for authenticating any request placed from a wireless network.
3. Whether a wireless signal is transmitted beyond the physical perimeter of the organization and additional security measures taken to prevent unauthorized access.
4. Whether an inventory of all resources accessible from a wireless network is available.
5. Whether there is a procedure for installing a new access point to the current network.
6. Whether all users of mobile computing devices keep their equipment protected with antivirus and antimalware software.

3

Software Security Issues

N THIS CHAPTER WE will learn about major software security issues that an information systems auditor should be concerned about. At the end of the chapter, we will be in a position to recognize the software security aspects that we need to include in our audit plan.

OVERVIEW OF TYPES OF SOFTWARE

In the course of an audit, the information systems auditor is likely to come across various types of software. In the following section, we have identified the common types of software most likely to be present in an auditee environment and the minimum control features that each of those software types should have.

System Software

System software is a set of instructions that perform the central control function for the computer system. It directs the way the computer responds to a program request and interfaces with other devices. When we switch on our laptop, the machine executes a series of commands before starting to load the operating system. Those commands form a part of the system software. Despite our installing different operating systems on our laptop, the series of commands it executes before commencing loading of the operating software remains the same. It is the system software that directs the laptop to the hard disk, DVD drive, USB drive, or network location to search for the operating software. In cases of complex systems, like large servers, the system software defines the borders of performance of the hardware.

Integrity of system software can be strengthened by adopting the following two measures:

1. Implementing strong access controls to system software and their handling facilities.
2. Implementing stringent human resource screening standards to select personnel for operation and maintenance of system software.

Operating Software

Operation of a computer—or a processor, to be specific—is managed by the operating system. Depending on the setup, operating systems may be selected by the hardware manufacturer or by the user. The total cost of the system may vary because of the operating system. In some cases, an operating system requires a specific hardware environment to be available. It has been observed that on one hand, operating systems are becoming more and more hardware hungry, while on the other hand there is a parallel movement wherein a lean operating system is loaded on minimum hardware requirements. Known as "thin clients," these installations draw their processing power from the main server with which they connect.

All operating systems generally have the following four components:

1. **Process management:** Deals with execution of computer programs.
2. **Input/output device management:** The operating system issues commands to input/output devices, detects interrupts, and handles errors.
3. **Memory management:** The memory manager keeps track of which parts of the memory are being used, allots memory to required processes, de-allocates memory when a process is complete, manages swapping between the storage devices and the main memory, and so forth.
4. **System file management:** System files contain programs, source and object codes, job procedures, text, and others. Operating systems make system calls to create and destroy files; read and write files; store, archive, and retrieve files; copy, sort, and merge files; and perform similar other tasks.

Increasing use and dependence on the Internet has given popularity to operating systems that are essentially designed to connect to the Internet in addition to executing some specific software and basic system commands. These operating systems are loaded on a basic hardware configuration, which is optimized for connecting to the

Thin Client

Thin clients are computers that draw the processing power from another powerful computer with whom it connects through a network. The thin computers may even lack storage space if they store the data on a remote storage. Thin clients essentially provide a user interface, leaving the computational task to the computer it connects to. Some thin clients may also have limited processing power and storage. Many educational institutions and particularly charitable institutions use computers, no longer used in commercial environments, as thin clients for educational purpose. With increased acceptance of cloud computing and use of handheld devices that can access Internet, the use of thin clients have seen an increase in recent years.

Computer Program

A computer program is a codified set of instructions that a computer can understand and execute. Some of the programs are available off the shelf while specific-purpose applications are required to be codified at the suggestion of the user. The choice of a platform to write the code depends on the operating system the computer uses. The program is usually stored on media and is loaded into the memory. The instructions are then sent to the processor for execution and results come back to the memory before being directed to the next step. The next step can be further processing or generation of an output directed to the screen, printer, or file.

Interrupt

Interrupt is a signal sent by a program or a hardware device notifying the main processor of an urgent event. The processor interrupts processing of the current code, saves it, and attends to the event. Once the event has been taken care of, the processor resumes the earlier processing from the saved state. Hardware interrupts are generated by hardware while a program generates software interrupts.

Memory

Memory is the physical device in the computer that stores, mostly on a temporary basis, the instructions to be run by the processor or output from it. In case of high memory requirements, the system often reserves a part of the physical storage system for use as memory, and this is known as "virtual memory." A part of the memory may be protected and no alterations are permitted. This is known as read-only memory (ROM).

Internet. The user connects to the Internet through a browser and works on resources such as a spreadsheet, word processing, and so on.

Memory Resident Programs

Memory resident programs retain control over processing resources of the system even after it appears to have completed its function. These programs, accidentally or by design, may cause loss of integrity of the processing in the system. An information systems auditor needs to inspect the software installed to ascertain installation and initiation of any unauthorized software. An examination of the processes running in the computer will allow the information systems auditor to verify whether there are any unknown or unauthorized processes running on the computer.

In a Microsoft Windows environment there are two tabs on Task Manager that provide detailed information about the processes and services running on the computer. Depending on the version of Microsoft Windows, this function can be accessed by pressing the keys Ctrl, Alt, and Delete simultaneously and selecting the Task Manager option. A list of processes running on the computer will be displayed on the screen, as may be seen in Figure 3.1.

It may be noted that all programs are loaded to memory for the purpose of execution. Memory resident programs are not made inoperative and continue to work in the background. One of the most common of these applications is an antivirus program that remains active after being initialized.

Utility Programs

Utility programs are specialized software used to manipulate data and programs. From the viewpoint of information systems auditor, they pose risks of various magnitudes as they are difficult to identify in the audit trail. It is to be noted that at times utility programs may be installed due to maintenance needs and a formal process must exist to distinguish between permissive and abusive installation.

Application Software

Applications are specific sets of software designed to accomplish one or more functions. In order to preserve availability, integrity, and confidentiality, the information systems auditor can check whether the following eight best practice controls are in place:

1. In case of integrated application and operating systems access control, the user ID and passwords should be maintained by the operating system and not by the application system.
2. Access structure should provide the minimum privileges necessary to perform a job.
3. Information that is replicated on multiple platforms must have similar access control all across. Absence of the same may allow a user who is not authorized to

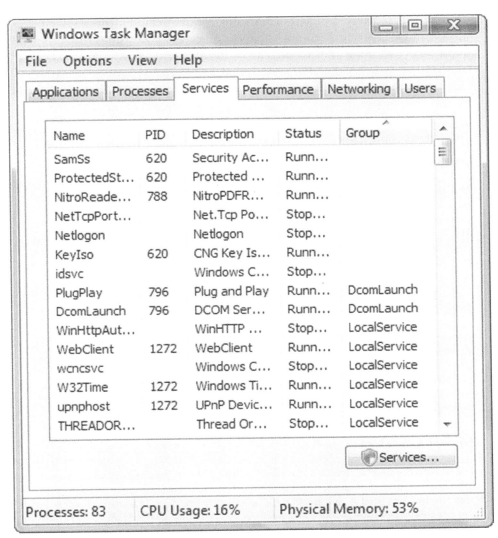

Name	PID	Description	Status	Group
SamSs	620	Security Ac...	Runn...	
ProtectedSt...	620	Protected ...	Runn...	
NitroReade...	788	NitroPDFR...	Runn...	
NetTcpPort...		Net.Tcp Po...	Stop...	
Netlogon		Netlogon	Stop...	
KeyIso	620	CNG Key Is...	Runn...	
idsvc		Windows C...	Stop...	
PlugPlay	796	Plug and Play	Runn...	DcomLaunch
DcomLaunch	796	DCOM Ser...	Runn...	DcomLaunch
WinHttpAut...		WinHTTP ...	Stop...	LocalService
WebClient	1272	WebClient	Runn...	LocalService
wcncsvc		Windows C...	Stop...	LocalService
W32Time	1272	Windows Ti...	Runn...	LocalService
upnphost	1272	UPnP Devic...	Runn...	LocalService
THREADOR...		Thread Or...	Stop...	LocalService

Processes: 83   CPU Usage: 16%   Physical Memory: 53%

FIGURE 3.1 Windows Task Manager

access the information from one system to get the same information from another system.

4. Accountability should be assigned specifically through user ID and time/date stamp.

5. The system should be provided with ownership information, whether individual or collective. This allows the system to evaluate an information access request.

6. Location control should be implemented to enforce additional restrictions at specific sensitive locations to prevent physical access to systems hosting sensitive data. The data center that hosts the main database is a common example of locations where such controls are usually enforced.

7. Critical transactions should have a dual control requirement. This ensures that a single individual cannot complete a process and requires involvement of at least one other individual. This is often referred to as "maker-checker" control.

8. Logs and reports of modifications/alterations/amendments of the database should be securely stored.

Audit Trail

The audit trail is a process of reconstructing an event for an auditor to understand the sequence of processes that lead to the event. In information systems this is achieved by maintaining sequential record of access and use of information assets. This is also referred to as an audit log. Many applications have an inbuilt audit log, whereas in some cases processes need to be built around the application to create an audit log. These records may be manual, for example, a record of entry into the server room.

Privileges

Privileges are activities that an authorized user is entitled to perform after securing access to an information system. These are the rights of an authorized user to perform various functions in the system. Privileges can be associated with a group of users or even with a single user and are closely linked with the access management system. More often than not when the user is authenticated, the applicable privileges are assigned.

Maker-Checker

The maker-checker control is a standard feature of financial transactions as well as processes involving creating new users on a system. In all such cases, a user initiates the process, that is, enters all data required to create a new user, and then the process supervisor reviews and approves it. It is only after approval that the process is completed and information recorded in the system.

Communication Software

Communication involves transmission of data from one point to another involving either a computer or communication hardware like switches and routers. In a telecommunication system, communication software performs major functions, including starting and stopping the network, changing the network configuration, allocating network resources, and handling functions of the network. Such software is often built into a system and may also be externally deployed. Many kinds of communication hardware also come with built-in software that is used to set up the equipment.

Switches

Network switches are physical devices that connect various components of a network. All the network components connect themselves with the switch and the switch manages all information requests that emerge from one component and are addressed to another component.

Routers

A router is a device in the network that forwards a data packet to another network component or to the destination that is connected to the router. Every data packet sent on the network comes with a target address, in the form of an IP address, and the routers determine the path to take. This is achieved by the host router querying the connected network components, including other routers, about the destination address and then forwarding the packet to the link that has responded positively. A router needs at least two networks to be present.

Database Management Systems

One of the most valuable information assets, a database is a collection of information that may be retrieved according to specified criteria. Though a database management system is a part of application software, considering its importance in the hierarchy of information assets, it should be identified independently. The following three additional controls are useful to protect databases from unauthorized access, modification, or destruction:

1. Database management systems controls must ensure that updating and retrieval of information preserve information integrity. There may be a need to align this with transaction control wherein the transaction privileges are used to define the right to update and retrieve.
2. Concurrency control should be established for shared databases, which defines whether users are allowed concurrent access to the database.
3. Physical and logical access control to information resources should restrict access to information management systems, applications, and other assets.

ELEMENTS OF SOFTWARE SECURITY

Software security may be ensured through five major controls, which are access control, operational control, protection against malicious software, information backup, and operator's log. These controls may be implemented over the following three phases:

1. Security implemented during design of software, wherein the designer apprehends threats that the software is likely to face and provides safety controls.

2. Security implemented for control over access and processing, wherein the user presents appropriate credentials to the software before the software carries out the request.
3. Operational controls, including those to be implemented during change and problem management. These controls seek to ensure that the desired level of security is maintained after completion of a major change request.

We will now discuss the broad types of controls identified earlier.

Access Control

Various aspects of access control that an information systems auditor needs to look into would include the following thirteen items:

1. **User access management:** Formal procedures should be in place to manage the entire process from allocation to revocation of access rights to information systems assets across all stages in the asset life cycle.
2. **Privilege management:** The allocation and use of privileges should be restricted and controlled through a formal authorization process. The process must provide for escalation and de-escalation of privileges based on specific need. Such situations often arise due to prolonged absence of the authorized user and during disaster, when quick response is necessary.
3. **User password management:** Passwords, being the most common tool of validating user identity, should have a formal management process governing their creation and allocation. Passwords should not be stored in an unprotected form. Other supplemental techniques such as biometric identification, hardware tokens, and the like should be considered for access to critical systems.
4. **Network access control:** This control ensures that users with access to networks and network services do not compromise the security of these network services. This not only involves access control but includes privilege management. Successful implementation of network access control requires an effective privilege management system.
5. **Operating system access control:** Operating system access control should be used to prevent unauthorized access to computer resources. These controls should be capable of the following:
   a. Recognizing and verifying identity of user and, if necessary, identity of the terminal or location.
   b. Recording successful and failed access requests received from all users.
   c. Providing appropriate means for authentication. Where password control system is used, the quality standard for passwords should be defined. The quality standard will include specifying the minimum number of characters the password must have, the composition of the password in terms of numbers and text, a compulsory change of password after a specific duration, and so forth.

d. Restricting connection time of users, depending on the nature of work performed, whereby the chance of leaving a logged-in system unattended is reduced. For example, in bank ATMs, after a specific time the user is requested either to log in again or to confirm whether more time is necessary to complete the function.

6. **Terminal log-on procedures:** A secured log-on system should control access to information services. The log-on procedure should not assist in information harvesting and disclose the least information about the system and authentication procedure. If a system requires a number of credentials to secure a login, it would be difficult for an intruder to enter the system and harvest information on access credentials.

7. **User identification and authentication:** All users of information systems should have a unique identity for their individual use to establish ownership of functions they perform on the system. User IDs ideally should not provide any indication of the associated privilege level, such as "administrator," "manager," or "supervisor." The auditor should confirm if such user IDs were part of the standard configuration provided by the vendor and wherever possible whether they were changed.

8. **Use of system utilities:** Most computer installations use system utility programs that can override system and application controls. The potential abuse of these utilities warrants a restricted and controlled procedure authorizing their use. Common examples of such applications include those that allow direct access to a database instead of routing through the application software.

9. **Terminal timeout:** Inactive terminals should be designed to shut down after a defined period of inactivity. After elapse of a scheduled duration of inactivity, any display on the terminal screen should be cleared and applications closed. This control is critical for sensitive applications and locations.

10. **Limitation of connection time:** High-risk applications should be provided with a limited duration of access beyond which the connection would be closed, requiring fresh log-in and authentication. This control reduces the window of opportunity for unauthorized access.

11. **Application access control:** Access to application systems must be restricted to authorized users. Controls that can be established include the following:
    a. Controls that ensure adherence to access control policy. In case the application system is supplied by a vendor and is nonconforming to the organizational policy, supplementary controls like physical access control and allied may be introduced to bridge the security gap.
    b. Protection against unauthorized access by any utility or operating system software that can potentially override system and application controls.
    c. Additional controls wherever resources are shared with other systems.

12. **Information access restriction:** Information access by the application system is to be restricted in accordance with business application requirements and information access policy. The application system connects to a database and is often

the gateway to data entry and retrieval from the database. The information systems auditor must ensure that users who are otherwise not eligible to have access to the information should not be able to retrieve such information by using the application software.

13. **Sensitive system isolation:** Sensitive systems ideally should be provided with a dedicated and isolated computing environment, commensurate with the sensitivity and criticality of the asset. If necessary, a dedicated system may be provided for sensitive applications that would share resources only with other trusted application systems. Sensitivity of a system refers to criticality of the system in view of the security.

Information Harvesting

Information harvesting refers to the act of collecting relevant information about a system for attack by a cybercriminal. The criminal collects such information to be able to build a profile of an identified authorized user and then attempts to secure access by posing as one. A common use of the technique is help-desk-based frauds in which the criminal collects information about an authorized user and then uses it for identification. On successful identification, the help desk operator shares intimate information about the target with the cybercriminals.

Operational Controls

Information systems auditors are required to review operational controls as an integral aspect of software security. Operational controls are mostly built-in as a component of application control. Two control techniques that are commonly used are the following:

1. **Completeness control techniques:** These techniques are used for controlling accuracy and include:

   a. **Automated matching:** Automated matching is a control technique wherein accuracy of input and processing is verified by the program using corroborative evidence available in the system. Naturally, in the absence of such evidence, an automated matching process cannot be implemented. A common application of this is evident when we type in the name of an airport while buying an airline ticket online. As we type in the name, the system progressively takes us to the exact match.

   b. **Batch totals:** This control compares manually computed batch totals that have been entered in the system with system-computed totals of the same elements. This control establishes accuracy of input, processing, and output. A common example of this control is found in some e-commerce websites where, after identifying the products we wish to buy, we are asked to enter the total amount we are paying. This is verified with the total value of the purchases made as computed by the portal.

   c. **Substantive check:** This control calls for checking of select data, usually those that are critical, with original input documents. For example, as in the earlier example, the total purchase value would be considered critical.

2. **Programmed edit checks:** Programmed procedures can be used to check the accuracy of data. The most common types of programmed edit checks include the following:

   a. **Reasonableness checks:** These are checks to verify whether the object data falls within predetermined parameters, for example, if the date of inbound travel is after the date of outbound travel.

   b. **Dependency checks:** This control tests whether contents of two or more data elements or fields on a transaction bear the correct logical relationship. This can be very useful to evaluate processing accuracy. For example, in cases of a discount being allowed to senior citizens, the discount rate provided will have to be validated by the age provided.

   c. **Existence checks:** This input control checks whether codes provided to identify a data element are available in the system. Often the control design prevents any erroneous entry by forcing the user to select an option from a list instead of entering it through the keyboard. This control can be seen in action while typing in the name of an airport on an online travel site.

   d. **Format checks:** These check whether the input is in the format necessary for processing. This may include verifying whether the data item is numeric, or a date, and so forth.

   e. **Mathematical accuracy checks:** This checks the calculations performed during processing of data.

   f. **Range checks:** These input and output controls check whether a value falls within a predefined range, for example, making an advance booking for a concert ticket from an online site where the tickets are sold only a specific number of days ahead of the show.

   g. **Check digit verification:** A check digit is designed to prevent an incorrect but valid match during input. The numbers are constructed in such a way that one of the digits bears a relationship to the other digits. This tool is often extended to text data. For example, the tax registration number may begin with the first letter of the surname of the assessee.

   h. **Document reconciliation:** This control technique is often used in online systems and involves checking the mathematical accuracy of entry of numerical data. For example, the total payment due shown in the payment gateway is reconciled with the cost of individual purchases made on another section of the website.

   i. **Prior data matching:** This validation technique is used for control of master file data amendments.

j. **Prerecorded input:** Errors frequently arise during input of a transaction. By preprinting or populating certain information fields, these errors can be reduced. For example, the tax registration number can be prerecorded in the invoice generation software.

k. **Audit trail:** The audit trail of the input system must record for every action committed on the application system information regarding the origin, contents, time of input, and other factors. The operations audit trail in the input system will record the resources used to process the data.

l. **Exception reports:** This control examines input and output data against a reference file and reports items that appear incorrect or out of the ordinary. The scope of the control may be beyond the data and include access controls. One of the common examples is access to a dormant bank account. It may be noted that exception reports are not analogous to error reports. Exception reports list those actions that are not ordinarily performed in the system and require special authorization. The exception report makes it difficult to exercise those special rights surreptitiously.

Protection against Malicious Software

The information systems auditor needs to be satisfied about the precautions taken to prevent and detect the introduction of malicious software, including viruses, malware, and so on, that have a potential to compromise data integrity and confidentiality, and even trigger the disruption of normal functioning. Controls are to be in place to detect and prevent its introduction. The following six controls should be considered:

1. Formal policy on induction of new software in the system with a specific focus on licencing and a zero-tolerance policy toward the installation of unauthorized software.
2. Formal policy on approving an external source as "trusted" and permitting subsequent acceptance of data from it for further processing in the system.
3. Installation and regular updating and upgrading of antivirus and antimalware software.
4. Defining a virus attack as a business continuity issue and training employees on recognition, containment, and resumption of normal functioning in the face of such attack.
5. Periodic review to identify installations and usage of unauthorized software.
6. Existence of a process for threat awareness, vulnerability assessment, and training.

Information Backup

The information systems auditor must verify the recoverability of all essential business information, software, and systems in the wake of a disaster. This may be ensured by implementing and maintaining adequate, effective, and efficient backup facilities. As a matter of abundant caution, multiple generations or cycles of backup information may be retained. However, this requirement may be complemented by maintaining multiple copies of recent backups that have been tested for completeness and recoverability. Backup media should be stored in an adequately secured environment different from that where the main data center is located. Such a location should ideally be set far enough away to ensure that both locations are not exposed to similar natural threats.

One of the neglected areas in backup processes is the restoration procedure. These procedures must be regularly checked and tested to ensure achievement of the target recovery objective. Every organization must define the retention period for business information and requirements for archiving, keeping in view the legal and business needs.

Operator's Log

Operational staff should maintain a log of their activities, which should generally include the following four items:

1. System boot and shut-down time.
2. System errors reported and corrective actions taken.
3. Audit trail to establish correct handling of data files and computer outputs.
4. Identity of person making the log entry, in case the log is maintained manually.

 **CONTROL ISSUES DURING INSTALLATION AND MAINTENANCE**

One of the activities that exposes an information system to severe compromise is installation and maintenance. The information systems auditor must be familiar with software procurement and implementation policies and practices of the auditee to understand the practices adopted during the installation and maintenance phase. The auditor should acquire the following information before commencing an audit of this area:

▪ Information technology infrastructure and environment.
▪ Resources available in the information technology department.
▪ Software products procured, externally or internally, and implemented during the period under audit.
▪ Status of the implementation of ongoing projects.
▪ Postimplementation problems, if any.
▪ Transaction processing errors, if any.
▪ Processing or implementation errors resulting in financial loss, reputation loss, regulatory noncompliance, and so on.

To review security during software implementation and maintenance activities, the information systems auditor must be well-versed with the following:

- Requirement identification and analysis process leading to procurement or modification of software.
- Software product and vendor selection criteria used by the auditee.
- Vendor selection process observed by the auditee.
- Contracting processes, practice, and agreement templates used by the auditee.
- Implementation practice adopted by the auditee.

The information systems auditor should examine the response of the auditee to the following questions to develop an opinion on the readiness of the auditee to preserve security of information assets during the implementation and maintenance phase. These questions are segregated over preimplementation and postimplementation issues.

Preimplementation Issues

1. Does the implementation plan cover data migration from a previous system?
2. Does the implementation plan address the following?
   a. Involvement and role of user departments
   b. Training needs covering user, system administration, acceptance testing, and others
   c. Role of the vendor, including terms and duration of support
   d. Adequacy of information systems infrastructure and development requirements
3. Is there an analysis of the risk involved in the implementation phase and mitigation strategy?
4. Are appropriate functional departments responsible for accuracy of key parameters and static data?
5. Have the physical areas that need to be accessed by the vendor during the implementation phase been identified?
6. Is it planned, wherever possible, to have a test environment to develop familiarization during the implementation process?
7. Is there a system of documenting errors identified during the implementation phase along with a procedure of vendor notification and root cause analysis?
8. Is there a system of separating operational and design flaws with a procedure of escalating the design flaws to senior management of software vendors and comparing the same with the request for proposal?
9. Are test packs developed by user groups, especially for testing customization, and are results of the test run verified by the same user group?
10. Is there a defined process for data integration when software is implemented?
11. Are test results properly documented?
12. Have system documents been changed appropriately to reflect customization?

13. Have all documents, including system documentation, data dictionary, installation manual, and user manual been handed over to the auditee by the vendor?
14. Are there proper archival systems for critical documents, especially in remote locations, to ensure retrieval in the event of a disaster?
15. Is a formal acceptance certificate signed by the user department and supervisor issued, marking the end of the implementation phase?

Postimplementation Issues

1. Whether required consequential action has been taken for backups and disaster recovery to reflect the altered environment.
2. Whether the information technology department has reassessed, if necessary, the database controls in consultation with user department.
3. Whether a problem-tracking system complete with escalation procedure and resolution recording has been implemented.
4. Whether vendor support is aligned with agreed service levels.
5. Whether responsibility for managing access to the system, backup, and enforcing database controls is assigned to identified individual.

LICENSING ISSUES

The information systems auditor must observe whether the auditee uses any unlicensed software or whether usage is beyond terms of the license granted by the vendor. The auditor needs to be satisfied on both of the following counts:

1. Only licensed or authorized software is used.
2. Conditions of the license agreements are met.

These assertions may be verified by reviewing the physical control of software inventory and periodic auditing of the information systems. It may be noted that as software is being increasingly sold with an option to download from the vendor website, instead of being delivered on a disk, for example, the physical control against installation of unauthorized software is being replaced by an access control.

Software licensing is a vital area that draws the special attention of an information systems auditor. The criteria for verification may be based on the size and complexity of computers. The auditor should note the following eight areas:

1. The kind of license being used for multiuser software:
   a. Site license
   b. Per-server license
   c. Per–personal computer license
   d. Number-of-users license

2. The maximum number of concurrent users on the system. Often the purchase of network-based software licenses depends on the number of employees who would use the software simultaneously.
3. In a client-server environment, it is a practice to buy a single copy of the software program and obtain a client license for each of the workstations. The server distributes floating licenses when a request is received from the client. The auditor needs to confirm usage to the terms of the licence.
4. Insurance requirements of the software and hardware devices.
5. Documented software reproduction rights and limitations.
6. Computer virus damage detection and prevention requirements.
7. Notification of unauthorized use, possession, or distribution of software.
8. Software and hardware maintenance requirements.

The auditee should ideally have a software antipiracy policy to protect it from legal action against the use of pirated software by an employee. The policy should include the following seven directives:

1. Prohibiting unauthorized access to software.
2. Prohibiting illegal copying and use of software.
3. Developing a software inventory and comparing the same with purchase orders and original diskettes, wherever physical copies were obtained.
4. Making illegal copying of software a ground for punitive action and employee dismissal.
5. Prohibiting copying of internally developed software.
6. Requiring all employees to sign a declaration committing not to use, bring, or install any illegal software into the organization.
7. Periodic checking to ensure no illegal software is copied into the system.

PROBLEM AND CHANGE MANAGEMENT

The information systems auditor must be satisfied on the existence of problem and change management control for software applications and related processes. To prevent unauthorized changes in the production environment, it is necessary to have a formal change control procedure that governs all changes, irrespective of whether they are major or minor, scheduled or emergency. The information systems auditor must examine existence of the following five practices as a part of change control procedure:

1. A formal change request and authorization process.
2. A testing and system acceptance procedure for each change.
3. A procedure for scheduling and documenting all approved change requests.
4. A method whereby all change procedures are accompanied with a defined and documented backup procedure, to allow restoration and rollback in the event of implementation failure.

5. A formal process of escalation of privileges that may be necessary to facilitate change and subsequent deescalation. Inappropriate use of such system privileges is a major contributory factor to the failure and breach of information systems security.

In any multiuser systems, allocation of privileges is controlled through a formal authorization process. The information systems auditor should confirm that the authorization process includes the following six best practices, unless not applicable:

1. Privileges are associated with each system component such as operating system, database management system, and each application.
2. Categories of staff who are granted such privileges are explicitly identified.
3. Privileges are allocated strictly on a need-to-use basis, ensuring that these are the minimum requirement for performing their functional role.
4. Privilege escalations are made on an event-by-event basis to facilitate performance of functions allotted to the individual.
5. Privileges are granted only after the prescribed authorization process is complete and the event is properly documented, even when the privilege request is turned down.
6. In case of multiple roles, special privileges are assigned to each additional user ID that is different from the user ID used for normal business.

4

Information Systems Audit Requirements

I N THIS CHAPTER WE discuss the critical requirements of an information systems audit in terms of both input and delivery. After reading this chapter, you should develop a comprehensive understanding of the general scope of an information systems audit, types of evidences, and areas that an information systems auditor must focus on.

RISK ANALYSIS

The scope of an information systems audit includes verifying the existence and performance of controls. The selection of the controls to test remains a critical decision for the information systems auditor and will have a major role in determining the quality of the audit. In order to ensure adequate coverage of testing, the auditor is required to prioritize testing of controls. Prioritization essentially depends on the corresponding loss exposure to the auditee in the event of the failure of a specific control. The likelihood of a control failing, and even being activated, is uncertain. This calls for a risk analysis exercise on the part of the auditor. Risk is the likelihood that the entity would face a vulnerability being exploited or a threat becoming harmful. Vulnerability is the inherent weaknesses of a system or process that can be exploited by a threat. Threats stand for uncertain events that can cause loss to the entity. The threats exploit the gap between the level of protection necessary and the degree of protection achieved. Once an entity is aware of the potential loss, it decides on a risk mitigation strategy. The likelihood of the risk resulting in an unfavorable exposure may be so low that the entity may decide to keep the risk unmitigated. On the other hand, in extreme cases the cost of mitigating a risk may be so high that the entity may opt to accept it. The information systems auditor keeps the risk strategy in mind while conducting the information systems audit.

People, processes, systems, and external events are all potential hazards to operations in an entity. Inadequacy or failure of any one of them can result in events that may cause loss. The loss may not always be described in monetary terms but may involve intangibles such as loss of reputation.

It must be noted that risks may materialize for various reasons. From the perspective of information systems audit, we are concerned only when these risks materialize because of failure of a control in the information systems. Risk factors inherent in business operations include the following nine examples:

1. **Access risk,** referring to the risk of an unauthorized user securing access to information assets.
2. **Business disruption risk,** or the risk of nonavailability of services from information systems resources.
3. **Credit risk,** such as the failure of a counterparty honoring their payment obligation.
4. **Customer service risk,** referring to the risk of customers being deprived of services.
5. **Data integrity risk,** or the risk of a possible compromise of data integrity that may arise for various reasons, including unauthorized access.
6. **Financial/external report misstatement risk,** referring to the risk that reports prepared by the entity contain misstatements and errors.
7. **Fraud risk,** referring to the risk of losses arising out of fraud committed using information systems resources.
8. **Legal and regulatory risk,** referring to risk of noncompliance to legal and regulatory requirements and consequences thereof.
9. **Physical harm risk,** referring to the risk of suffering from bodily harm.

The auditor needs to understand how control failure in information systems can lead to a vulnerable environment. In order to successfully conduct risk analysis, we need to understand the concepts of threats, vulnerabilities, exposure, likelihood, and attack in an information system.

THREATS, VULNERABILITY, EXPOSURE, LIKELIHOOD, AND ATTACK

Understanding threat, vulnerability, exposure, likelihood, and attack forms the basis of an information systems audit requirement.

- A **threat** is the potential event that could exploit vulnerability in a system, leading to the entity being exposed to chances of suffering a loss. The harm to an information system may be in the form of a compromise in the confidentiality, integrity, or availability of an information systems resource.
- **Vulnerability** is the weakness in the system that can potentially be exploited by threats. The weakness may be in design, technology, implementation, or any other aspect of the information systems assets. For example, a poor access control method—the vulnerability—may allow a hacker—the threat—to obtain illegitimate access—the risk. Extent of safeguards implemented often determines the level of vulnerability. Determining vulnerabilities involves security evaluation of the system, including inspection of safeguards implemented, testing their response, and conducting penetration analysis.
- **Exposure** is the extent of loss an entity is likely to face when a risk materializes. The loss may not be restricted to the immediate future but may also occur in the long run. Examples of loss include loss of business, loss of reputation, compromise of privacy, and even injury or loss of human life.
- **Likelihood** is an estimation of the probability that the threat will attempt to exploit the vulnerability and, upon being able to successfully exploit it, cause loss to the entity. The presence and strengths of threats, and the effectiveness of safeguards, influence the likelihood of the threat successfully exploiting the vulnerability.
- **Attack** is the act of the threat seeking to exploit the vulnerability through a set of actions to compromise confidentiality, integrity, and availability of an information systems asset. Attacks seek to overcome the safeguards and controls implemented by the auditee. The extent to which the safeguards are compromised by the attack will determine the extent of consequential loss.

INFORMATION SYSTEMS CONTROL OBJECTIVES

Information assets have a value in the entity and are required to be suitably protected. In fact, in light of the growing importance of intellectual property in commerce, there is an increased awareness about the value of information assets. This is more relevant in service industries, where the majority of the services provided are essentially information driven.

Information security has the following three characteristics:

1. **Confidentiality:** Ensuring accessibility only to those authorized to have access.
2. **Integrity:** Ensuring that information is accurate and complete throughout the cycle of input, processing, and output.
3. **Availability:** Ensuring need-based access to information for all authorized users.

In order to ensure that security of information systems is preserved, the entity needs to ensure that usage of information systems assets and related processes, whether computerized or manual, is governed by an internal control system. Information systems control objectives include the following:

- Safeguarding information systems assets
- Compliance with corporate policies, and regulatory and legal requirements
- Assuring system reliability
- Maintaining data integrity
- Assuring system security
- Assuring system availability
- Maintaining system controllability
- Assuring system maintainability
- Assuring system usability
- Assuring system effectiveness
- Maintaining system economy and efficiency
- Maintaining system quality

INFORMATION SYSTEMS AUDIT OBJECTIVES

The goal of an information systems audit is to achieve the following nine objectives:

1. Ensure adequacy and effectiveness of internal controls.
2. Ensure that resources are allocated to constituents of information systems in an efficient and effective manner.
3. Provide assurance that systems-related assets are safeguarded.
4. Ensure that information is accurate, available on request, and reliable.
5. Provide reasonable assurance that all errors, omissions, and irregularities are prevented, detected, corrected, and reported.
6. Review the systems to ensure compliance to policies, procedures, standards, and legal requirements.
7. Review application and operation systems to ensure that needs of the users are met, necessary compliances are achieved, audit trails are incorporated, documentation is completed, and systems data integrity and security are maintained.
8. Identify and recognize potential threats that can compromise confidentiality, integrity, and availability of information assets.
9. Ensure that management takes appropriate detective, corrective, and preventive actions.

SYSTEM EFFECTIVENESS AND EFFICIENCY

During the course of information systems audit, an auditor is often required to comment on the effectiveness and efficiency of a system. An information systems auditor is required to know the difference between the two, which is described below.

1. Effectiveness evaluation determines whether the system is achieving its objectives and whether the system should be continued, modified, upgraded, or scrapped. Effectiveness analysis may be done at the design stage to ensure that user needs are being fulfilled and the system is achieving its implementation objectives.
2. Efficiency of a system is reflected by usage of the minimum amount of resources to achieve its objectives. The resources may be of different kinds, including machine time, peripherals, system software, application software, and human resources.

 ## INFORMATION SYSTEMS ABUSE

Information systems abuse may manifest itself in various ways. This may include the following:

1. **Destruction of assets:** Hardware, software, networking infrastructure, data, facilities, documentation, files, and so forth may be destroyed.
2. **Theft of assets:** Illegal removal of hardware, software, data, documentation, or peripherals may take place.
3. **Modification of assets:** Unauthorized access and modification of hardware, software, data, or documentation may affect safeguarding and security of information systems assets. Often unauthorized modification of assets may lead to unknown incompatibility with other components, which can seriously compromise functionality of the system.
4. **Privacy violation:** Privacy of data relating to a person or an organization may be compromised, which could have a far-reaching impact, including loss of business. One of the most common examples is compromise of confidentiality of customer data.
5. **Disruption of operations:** Day-to-day operations of the information systems functions may be disturbed, and at the extreme this could temporarily disrupt the working of the entire system.
6. **Unauthorized use of assets:** Hardware, software, data, facilities, documentation, peripherals, or supplies may be used for unauthorized purposes that may cause losses to the organization. A common example is the unauthorized download of music or a movie, creating a network load and slowing down network performance for legitimate usage.

Activities that could result in any of the above or similar incidents would be considered as threats to information systems and the auditee's organization must have safeguarding mechanisms in place to prevent such occurrences.

ASSET SAFEGUARDING OBJECTIVE AND PROCESS

One of the primary problems associated with safeguarding information assets is identification of the same. With increased usage of distant computing facilities and wide-area networks, the information assets are spread across geographical boundaries. The problem of identification is accentuated by the fact that often these assets are intangible in nature. The task of having an information systems asset safeguarding mechanism in place involves a series of functions and procedures, including the following four areas:

1. **Compiling a functional information technology asset list:** All information technology systems assets used to perform various functions in an organization are to be listed, regardless of whether those systems are managed by the user department or by the information technology department. Special note should be made of mission-critical functions and assets.
2. **Information technology systems detailing:** Detailed information includes names of hardware, software, network platform, applications with vendor details, installation location, year of installation, major upgrade history, and so forth.
3. **Asset safeguarding:** This process focuses on whether information systems assets could be used or have been used for unauthorized purposes and the consequent losses that have occurred or could have occurred. It is important to identify events that might not have caused any loss but potentially could have. These create increased awareness about possible future loss events and the organization can take preventive steps.
4. **Assigning probabilities:** The entity needs to assign probabilities to different losses that could arise out of failure or a compromise of safeguarding mechanisms of the information assets. Assignment of probabilities may be based on past experience. Opinion of experts may also be used as a basis for determining such probability. Independent probabilities can be assigned to various magnitudes of loss and a singular value for estimated loss may be computed.

CASE STUDY

A company seeks to find out the expected loss arising out of the failure of an internal network. Based on past experience, it was believed that there is a 50 percent probability that an event involving losses amounting to 1 million currency units will take place. Similarly the respective probability of loss events of magnitudes of currency units of 2 million, 5 million, 8 million, and 10 million are 20, 15, 10, and 5 percent, respectively. The expected value of loss can be computed in the manner shown in Table 4.1.

TABLE 4.1 Computation of Expected Loss

Probability	Loss Amount	Expected Loss
A	B	C = A × B
50%	1,000,000	500,000
20%	2,000,000	400,000
15%	5,000,000	750,000
10%	8,000,000	800,000
5%	10,000,000	500,000
Expected value of loss		2,950,000

Expected value of loss is the sum total of the weighted loss. Individual weighted loss is the product of probability and loss amount. Please note that the sum total of value of probability assigned to various scenarios will add up to 100 percent.

EVIDENCE COLLECTION AND EVALUATION

An area of concern for an information systems auditor is collection of evidence during audit. Very often internal controls used in the information systems are built into the system. For example, a bank teller will not get payment authorization against a presented check if the available balance is not sufficient. This internal control is built into the application software. Consequently, auditors have to interact with the system to collect necessary evidence of the existence and efficiency of internal controls. The auditor has to evaluate whether a control is acting reliably, and assess impact of its functioning through the system. It may be noted that the evidence in case of information systems auditors would reflect in terms of working of the system and processes and not necessarily in terms of financial impact. Though the information systems auditor may use the same set of tools and techniques that are employed by the financial auditor for the purpose of extracting data, the scope of application of these tools will be quite different.

It must be appreciated that the financial system is intensely connected with the information systems in almost all organizations. Thus there can always be certain controls that perform a dual role in terms of satisfying the control requirements of both financial systems and information systems. In other words, the financial systems audit can supplement the information systems audit, and vice versa.

Techniques of Audit Evidence Collection

Various techniques may be used by the information systems auditor to gather audit evidence, including the following five methods:

1. Reviewing organization structure, documentation, standards, and practices.
2. Interviewing appropriate personnel and observing processing and operations.
3. Using audit documentation techniques such as flowcharts, questionnaires, system narratives, decision trees, decision tables, and control grids.
4. Applying analytical review procedures and sampling techniques.
5. Using software tools to analyze logs and audit trails built into the system.

Categories of Audit Evidence

An information systems auditor may select the appropriate methodology for collection of evidence from the 10 categories listed below:

1. **Physical examination:** Physical inspection for presence of tangible information systems assets. The information systems auditor may physically count and inspect for the presence of kinds of computer equipment, such as terminals, printers, and so forth.
2. **Confirmation:** A response from an independent third party, mostly written and provided at the request of the auditor, verifying a fact or the accuracy of information.
3. **Documentation:** Examination of documents and records to substantiate information, especially those involving the designing and functioning of software and network. For example, a review of service agreements will substantiate the service entitlement claims made by the auditee.
4. **Observation:** This involves observing the conduct of specific activities. For example the auditor may verify whether a particular operation is performed under dual control. Observations usually require corroborative evidence to be substantiated.
5. **Inquiry:** Herein evidences are created through obtaining written and oral information from the auditee against specific queries. Additional corroborating evidence is required since the responding person is not an independent entity.
6. **Processing accuracy:** Processing accuracy involves rechecking a sample of activities performed by the auditee for confirming processing accuracy. For example, an information systems auditor can test processing accuracy of computations with use of appropriate software, observing logs, or by reviewing data in certain fields in the object data file.
7. **Screenshots:** The auditor may take screenshots of errors that are observed during the audit. Various operating systems provide different methodologies to obtain the screenshot.

8. **Log files:** Access logs, transaction logs, fault logs, and other audit trails provide corroborative evidence to errors.
9. **Testing software results:** Where software has been used for testing, for example, network security testing, the output reports generated by such software provide evidence of errors in the system.
10. **Analytical procedures:** These involve the use of comparisons and relationships to determine the reasonableness of the processes and activities being audited. For example, an information systems auditor may examine the number of times during two audit periods that accounts were locked out because of inaccurate passwords and form an opinion on whether there has been an increased attempt of access violation.

LOGS AND AUDIT TRAILS AS EVIDENCE

An information systems auditor may use audit trails and system logs as evidence. These are discussed next.

Audit Trails

Audit trails are records of an activity that can be used to reconstruct the performance of the activity. An audit trail is essentially a detective control, but it can also be designed to act as a preventive control.

1. For adequacy of audit trails in the system, one may ensure the presence of audit trails, at least under the following circumstances:
   a. When access is granted to a sensitive information asset.
   b. When network services are accessed.
   c. When override system controls are used.
   d. When unsuccessful attempts are made to access sensitive information or use network services.
2. Wherever practical, audit trails should be able to perform at least the following:
   a. Identify the user.
   b. Identify the functions performed, and the resources and information used or changed.
   c. Provide a date and time stamp, including time zone to establish the local time.
   d. Record address of the workstation accesses and network paths used.
   e. List specific transaction committed or program executed.
3. An audit trail can be designed to act as a preventive control to generate a real-time alarm for significant security-related events, including the following:
   a. Attempt to violate access control rules.
   b. Attempts to initiate processes or access information that are not authorized for the privilege level of the user.

c. Attempt to secure multiple log-on from different workstations especially when such log-on is prohibited.
d. Attempt to make changes in the security profile to grant unauthorized privileges.

In order that audit trails are effective as detective and preventive controls, the entity should perform management reviews of the audit trail information on a regular basis. Audit trail information must be preserved for an appropriate period of time, matching business and legal requirements.

AUDIT TRAIL

A view of an audit trail from Microsoft Windows is shown in Figure 4.1. You can see this for yourself by clicking on the "Event Viewer" option under "Administrative Tools," found in the "Control Panel" icon.

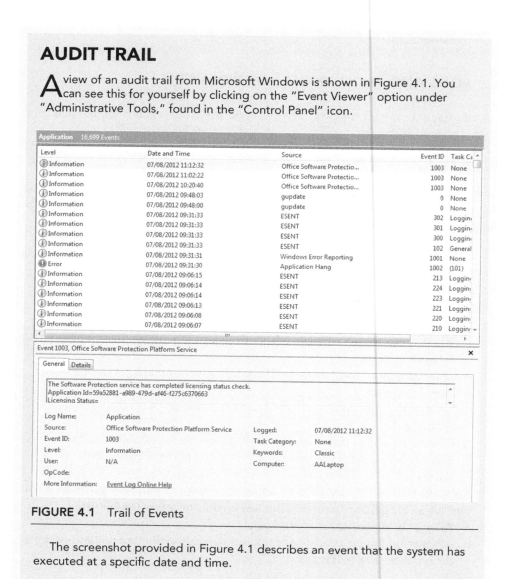

FIGURE 4.1   Trail of Events

The screenshot provided in Figure 4.1 describes an event that the system has executed at a specific date and time.

System Logs

Four system logs that are useful to the information systems auditor are listed here:

1. **Control total verification:** Control totals such as record counts, line item counts, financial totals, quantity totals, and hash totals, for example, of account numbers, can be used to verify the accuracy of input, processing, and output.
2. **Transaction logs:** Transaction logs act as a processing control and provide an audit trail. They are useful for file reconstruction and error tracing when

ERROR LOG

Figure 4.2 is a screenshot showing detailed information about an error the system had logged.

FIGURE 4.2 Error Log

The bottom part of the screen in Figure 4.2 describes the kind of error encountered by the system.

an error occurs in updating online files. It is very useful in recovering from a disaster.

3. **Operator logs:** Operational staff should independently maintain a log of their activities unless it is automatically maintained by the system. Logs should include, wherever appropriate, at least the following:

   a. System log-in and log-out times.
   b. System errors observed and corrective actions taken.
   c. System-based confirmation of correct handling of data files and computer output.
   d. Name of the person making the log entry.
   e. Result of the comparison of the operator's logs against operating procedures.

4. **Fault logs:** All faults encountered by users or systems should be reported. A log of such events along with corrective actions taken should be maintained. There must be clearly defined rules for handling reported faults, with special focus on the following:

   a. Review of faults logs to verify fault resolution.
   b. Review of corrective measures to verify
      i. Whether controls have been compromised.
      ii. Whether corrective actions taken were authorized.
   c. Analysis of fault logs to decide whether the faults should be included in the risk registers even when they were successfully resolved.

The audit trails generated by the system are an excellent repository of logs. Depending on the extent of details recorded, these logs can also be useful as fault logs.

CHAPTER FIVE

Conducting an Information Systems Audit

I N THIS CHAPTER WE learn about the process of conducting an information systems audit. An overview of an audit program is offered: the plan and procedure, compliance and substantive testing, testing tools, and the process of reporting. An audit workflow is presented in detail at the end of the chapter. This chapter enables us to be in a position to understand how the entire auditing process is conducted.

AUDIT PROGRAM

Preparing an audit program is the first step of conducting an information systems audit. The various activities involved in defining an audit program include the following procedures.

Audit Checklists

Audit checklists are necessary to perform an effective and efficient audit. Audit checklists are essentially lists of various tests that auditors must perform in order to determine whether key controls intended to mitigate significant risks are functioning as designed. The ISecGrade framework involving usage of such checklists is provided in Chapter 12 of this book. Based on the results of the tests performed, the information systems auditor would be able to conclude on the adequacy of controls over a particular process or the system in its entirety.

Resource Planning

Audit programs help the information systems auditor to plan for required resources. After identifying the checklists necessary for conducting the audit, the information systems auditor may proceed to estimate the total number of hours needed to perform the audit. This estimate is based on the expected amount of time required to perform each of the steps mentioned in the audit checklists. Past experience of the auditor is useful while making estimates.

Consistency

The use of audit programs and checklists helps to promote consistency in tests that are performed while auditing a specific process or the entire system from one cycle to the next. Audit programs also promote uniformity in tests performed on common process controls. This allows comparability of reports of two audit events conducted at different points of time.

The audit programs may be grouped into the following six categories based on the information system controls examined by these audit programs:

1. Organization and administration
2. Program maintenance and system development
3. Access to data files and databases
4. Application controls
5. Network controls
6. Continuity of operations
   a. Physical and environmental protection
   b. Physical and logical access control
   c. Personnel policies
   d. Insurance
   e. Backup procedures
   f. Disaster recovery plans

■ AUDIT PLAN

The audit plan is characterized by various activities, which are discussed in the following sections.

Engagement Letter

At the planning stage the external auditor decides whether the engagement should be accepted. If the decision is to accept the engagement, the auditor is required to obtain an engagement letter that clearly defines the scope of the assignment. It must be noted that an information systems audit may cover a wide area of operations and activities across several information assets. The information systems auditor makes an assessment of the audit risk involved and considers whether to accept the audit assignment. The engagement letter must include the following:

1. **Information processes to be audited:** This will specify the scope of the audit in terms of processes involved. For example, the audit may involve reviewing a software either in its entirety, such as an enterprise resource planning solution, or by examining only a specific process, such as security controls of an enterprise resource planning solution.
2. **Information assets to be covered:** Any information system process may involve multiple information assets. The audit engagement should specify the assets to be included in the scope of the audit. For example, an audit may encompass security of an entire data center or only the security of data exchange with external agencies.
3. **Object of the audit:** An audit is ultimately an expression of opinion by the auditor. Thus the terms of engagement should specify which aspects of information system are required to be commented upon. For example, the audit may involve expressing an opinion on the security aspect of systems or on conformity with expressed capabilities.

Audit Risk

Audit risk is the risk of the auditor providing an opinion that is incorrect in view of the existing facts and has come about because the evidences did not surface during the sample check made by the auditor. All auditors face this risk and should they feel that the chances of such wrong opinion are high, they may refuse the engagement.

Inherent Business Risks

Inherent business risks are the risks that are inherent to any business and process and remain unmitigated irrespective of all risk mitigation measures taken. An entity has to accept these risks in order to use the process. For example, hacking is a risk that all online information assets are exposed to. No matter what technology-driven mitigants are used to reduce the possibility of the threat materializing, this threat will always be there. If the auditee is not willing to accept this risk, online presence will have to be discontinued.

(Continued)

> ## Control Risk
>
> All entities employ a host of techniques to ensure that processes are within the level of their target operating efficiency. These controls are designed to reduce the possibility of a threat exploiting vulnerability and inflicting damage. There is a risk of the control failing or having an inadequate design. For example, every online information system uses access control as a management control against unauthorized access. The ability of an intruder to compromise the access system is an example of control failure.

Background Overview

The auditor looks into the background information about the client, the legal obligations, the business, and the industry. The auditor understands the objectives of the assignment, obtains background information, assigns appropriate staff, and identifies the areas of audit risk. Analytical review procedures are performed to understand the client business, the relationship of data, and the risk involved in the audit. The auditor needs to have special emphasis on the history of the information technology infrastructure of the client. Recent additions to the information assets, migration from one platform to another, or major upgrades are instances that will require the auditor to enhance the variety and scope of testing procedures.

Materiality Level

Materiality level is set after making a decision about the level of desired or acceptable audit risk. Some areas and some units may be more susceptible to errors, irregularities, ineffectiveness, and inefficiencies. The underlying factor influencing the degree of materiality is the sensitivity of the object of audit to functioning of the entire process. If tolerance level is set high, that would mean that the process is more tolerant to deviations from expected. This might include instances of using printing paper not conforming to exact dimensions specified. If a process has low tolerance level, or a low materiality threshold, even a small deviation is considered significant. Failure of power backup to supply power in the event of power failure is an example of processes with low tolerance. The auditee may have a zero-tolerance policy for critical functions and statutory requirements.

Techniques Used for Information Systems Planning

Various techniques used by the auditors include audit area selection, simulation and modeling, scoring, and competency center.

- **Audit area selection:** This technique is applicable in multilocational complex computer systems. It helps the auditor to identify the areas where the audit would require the maximum attention. This helps to optimize the use of limited resources effectively in potential problem areas. For example, the data center is an area of importance for the audit wherever the auditee uses a centralized operation. Key indicators of business risk and control risks are identified and placed in the form of a matrix. The resource requirement for the audit is compared with available resources, and wherever the latter falls short, specific areas are to be selected for detailed examination. The areas with high business risks and high control risks are what the audit procedures will focus on.

■ **Simulation and modeling:** This audit procedure is used to monitor selected transactions on a continuous basis. A comparison is made between the expected results and the actual results from the process. Expected results are derived by simulation of the process. Differences between the expected and actual results help to identify areas where deviations have taken place. This technique also identifies problem areas that require the auditor's attention. A common application of the technique is monitoring the network load. If the network load is higher than expected on a consistent basis, the auditor will accord a higher priority to review of the same.

■ **Scoring:** In this technique, the characteristics of a computer application system are identified and quantified. A score is awarded for each of the characteristics and a weighted score is derived. A total of the individual weighted scores gives us the score of the system. The ISecGrade methodology described in Chapter 11 of the book explains the scoring technique in detail.

■ **Competency center:** In a computerized system spread over many locations, an alternative technique is the centralized audit approach. The audit is conducted from a centralized location using auditing software and other processes. Other locations are visited on a selective basis to evaluate controls that require physical verification. Multisite audit software is used while adopting this technique. Effective use of this technique requires the computer system at different sites to be same or almost identical, for example, the software used in banks.

AUDIT PROCEDURES AND APPROACHES

Information systems auditors play a major role to identify risks and to evaluate the adequacy of controls in critical information systems in an organization. Various steps involved in an information systems audit process are described next:

1. **Obtain the background information:** Information about the organization, including its operations, work, document flow, and computing system, is obtained by the auditor at the outset of the audit. This background information allows the auditor to form an opinion about the maturity of the system users.

2. **Understanding the controls:** The auditor makes an evaluation of controls, their strengths and weaknesses, and the overall reliability of the system. Administrative controls to maintain data integrity and safeguarding of assets may

even be built into the system. An auditor looks into the design of controls and functional areas to which they relate. Internal controls normally include the following components:

a. **Control environment:** The control environment consists of the management's philosophy, responsibility, and authority assignments, structure and functioning of the audit committee, and methodology of performance measurement and monitoring. Design of control, definition of level of materiality, and sincerity in enforcement of control tools are all dependent on the control environment.

b. **Risk assessment:** It is a process of identification and analysis of risks and exposure of the auditee and ways in which risk can be managed. This assessment will assist the auditor in identifying risk areas with high overall adverse exposure and prioritizing the same in the audit plan.

c. **Control activities:** This includes access, authorization, duties, segregation of jobs, documentation, maintenance, safeguards of assets, checks on performance, and so forth. However, it must be noted that mere existence of controls does not validate whether the internal control system is efficient. Adequacy and effectiveness of the controls also need to be assessed.

d. **Information and communication:** This includes existence of defined roles and responsibilities for information generation and exchange control.

e. **Monitoring:** Continuous monitoring and analysis of operation of internal controls is an integral part of an effective system of internal control. The feedback arising from monitoring activity helps to strengthen the internal control environment.

3. **Developing the audit plan:** Development of an audit plan and audit program to schedule an audit is a critical component of the audit process. Much more than a procedural exercise, as it is often alleged to be, the audit plan defines the boundaries of effectiveness of an audit. An inefficient audit plan is likely to cause an inefficient audit exercise, regardless of the quality of audit staff and process.

4. **Compliance test of controls:** This process involves testing the general controls. Relevant checklists under the ISecGrade framework have been provided in Chapter 12. Compliance reviews and tests provide a reasonable assurance that the system controls are functioning as intended and are in line with the auditee's plans, programs, policies, procedures, standards, guidelines, government laws and regulations, and other regulatory agency requirements.

5. **Use of analytical review procedures:** Various ratios, trends, and relationships among data items may be reviewed using mathematical procedures to identify areas that would require further audit work. Focus of the analytical tests is on various parameters of information system functioning such as network load, connection speed, transaction per second, and allied. The analytical procedure will identify if any parameter is reporting values out of normal range given the activities performed on the information system.

6. **Substantive tests of details of transactions:** The extent of substantive reviews and tests to be performed are designed based on the degree of satisfaction and reliance derived from the results of the compliance tests. This would include review of the authentication devices, application software, database management system, network, utility software, legal compliances, and so forth.

7. **Summary of evidences:** The information systems auditor then summarizes the audit evidence collected during the audit.

8. **Evaluation and opinion:** Upon evaluation of the test results the auditor will form an audit opinion. This will be discussed with the auditee to confirm its acceptance or disagreement. Subsequent to considering the response of the auditee, the auditor will issue the audit report.

 ## SYSTEM UNDERSTANDING AND REVIEW

The auditor should familiarize himself or herself with various components and functions of the information systems and be conversant with how they work. The auditor needs to study various inputs, their flow through the system, the processing of data, and the generation of various outputs.

The focus of the auditor should not be the operating aspects of technology unless that is the audit objective. One of the common errors in an information systems audit is to change the same into a technology audit wherein only the effective usage of technology is evaluated. While this may be one of the areas of examination, the concentration should be on attainment of the information systems objectives, understanding the flow of data, ascertaining control effectiveness, and identifying audit evidence. Information systems audit is to be treated as a management control, and technology should be reviewed as the enabler and not the central theme.

In addition, the auditor needs to perform an overall study of the organization, the operations, the work, the document flow, and the computing system. This study would include assessment of the risks that the auditee is exposed to, threats to the assets, vulnerability to specific threats, likelihood of the threat materializing, and their potential impact. The auditor would need to look into the statutory, regulatory, and contractual requirements that the auditee, its associates, contractors, and outsourced service providers need to satisfy. The auditor also needs to assure conformity with the principles, objectives, and requirements for information processing developed by the entity.

 ## COMPLIANCE REVIEWS AND TESTS

Test of controls: Controls help to prevent and detect errors, omissions, and irregularities and assist in reducing adverse impacts of exposure to risks. Auditors test controls to evaluate whether specific controls are adequate and reliable. Controls may be either general controls or application controls.

The standards, policies, procedures, and guidelines of the auditee entity should be considered at this point as they have an influence on the control structure. The auditor should include the following five areas while conducting compliance review and testing:

1. A study of internal control principles of the auditee, operating and administrative standards for manual and computerized operations, and policies and procedures. Special focus should be provided for activities that have complementary manual and computerized controls, for example, physical- and password-based access control system.
2. An overview of the application system development process along with maintenance methodology and technical standards followed by the auditee. In the event a standard is followed, the auditor needs to be acquainted with the said standard and use the specifications of the standard as a benchmark for the audit.
3. Industry standards (nature and type) and legal, taxation, and regulatory requirements, if any, need to be listed.
4. An outline of the computing standards, data processing norms, and auditing standards followed should be reviewed.
5. The control philosophy of the auditee and tolerance to risk levels and exposures must be assessed and taken note of by the auditor.

Once the tests of controls are made the auditors would reassess the control risk and decide on further procedures for the audit and the nature, extent, and timing of carrying out substantive testing. In an extreme case where the tests of controls are conclusive, the auditor may form an audit opinion at this stage.

Test of transactions: Samples of material transactions are traced from their initiation to the end to analyze the impact of various application controls and their efficiency and reliability. The focus of such testing is not to assess any financial implication but to understand the process flow through the system. If the results of tests of transactions indicate that material errors have occurred or might occur or that information provided by the system is or might be materially misstated, the extent of substantive tests of the process segment or overall process will be increased. For example, an observation that enterprise resource planning software is allowing a negative balance of inventory will lead to detailed testing of the process and associated controls to identify how this was permitted.

Overall tests: Before forming the final opinion on the extent of errors, misstatements and weaknesses in the system, failure to safeguard assets, and failure to maintain data integrity, the auditor will conduct tests considering the system as a whole. These tests would range from physical counts of information assets, assessment of the access and security norms, work study, overview of the organizational structure, and so forth.

Audit trails: The audit trail provides a trace from the initiation of a transaction to its disposition through all the intermediate points. In a computerized system it includes source documents, tracing of all processing activities, and outputs. The audit trails determine accountability, show what actions were taken by people and the system, and provide the ability to reconstruct events or processes and thus help to reduce errors, omissions, and frauds. Audit trails may include the following eight items:

1. **Document number** that is preassigned or assigned by the user in the form of a batch number or a transaction number allotted by the computer. These numbers help to identify a particular transaction.
2. **Transactions logs** include database logs, application transaction logs, access logs, console logs, usage logs, telecommunication logs, change logs, job allotment logs, and maintenance logs. These logs capture data about system activity that can be used for tracing, audit analysis, and substantive reviews.
3. **Control totals** include quantitative totals, hash totals, and record counts. They help in verifying the accuracy of processing and the integrity of data.
4. **Error logs** help an auditor to identify mistakes that took place in the system and corrective measures employed. They describe the types of errors and the application where it occurred. Auditors analyze the impact of the errors and determine the level of risks the auditee is exposed to.
5. **Control grids** form a matrix with the risks on one axis and the exposures on the other. A grid may also be designed to show the threats, risks, or exposure on one axis and the controls that minimize or eliminate such threats, risks, and exposures on the other axis. These control grids help the auditor in understanding the relation between compensating and complementary controls.
6. **Access rules** define the authority of a user to carry out specific functions, such as make changes, delete records, and retrieve data. The rules may also define whether any devices or processes are to be used while conducting such functions. For example, an access rule may require physical identification of the user and a password to be keyed in, or it may require the swiping of an identity card on a device along with the manual entry of a password. This restricts unauthorized persons from accessing system resources, including data and application.
7. **Run-to-run control totals** of computer records or data fields of significance could be designed where totals from source application are verified by destination application. For example, an Internet banking application system may verify the availability of funds for a transaction request and present these credentials to the database management system while completing the transaction. System-driven verification of reports generated by the application system would help in assuring data integrity and accuracy of processing logic.
8. **Exception and statistical reports** identify deviations from standards. This information can be used to analyze situations leading to the deviations.

SUBSTANTIVE REVIEWS AND TESTS

Substantive tests determine the validity of classes of transactions and information generated by the system. They involve a detailed scrutiny and investigation of the system in terms of the methods and controls applied to ensure effectiveness, efficiency, and accuracy of inputs, processing, and outputs. The auditor selects a process or transaction and traces it back to its source to determine whether it was processed in the designed manner. Substantive testing also identifies ineffective system design even though there was no processing error. Substantive tests further include analytical reviews and investigation into significant deviations.

The nature of the substantive procedure depends on the audit object being verified. Examples of such procedures include confirmation, inspection, reperformance, cut-off testing, vouching, analysis of fluctuations, analysis of trends and ratios, reconciliation, transaction analysis, and observation. Five of these procedures are described in the following list:

1. **Confirmation:** The verification of facts or conditions through correspondence with a third party, such as vendors. For example, claims of the auditee about service arrangements may be verified with the service provider.
2. **Inspection:** This involves physical counting and/or examining information systems assets. This substantive test is typically applied to the information asset and other resources.
3. **Reperformance:** In many instances, information provided by the system arises as a result of computations, comparisons, and conclusions drawn by the information system. The auditor may repeat these procedures and confirm the results being produced by the original system. Often such reperformances are conducted on a test environment by using a test pack. If necessary, such reperformance may also be conducted on the production system where it does not irreversibly compromise data integrity. For example, the effectiveness of an access-locking system can be tested by entering a wrong password against a user ID on the main system.
4. **Document review:** Document review is the examination of evidence supporting a process or item to determine its validity. This may include review of the procedures for generating supporting documentation, examining the supporting documents, and review for unusual items. For example, the layout of the data center may be verified to find out whether the designed emergency escape plan can be actually implemented.
5. **Reconciliation:** Reconciliation consists of identifying and accounting for any differences between two values that should agree. These reconciliations may be required when differences are identified during verification of assets, or of processing results from actual, or between the transaction file and the corresponding update to the master file, and so forth. For example, the total space on a storage system must reconcile with the report of space usage and free space available on the system.

AUDIT TOOLS AND TECHNIQUES

The commonly used tools in performing an information systems audit include the following seven items:

1. Audit checklists
2. Interviews
3. Observation
4. Internal control questionnaires
5. Statistical and judgmental sampling
6. Application system and program flowchart
7. Audit software

In addition to this list, there are a number of specialized techniques using computerized auditing tools to test computational routines, program logic, or whole application systems in order to determine the effectiveness of controls, accuracy of computer processing, and compliance with specified processing procedures. Some of these techniques are discussed in the following sections.

Testing Computer Application Program Controls

Various techniques that are deployed for testing computer application program controls include the following four:

1. **Test data method:** This method verifies accuracy of processing by application programs. This is achieved by executing these programs using manually prepared sets of test cases, and test data whose standard results from processing are known. The results from processing are compared with the expected results to verify whether the program logic is correct and consistent.
2. **Base case system evaluation:** This is a technique that applies standardized body of data, inputs, parameters, and output called the base case to the computer application program. Results of the system are judged based on set criterions. It is an extension of the test data method except that the base case is a standardized set. It is extremely useful in cases of testing effectiveness of different software against a specific application.
3. **Integrated test facility:** This is a technique to review application program logic and functions to provide the auditor with evidence of observed operating procedures and error-handling conditions. The auditor provides test input data for a fictitious entity and the outputs of processing such data are compared with precalculated and standard test results. Here, the auditor's data are processed together with the normal production data.
4. **Parallel simulation:** The parallel simulation method processes live data through test programs. Parallel simulation programs include the application

logic, calculations, and controls that are relevant to the specific audit objective. This allows the auditor to have a detailed understanding of functioning of the application.

Selecting/Monitoring Data Processing Transactions

There are various techniques for selecting or monitoring data processing transactions. Three common techniques used are the following:

1. **Transaction selection:** This method enables the auditor to examine and analyze transaction volumes and error rates and to statistically sample specified transactions. One of the common applications would be to review the volume of data lost during transmission and the standard rate for such data loss.
2. **Embedded audit data collection:** Specially designed data collection modules are embedded in the computer application system to select and record data for subsequent analysis and evaluation. This technique is intended to highlight unusual transactions and subject them to audit review and testing. Computing the number of times an item is withdrawn from the inventory will be an instance of such testing, as these data will highlight any unusual movement.
3. **Extended records:** The extended record includes all the significant data from all computer application systems that contributed to the processing of a transaction, which the auditor may use for audit review and analysis. This can be very useful for developing an audit trail; an example of such a record is the history of interest rate revisions in banking software.

Data Verification

Common tools that are deployed for data verification during an information systems audit include the following three:

1. **Generalized audit software:** These programs assist auditors to extract and analyze data. The advantages include the ability to read an entire file instead of samples; to extract all exceptions instead of statistically projecting the rate of exceptions in a given application file; and to determine data characteristics and data profiles. Though used extensively for financial audits, these kinds of software allow an information systems auditor to form an overall understanding of the data flow across the system. It assists the auditor to form an idea of the effectiveness of controls built into the system, such as reasonableness test and range test.
2. **Terminal audit software:** A terminal audit software accesses, extracts, manipulates, and displays data from online databases, including log and event databases, using remote terminal inquiry commands. It provides direct access to data files for audit examination without extensive setup procedures or separate processing. This software allows auditors to identify exceptional events that might have been caused by a control failure.

3. **Customized audit programs:** These programs are specially developed to extract and report data from a specific application system's data file and access records.

Analyzing Application Programs

Analysis of application programs involves various techniques. Four of the popular techniques are discussed here.

1. **Snapshots:** A technique that extracts data residing in the computer memory that may contain data elements involved in a computerized decision-making process. This snapshot is usually obtained at the time the decision is made to record the underlying variables used by the system to make the decision. Input transactions are tagged and written to an audit log file with date, time, and indication of the point in the program at which the snapshot was taken.
2. **Tracing:** An audit technique that provides the auditor with the capability of performing an electronic walkthrough of computer applications. The basic methodology involved is to follow a process or transaction from inception to eventual disposal as it moves through the system. This exercise identifies various system components used by the application along with the controls that are built into the process.
3. **Mapping:** This is performed by software performance measurement tools that analyze a computer program during execution and indicate which program statements have been executed and the CPU time consumed by each segment of the program. Wherever the audit scope requires ascertainment of application performance or comparing against a benchmark, this technique is extremely useful for the auditor.
4. **Control flowcharting:** A graphical technique or a flowchart for simplifying the identification and interrelationships of controls can be of great help in evaluating the existence and adequacy of those controls. They further assist in assessing the impact of system changes on the overall control profile.

Other Tools and Techniques

In addition to generic control-driven tools and techniques, there are several other tools and techniques that are used by information system auditors. Two of the common ones are discussed here.

1. **Utility programs:** Utility programs can be used to check the status of communication ports, volume of network traffic, incidence of specific data requests, search for deleted files, and so forth. These tools allow the auditor to form an idea of involvement of various systems components in normal activities of the auditee. Many installed applications automatically search for updated versions and establish a communication line. Utility programs are an excellent way of identifying

such instances, and the auditor can verify whether such access was permitted by the auditee.

2. **Query language software:** These are user-friendly tools written for nonprogrammers with menus and prompting screens that accept the queries and requests from users. These are useful to extract specific data from large log files that are not possible to review manually.

SAMPLING TECHNIQUES

Auditors often perform tests of control for the purpose of estimating rate of deviation from control policy or procedure. Such tests allow the auditor to ascertain the frequency of such deviations. Sampling is a useful technique to make a bias-free assessment without verifying every single instance of process usage. Application of the technique of sampling requires the auditor to make some decisions, such as the following five:

1. Auditors must define the problem adequately to be able to identify what to measure, the relevant information requirement, and the testing procedure to be used.
2. Auditors need to ascertain the population size and characteristics. For example, in the case of a help desk database, the population will be the number of complaints and the characteristics will include the nature of a complaint, the assets involved, and the time taken for resolution of the problem.
3. Auditors need to study both strengths and weaknesses of the internal control systems. The audit areas suitable for sampling must also be determined. For example, the auditee may follow a policy of achieving a 24-hour turnaround time for problem resolution and seeks to achieve the same through an internal control system designed to escalate help desk calls remaining unresolved after 18 hours. The auditor may verify functioning of the system by selecting help desk calls and computing their resolution time.
4. The maximum error rate that is acceptable to the auditor must be decided. Since sampling technique by design is open to errors, the auditor must agree on the error tolerance. If the error tolerance is low, the sample size will have to be increased.
5. Conclusions about the population would be drawn from sampling results.

The sample selection procedure used to draw the samples may be of different types or even a combination can be used. Three of the procedures include:

1. **Statistical sampling:** random sampling, systematic sampling, and cluster sampling
2. **Nonstatistical sample selection methods:** haphazard selection, block selection, and judgment selection
3. **Stratified sampling:** a combination of the statistical and nonstatistical methods.

AUDIT QUESTIONNAIRE

Questionnaires are checklists that the auditors use while querying the auditee. The use of standardized checklists ensures consistency of judgment on the reliability of controls over the application system. The questionnaire breaks up the process of review into defined steps, ensuring that the auditor undertakes all steps before forming any opinion about functioning of a control. There are three major aspects of the questionnaire design:

1. **Design of questions:** This involves identifying the aspects of audit that are to be covered by the questionnaire.
2. **Design of the response scales:** The response of the auditee may be objective or subjective. Even when the responses are objective in nature, they may be binary—yes or no—or scaled, for example, a scale of 1 to 5, where 1 denotes complete agreement with the question and 5 denotes complete disagreement.
3. **Design of the layout and structure of the questionnaire:** The questionnaires can be designed to correspond with either the auditee's processes or applications. For example, one may have questions on the process of access control, which is applicable across all applications, or one may also have questions regarding a specific application.

A detailed questionnaire covering various domains of information systems has been provided in Chapter 12.

While designing questionnaires, the following four guidelines may be kept in mind:

1. **The characteristic of the user group:** If auditors are the questionnaire users, the questions should be specific, terms can be left undefined, and instructions for completing the questionnaire can be minimized.
2. **The nature of the information sought:** The auditors may use questionnaires to elicit either facts or opinions. The questionnaire designer may provide different kinds of information on the questionnaire to ensure that the respondent understands what facts are required. Ambiguous questions, use of technical language, questions that lead to a preferred response, questions based on any presumption, hypothetical questions, embarrassing questions, and those that involve extensive recall ideally should be avoided.
3. **Methodology of administering the questionnaire:** This consideration defines the extent to which the questions need to be self-explanatory. If auditors administer the questionnaires, it may be assumed that the auditors are capable of answering queries and clarifying any ambiguities that arise. In the event that the questionnaire is administered by nonspecialists, the questions need to be self-explanatory so that the administrator is not required to respond to technical queries of the respondents.

4. **Choice of the layout and structure:** The objective of designing a questionnaire is to achieve a layout and structure that is simple, logical, and visually appealing. The length of the questionnaire affects the morale of respondents. The questionnaire should look uncluttered with the questions and various sections of the questionnaire spaced adequately.

AUDIT DOCUMENTATION

During the course of an information systems audit, the auditor examines various records, studies various information and data, observes work procedures including screen display, and interviews various personnel. These processes generate evidence that the information systems auditor evaluates to form an opinion on the adequacy and effectiveness of internal controls, and their efficiency and other factors under the scope of systems audit. It is imperative that the auditor document and securely store these evidences for future retrieval.

Audit documentation is also referred to as audit working papers. Audit working papers are usually maintained across two files—the permanent file and the current file. The permanent file may contain, among other material, the following:

- Organization structure of the auditee entity
- Information systems policies of the auditee
- Historical background of the information systems in the auditee entity
- Extracts of copies of relevant legal documents
- Report of evaluation of internal controls related to information systems
- Copies of past information systems audit reports and observations

The current file primarily contains working papers and evidences that the information systems auditor gathers during the audit. The current file usually contains the following:

- Engagement letter.
- Audit program.
- Report that includes the nature, timing, and extent of auditing procedures performed, and the results of such procedures.
- Copies of communications and minutes of meetings with the auditee.
- Representation and confirmation received from the auditee.
- Observation and conclusion of the auditor on significant aspects of audit. This should also include opinion of the auditee and subsequent resolution of queries involving exceptions and unusual incidents observed by the auditor.
- Extracts, including screenshots, of data and system reports being used to form the audit opinion. In view of the transient nature of some evidences, particularly those observed on the screen, it is imperative for the auditor to collect the evidences or confirm their existence with the auditee. Such confirmation may be in

the form of minutes of a discussion with the auditee or in the form of a certificate from the auditee.

For audit documentation to be useful and acceptable as evidence, it must satisfy certain broad criteria, including those pertaining to the following seven areas:

1. A record of points discussed in an interview should specify the following:
   a. Topic of discussion.
   b. Person interviewed along with his or her designation and role in the auditee organization.
   c. Time and place of the interview.
   d. If there was a specific response, the question that prompted the response.
2. Physical observations made by the auditor should specify the following:
   a. Time and place of the observation.
   b. Background of the observations, including whether the observation was part of a conscious process of verification.
   c. Comments of the auditor.
   d. People and resources involved in observation.
   e. Circumstances that led to the observation so that the incident can be re-created.
3. Reports and data obtained from the system should have the following information:
   a. Source of the procurement—auditor or staff of auditee.
   b. Source of the report.
   c. Date and time of the acquisition of the evidence.
   d. Steps observed to acquire the same that can act as an audit trail.
4. Auditors may clearly mark their comments and outstanding queries on the documentation. Once the queries are answered, the remarks should include how and where they were resolved.
5. Remarks and approval of a senior or peer, if any, who reviews the report should form a part of the documentation.
6. The documentation must maintain version control and maintain time-stamped copies of draft and final reports. Once part of a report is modified, ideally the earlier version should also be preserved and the reason for modification stated.
7. Wherever the evidence was obtained in the presence of the auditee, the auditor should try to obtain endorsement of the auditee in the documentation. Such endorsement should be specifically obtained if the evidence is system based and transient in nature.

AUDIT REPORT

The audit report is the formal written communication of the auditor with the auditee and its management. Since the audit report provides a concise statement on what was found and forms an opinion arising from the audit exercise, the audit report is the focal point for an auditor and for all those who rely on the auditor's work.

The structure of the audit report is critical for effective communication of audit results. Without a well-defined structure, it is difficult for the auditee to evaluate, compare, and act on the report. The audit report should include the following eight elements:

1. An executive summary of findings that does not require any technical knowledge for understanding
2. Identification of the scope of work and objectives that are to be achieved
3. Identification of the functions and operations reviewed
4. Background or an introductory statement
5. Expression of an opinion on the effectiveness, security, efficiency, and integrity of systems reviewed
6. Detailed findings supported by evidence
7. A list of findings that require either technical knowledge or expertise of operations
8. A conclusion highlighting the achievements of the audit

Opinions expressed in the audit report may be of the following four types:

1. **Disclaimer:** The information systems auditor feels that due to insufficient evidence, no opinion can be expressed.
2. **Adverse:** The information systems auditor opines that the auditee has failed to demonstrate its competence in line with the audit objective. For example, if the objective of the audit was to assess security preparedness, then the auditee could not demonstrate adequate preparedness.
3. **Qualified:** This opinion indicates that the auditee conforms to the audit objective with some deviations. These deviations are not as critical to warrant an adverse opinion but can potentially compromise achievement of the objective.
4. **Unqualified:** The auditor opines that the auditee has demonstrated competence in the achievement of the audit objective.

When the auditor makes any qualified audit opinion, the reasons should be included in the report, stating the condition, impact, origin, preventive measures necessary, and other such recommendations that the auditor may deem prudent to include.

As adopted by the ISecGrade framework, which is included in Chapter 11, the opinions may be written in one of the following four ways:

1. **Disclaimer opinion:** Based on the information provided, explanations given, and evidence found and evaluated by us, we are **not in a position to opine** whether the information systems and the environment adequately safeguard

assets, maintain data and system integrity, provide relevant and reliable information, consume resources efficiently, achieve information system goals effectively, and provide a reasonable assurance that the auditee's operational and control objectives will be met.

2. **Adverse opinion:** In our opinion, based on the information provided, explanations given, and evidence found and evaluated by us, the information systems and the environment **do not** adequately safeguard assets, maintain data and system integrity, provide relevant and reliable information, consume resources efficiently, achieve information system goals effectively, and provide a reasonable assurance that the auditee's operational and control objectives will be met.

3. **Qualified opinion:** In our opinion, based on the information provided, explanations given, and evidence found and evaluated by us, and **subject to some observations**, the information systems and the environment adequately safeguard assets, maintain data and system integrity, provide relevant and reliable information, consume resources efficiently, achieve information system goals effectively, and provide a reasonable assurance that the auditee's operational and control objectives will be met.

4. **Unqualified opinion:** In our opinion, based on the information provided, explanations given, and evidence found and evaluated by us, the information systems and the environment adequately **safeguard assets**, maintain data and system integrity, provide relevant and reliable information, consume resources efficiently, achieve information system goals effectively, and provide a reasonable assurance that the auditee's operational and control objectives will be met.

At the conclusion of an audit, an information systems auditor should provide the auditee with a report documenting control weaknesses the auditor has identified, potential consequences of these control weaknesses, and some recommendations for remedial actions.

AUDITING APPROACHES

The information systems auditor, subject to the scope of audit, may adopt an audit approach that suits the audit requirement. The following three sections outline the most common audit approaches available for an information systems auditor.

Auditing around the Computer

This is an indirect approach of audit wherein the auditee system is examined based on the input and output. The auditor bases the examination and evaluation on printed copies of the input and outputs and the level of management control implemented. Internal processing by the system is deduced from the evolution of the output from the input data. The computer is thus treated as a black box.

Such an audit technique can be used in cases where the following six conditions apply:

1. The system is simple and essentially involves repetitive functions.
2. Inherent risk is low.
3. Processing logic is simple and bereft of complexities.
4. Separation of duties and management supervision is built primarily into the input process, as is common with any manual system.
5. Processing generally consists of input of data and updating a master file, for example, the system for managing a store's inventory.
6. Audit trails are clear and modifications to the system are few, if any.

The auditor uses this technique to verify the reliability of the system-generated information by observing the following two-step approach:

1. The auditor calculates expected results from transactions entered into the system.
2. Then, the auditor compares these computed values with the results of computer processing.

In the event that the results are accurate and valid, the auditor can legitimately assume that the system controls are effective and the system is operating properly. In fact, to test the robustness of control, the auditor may include erroneous or extreme condition data in the test pack.

However, this approach has major limitations, including the following three caveats:

1. This is useful only for very simple systems.
2. This method does not test the ability of the system to cope with changes and non-standard input.
3. This verifies output-based accuracy but does not determine whether the program logic is correct and efficient.

Auditing with the Computer

The approach of auditing with the computer is a mix of various techniques and tools that are commonly referred to as computer-assisted audit techniques (CAAT). CAAT involves using computers to aid auditors to improve their observations and collect evidence for forming an opinion. Though utilization of CAAT can enhance audit effectiveness, use of such tools is primarily restricted to substantive tests. It may be noted that use of these tools is subservient to the audit strategy and is not obligatory.

It may also be noted that common CAAT software is designed primarily for financial audits. There are few choices of software for the purpose of an information systems audit, which mostly focuses on the testing of the security aspect of a system. The auditors are often required to design their own CAAT to be used in an information systems audit.

Auditing through the Computer

Computers are used to test processing logic and the accuracy of records produced by the information system. This technique is used where processing and operations are complex; there is a large volume of transactions, making manual checking difficult; internal control measures, checks, and validations are built into the system; and the parameters of computation are system based. The technique focuses on testing program logic and reviewing routines and programmed controls. It embraces a family of techniques, including test data, parallel simulation, integrated test facilities, and embedded audit modules. Finally, this approach draws extensively from the tools and techniques used in both auditing with and without with the computer.

SAMPLE AUDIT WORK-PLANNING MEMO

The following is a sample audit work-planning memo that the information systems auditor may prepare at the commencement of the audit. The work plan would provide an overview of the workflow and resource allocation. The memo should form a part of the current file of the information systems auditor.

Audit Objectives and Scope

In this section the information systems auditor would detail the scope of the assignment and the objective that the audit is trying to achieve. This may vary from one audit to another and may range from providing an opinion on the security of network access to a system for document backup.

The review will cover the following nine areas:

1. Utilization objective of information system assets.
2. Security objectives for information system assets.
3. Security settings for individual users as well as groups.
4. Account policies governing privileges associated with a type of account.
5. Local policies defining the operating environment provided on a system.
6. User rights assigned to individual users or groups.
7. Security options available and the rationale behind selecting those implemented.
8. Passwords policies along with implementation status.
9. User training and awareness.

Audit Process

An information systems audit process comprises distinct steps including the following nine:

1. Conduct an opening meeting with the auditee to reiterate the audit objective and define resource requirement.
2. Finalize audit plan and confirm it with the auditee.
3. Conduct risk analysis exercise to identify areas that need special focus.

4. Identify, test, and evaluate adequacy and efficiency of controls.
5. Conduct risk assessment based on preliminary risk assessment and test of controls.
6. Initiate substantive testing-based risk assessment.
7. Draft report and discuss the same with the auditee.
8. Conduct closing meeting.
9. Finalize and issue the audit report.

Testing Techniques

Various techniques may be used in testing and evaluating controls, including the following seven:

1. Interviews and inquiry.
2. Inspection of documents including policies and procedures.
3. Selective confirmation of documents, particularly those pertaining to external agencies.
4. Observation of procedures including outcome.
5. Reperformance of procedures to ascertain or verify that the generation of outcome is the same or similar to the original outcome.
6. Performance of selected tests on critical transactions and activities. The issue of criticality may not be determined based on single transaction exposure alone but on combined impact of several transactions.
7. Performance of analytical procedures to assess technical efficiency wherever applicable. Examples may include throughput time and mean time between failure.

Audit Team Assignment

Allocation of audit team members to specific tasks can be documented using the template provided in Table 5.1.

Activities and Deliverables

The deliverables from each activity can be documented using the template provided in Table 5.2.

Five best practices with regard to these activities are described here:

1. Once the audit is complete, prepare a draft audit report including the audit opinion and all findings. Subject to scope of audit, the report may include recommendations to improve controls and enhance efficiency.

TABLE 5.1 Audit Team Assignment

Name	Role
	Information systems auditor
	Network expert
	Assistant

TABLE 5.2 Activities and Deliverable Listing

Activities	Preliminary Dates	Deliverables
Audit preparation and planning		
Fieldwork and review		
Draft report		
Final report		

2. Categorize audit findings as high risk, medium risk, and low risk, signifying their potential to compromise the confidentiality, integrity, and availability of an information systems asset. The classification will be based on the impact potential and probability of occurrence.
3. Discuss the draft report with the auditee and consider additional evidence in support of any claim that the auditee may make.
4. Finalize a schedule of modification at the closing meeting, noting the acceptance of submissions by the auditee or dissent of the auditee. The dissent may not form a part of the audit report though an annexure with the management response may be included. Much as the auditor has a right to accept any submission of the auditee, the right of the auditee to disagree with the opinion and interpretation of the auditor needs to be respected and acknowledged.
5. Issue the final report.

SAMPLE AUDIT WORK PROCESS FLOW

An outline of the work process depicting the application of general methodology is provided here for instant reference:

1. Commencement of audit work.
2. Review background information, policies, and previous audit reports, and so forth. Complete the following checklists (provided in Chapter 12):
   a. Business strategy.
   b. Long-term information technology strategy.
   c. Short-term information technology plan.
   d. Information systems security policy.
   e. Implementation of information systems security policy.
3. Do preliminary assessment of general controls based on inquiry, observations, and walkthrough. Complete the following checklists (provided in Chapter 12):
   a. Logical and physical access control.
   b. Parameter settings.
   c. Application development and change control.

      d. System software controls.
      e. Segregation of duties.
      f. Disaster recovery plans.

4. Determine if controls are effective:
      a. If controls are not effective, perform the following:
         i. Make a control risk assessment.
        ii. Determine extent of performance of application testing.
      b. If controls are effective, perform the following:
         i. Carry out a detailed test of other general controls.
        ii. Use the following checklists (provided in Chapter 12):
            ■ Physical environment
            ■ File and directory protection
            ■ Peripherals and storage devices
            ■ Maintenance
            ■ Problem management
            ■ Change management

5. Perform application testing. Use the following checklists (provided in Chapter 12) for this purpose:
      a. Client-server
      b. Authentication devices
      c. Application software
      d. Database management
      e. Antivirus
      f. Software licensing
      g. Communication software
      h. Data communication
      i. Electronic fund transfer
      j. Internet security
      k. Local area network (LAN)
      l. Legal compliance
     m. Management control system
      n. Operating system
      o. Packaged software implementation
      p. System conversion and reconciliation
      q. Transaction processing
      r. Utility program

6. Perform information technology risk assessment using the grading system provided under ISecGrade methodology in Chapter 11.
7. Prepare draft audit report.
8. Discuss with the auditee.
9. Finalize and issue audit report.
10. Update permanent and current file.
11. Completion of audit.

SAMPLE: SCOPE OF AN INFORMATION SYSTEMS AUDIT OF A BANK

Secured Future Bank invites a competent information systems auditor to carry out an information systems audit in its bank. The scope of the audit is detailed below, and it must be noted that the details provided in the scope are not exhaustive and additional scope may be included if circumstances so demand.

1. Audit of information security architecture and implementation of information security policy with specific reference to the following areas:
   1.1. Information security organization structure
   1.2. Roles and responsibilities
   1.3. Data classification policy
   1.4. Application security policy
   1.5. ATM application security
   1.6. Password security policy
   1.7. Internet banking policy
   1.8. Data center security and monitoring
   1.9. Virus control policy
   1.10. Backup policy
   1.11. Network policy
   1.12. Physical security policy
   1.13. Environment security policy
   1.14. Incident management policy
   1.15. Business continuity and disaster recovery plan
   1.16. Internet usage policy
   1.17. E-mail usage policy
2. Information systems audit of key information technology systems and resources:
   2.1. Network management and security audit
       2.1.1. Network security architecture including:
           2.1.1.1. Audit of redundancy for links and devices in core banking software (CBS) setup.
           2.1.1.2. Analysis of the network security controls, which includes a study of logical locations of security components, such as firewall, IDS/IPS, and so forth.
           2.1.1.3. Access control for militarized zone, de-militarized zone, network operation center, and wide area network and for specific applications of the respective zones.
           2.1.1.4. Review of all types of network-level access controls and logs for ensuring their sufficiency and security of creation, maintenance, and backup.
           2.1.1.5. Secure network connects for CBS, ATM, and Internet banking including client- and browser-based security.
           2.1.1.6. Evaluate centralized controls over routers installed in branches and their password management.
           2.1.1.7. Virtual LAN trunk protocol (VTP) security and VTP modes

(Continued)

2.1.2. Configuration audit of network devices including the following:
- 2.1.2.1. Routing protocol analysis.
- 2.1.2.2. Analysis of load balancing mechanism.
- 2.1.2.3. Analysis of latency in traffic across various links.
- 2.1.2.4. Understand and evaluate the loopholes in the configuration, if any.
- 2.1.2.5. Encryption of password on the routers/switches and their compliance with the requirement of a minimum number of characters.
- 2.1.2.6. Restriction on local and remote access to the networking devices.
- 2.1.2.7. Version of internal operating system and known vulnerability issues.
- 2.1.2.8. Port duplex and speed-setting verification.
- 2.1.2.9. Validation of the following services for security, effectiveness, and efficiency on all network devices:
  - 2.1.2.9.1. IP-directed broadcasts
  - 2.1.2.9.2. Incoming packets at the router sourced from invalid addresses
  - 2.1.2.9.3. All source routing
  - 2.1.2.9.4. Standardized SNMP community strings used
  - 2.1.2.9.5. Logging and auditing
  - 2.1.2.9.6. Banner checking

2.1.3. Vulnerability assessment of network and ensuring compliance of the security goals:
- 2.1.3.1. Port scanning of the servers, network devices and security devices/applications.
- 2.1.3.2. Analysis and assessment of vulnerabilities of entire network.
- 2.1.3.3. Observance of network traffic to verify existence of important and confidential information, such as username, password in clear text, and so forth.
- 2.1.3.4. Comprehensive scanning of all IP address ranges in use to determine vulnerabilities that may exist in network devices and servers, and to audit all responses to determine if any risks exist.
- 2.1.3.5. Check for the known vulnerabilities in the operating systems and applications, such as CBS, browser, e-mail, web server, web application server, and FTP.
- 2.1.3.6. Review of specific controls against web defacing and of uploading of Trojan/virus/malware/spyware, and so forth, at the core banking and Internet banking web server.
- 2.1.3.7. Review of control against spread of network-based virus to clients/connected machines.
- 2.1.3.8. Attempt to guess passwords using password-cracking tools.
- 2.1.3.9. Check for unnecessary services/applications running on network devices/servers/workstations.
- 2.1.3.10. Unauthorized access into the network.

2.1.3.11. Unauthorized modifications to the network and the traffic flowing over network.

2.1.3.12. Possibility of web defacing, SQL/XPATH injection, cross-site scripting, information leakage, cookie handling, IP spoofing, buffer overflow, session hijacks, farming, phishing frauds, sniffing, SQL query in parameter value, and so forth.

2.1.3.13. Controls against possibility of DoS, DDoS attacks, spoofing, DNS poisoning, and so forth.

2.1.3.14. Effectiveness of virus control systems in e-mail gateways.

2.1.3.15. Possibility of traffic route poisoning.

2.1.3.16. Checking spanning tree topology; check whether all switches are free from spanning loops.

2.1.3.17. Checking fault tolerance.

2.1.3.18. MAC spoofing.

2.1.3.19. Communication controls.

2.1.3.20. Firewall /ACLs (access control list) compromise.

2.1.4. Network traffic analysis and performance:

2.1.4.1. Understanding the traffic flow in the network at LAN and WAN level.

2.1.4.2. Network performance analysis.

2.1.4.3. Network traffic analysis.

2.1.4.4. Adequacy of base line configurations.

2.1.4.5. Proper usage available of bandwidth.

2.1.5. Vulnerability of delivery channels:

2.1.5.1. Assess flaws in web-hosting software, for example, security of web server and e-design of the applications.

2.1.5.2. Tool-based or guess-based password-cracking.

2.1.5.3. Search for back-door traps in any of the software.

2.1.5.4. Attempting penetration through perceivable network equipment addressing and other vulnerabilities.

2.1.5.5. Functioning of the SSL certificate and PKI verification.

2.1.5.6. Reliability of solution architecture to provide 24 × 7 availability.

2.1.5.7. Time synchronization with central NTP server.

2.1.5.8. Vulnerability analysis of remote server, management software, web logic server.

2.1.5.9. Proper configuration of rule base in Firewall.

2.1.5.10. Ascertain effective IDS configuration, monitoring, and reporting.

2.1.5.11. Make checker control system parameters change.

2.1.5.12. Use of proxy server between Internet and proxy systems.

2.1.5.13. Logging and reporting of computer access and security violations.

(Continued)

2.1.5.14. Effectiveness of system monitoring tools against intrusions and attacks.

2.1.5.15. Check for the known vulnerabilities in other applications, such as automated clearing system, electronic fund transfer, remittance, e-mail security, e-statement generation, loan application processing system, call center services, IVR, and SMS alert services.

2.2. Data center:

2.2.1. Information systems audit of data center operations for core banking system:

2.2.1.1. Physical and environmental security

2.2.1.1.1. Access control systems.

2.2.1.1.2. Fire/flooding/water leakage/gas leakage, and so forth.

2.2.1.1.3. Assets safeguarding and handling of movement of staff/materials/media/backup/software/hardware/information during disaster.

2.2.1.1.4. Air-conditioning of data center, humidity control systems.

2.2.1.1.5. Electrical supply, redundancy of power level, generator, UPS capacity.

2.2.1.1.6. Surveillance systems of data center.

2.2.1.1.7. Physical and environmental controls.

2.2.1.1.8. Pest and rodent prevention systems.

2.2.1.2. Operating system

2.2.1.2.1. Setup and maintenance of operating systems parameters.

2.2.1.2.2. Operating system change management procedures.

2.2.1.2.3. Use of "root" and other sensitive passwords.

2.2.1.2.4. Use of sensitive systems software utilities.

2.2.1.2.5. Vulnerability assessment and hardening requirement of operating systems.

2.2.1.2.6. Management of users and groups created, including all types of users, ensuring password complexity, periodic changes, and so forth.

2.2.1.2.7. File systems security of the operating system.

2.2.1.2.8. Review of access rights and privileges.

2.2.1.2.9. Services and ports accessibility.

2.2.1.2.10. Review of log monitoring, its sufficiency, security, maintenance, and backup.

2.2.1.2.11. Interfaces with external applications such as other electronic channels in the case of CBS and ATM switches, clearance system with Central Bank.

2.2.1.2.12. Search for back-door traps in the operating systems.

2.2.2. Application review of core banking software and other applications and interfaces thereof:

    2.2.2.1. Authorization control, such as maker checker, exceptions, overriding exceptions, and error conditions.

    2.2.2.2. Authentication mechanism.

    2.2.2.3. User management and password management.

    2.2.2.4. Parameter maintenance.

    2.2.2.5. Access rights.

    2.2.2.6. Access logs/audit trail generation.

    2.2.2.7. Change management procedures including procedures for testing.

    2.2.2.8. Documentation of change management.

    2.2.2.9. Documentation of data center operations.

    2.2.2.10. Review of all controls including boundary controls, input controls, communication controls, database controls, output controls, interface controls from security perspectives.

    2.2.2.11. Review of all interfaces of application with other systems and interfaces of other systems with applications for security, accuracy, consistency, and safety.

    2.2.2.12. Identifying critical risk areas, control weakness in application systems and recommended corrective actions from security prospective.

2.2.3. Backup and recovery testing:

    2.2.3.1. Audit of backup and recovery testing procedures.

    2.2.3.2. Sufficiency checks for backup process.

    2.2.3.3. Audit of access controls, movement, and storage of backup media.

    2.2.3.4. Audit of media maintenance procedures.

    2.2.3.5. Security of removable media.

    2.2.3.6. Controls for prevention of data leakage through removable media or other means.

    2.2.3.7. Media disposal mechanisms and database archival and purging procedures.

    2.2.3.8. Synchronization between data center and recovery center databases.

2.2.4. DBMS and data security

    2.2.4.1. Secure use of SQL.

    2.2.4.2. Control procedures for changes to parameter files.

    2.2.4.3. Logical access controls.

    2.2.4.4. Control procedures for sensitive database passwords.

    2.2.4.5. Control procedures for purging of data files.

    2.2.4.6. Procedures for data backup, restoration, recovery, and readability of backed up data.

2.3. Disaster recovery (DR) site in line with business continuity plan (BCP):

2.3.1. Audit of DR site including verification of systems/control assessment of environment and procedures at the DR site, parameter management, adequacy of infrastructure, fallback procedures,

(Continued)

assessment of access control, comparisons of DR site setup with data center with respect to infrastructure (hardware, application software, systems software, and so forth), and physical security.

2.3.2. DR services to be available for branches, as per recovery time objective of business continuity policy.

2.3.3. Review of DR drills undertaken and reports thereof as per business continuity plan and business impact analysis.

2.4. IT products:

2.4.1. ATM switch, card and PIN management system:

2.4.1.1. Audit of ATM switch covering application, network security, switch functionality, interface, audit trails, transmission security, authorization, fallback/fail over procedures, status update.

2.4.1.2. PIN management (generation and regeneration, and so forth) of the ATM.

2.4.1.3. Connectivity to partner networks and two-way authentication between bank's server and third party's server.

2.4.1.4. Card management including delivery of cards/PIN, hot listing of cards, and reconciliation with settlement agency.

2.4.1.5. ATM switch operational controls and consortium issues,

2.4.1.6. Customer dispute resolution.

2.4.1.7. Reconciliation within the bank and with settlement agency/banks.

2.4.1.8. ATM switch reconciliation.

2.4.1.9. Vulnerability analysis of ATM Network.

2.4.1.10. Database controls.

2.4.1.11. Backup and recovery.

2.4.1.12. Analysis of administrative procedures.

2.4.1.13. Review of ATM sharing arrangements with other banks/Visa/MasterCard and other agencies and compliance to the terms of sharing.

3. General scope:

3.1. Review of privileges available to systems integrator and outsourced vendors.

3.2. Evaluation of role, responsibility, and accountability of information technology process owner.

3.3. Audit of service level agreement for all kinds of services like data center, DR site, ATM switch, physical security, facilities management, and so forth.

3.4. Check for appropriate and valid licenses for all the operating systems, databases, network systems, and all other software being used.

3.5. Audit of incident management and handling processes, roles and responsibilities, incident response procedures, verification of incident reports and effectiveness measurement, awareness of security incidents and events.

3.6. Security management, including patch management and audit of antivirus protection at host and at desktop levels, procedure of antivirus updates at data center, servers, desktops, and at gateway level protection.

CHAPTER SIX

Risk-Based Systems Audit

THIS CHAPTER INTRODUCES THE concept of a risk-based information systems audit. Under the situation of resource constraint, an information systems auditor may be required to selectively review some functions of the auditee. In fact, even when there is no paucity of resources, the auditor may need to achieve optimal use of the resources deployed. Upon completing this chapter, we should be able to prioritize various functions in terms of their risk criticality and design the audit program so that we can focus more on the critical areas.

CONDUCTING A RISK-BASED INFORMATION SYSTEMS AUDIT

A risk-based information systems audit includes, in addition to testing of logic and transaction, an evaluation of risk engrained in management systems and control procedures established in various operations. Under a risk-based information systems audit, the focus shifts from exhaustive testing to a system guided by risk identification, prioritization of audit objects based on identified risks, and allocation of audit resources in line with risk assessment. Thus, the criteria for selecting an audit object shifts from the functionality of such an object to the risk associated with its failure. An information systems audit under a risk-based approach results in greater assurance that the entity is adequately geared to face the risks its information systems is exposed to.

A risk-based information systems audit consists of the following five steps:

1. **Profiling of risks:** The information systems auditor starts the audit process with risk-profiling various functional areas of the auditee. The profiling is based on available records and information from various sources including, but not limited to, the following:
   a. External and internal audit reports.
   b. Industry trend and other environmental factors.
   c. Amount of time lapsed since the last audit.
   d. Proposed changes in business line that may introduce new risks that the auditee has not yet encountered.
   e. The auditor would evaluate the probability and exposure to risks the auditee is facing by looking into the following:
      i. Previous audit reports.
      ii. Prior audit findings and action taken on them.
      iii. Volume of business.
      iv. Internal controls and control environment.
      v. Quality and experience of the management.
      vi. Complexity of business handled by the auditee.
2. **Conducting risk assessment:** The risk-based information systems auditor would undertake risk assessment essentially to develop the plan for a risk-based information systems audit. The risk assessment function would otherwise, as an independent activity, review various processes in place to identify, measure, monitor, and decide on acceptable level of risks. The auditee should internally devise a risk assessment methodology, with approval of the board of directors, keeping in mind the size and complexity of the business undertaken by the organization. In the event a risk assessment methodology is in place, the information systems auditor may use the same after being satisfied on the effectiveness of design and operation of the process. The risk assessment process would include, at minimum, the following:
   a. Identification of inherent risks in various systems and activities undertaken by the auditee. Inherent risks are those risks that the organization must accept in order to carry on the line of business or service.
   b. Evaluation of effectiveness of control systems designed to monitor and manage the identified inherent risks. All business formulates an internal strategy to face the risk, which includes the establishment of control mechanisms to keep the risk exposure within a defined limit. For example, the auditee may decide that it will seek to maintain the maximum duration of a network failure to one minute. In order to achieve the same, the auditee invests in a parallel secondary network connectivity that will be activated if the primary network goes

down. The fact that a primary network can go down is an inherent risk and setting up the redundant line is a control mechanism to limit exposure to the risk. The possibility that the parallel network connectivity may fail simultaneously is an example of residual risk. The formal study of likelihood of such control failures is known as control risk assessment.

   c. Populating a risk matrix involves using inherent business and control risks as the horizontal and vertical axes of the matrix. Various underlying risk exposures are plotted against these axes. A commonly used scale is of three—high, medium, and low—though an organization can use a further granulated scale. In this context, it is important to detail specification of the basis of stratification of inherent risk and control risk into the high, medium, and low categories. Various cells of the matrix describe the risk factors in terms of their probability of emergence. An information systems auditor will prioritize the risk factors that have high inherent risk and high control risk as critical and will proceed toward the least critical factors described by low inherent risk and low control risk. It may be noted that a risk matrix can also be populated using different components. A detailed discussion on creating a risk matrix is provided later in the chapter.

3. **Audit prioritization:** The annual audit plan should be approved by the top management. The plan should include the following:

   a. Schedule and rationale for the audit work planned.

   b. Recognition of risk areas.

   c. Audit prioritization of risk areas based on the level and direction of risk. The direction of risk is assessed by comparing the risk matrix of two different periods and reviewing their movement from one cell to another. For example, if a risk factor moves from a high–high coordinate of the risk matrix to a high–medium coordinate, the risk trend will be described as "decreasing."

   d. The basis of classification of trends of business and control risks in categories such as increasing, stable, and decreasing must be clearly enunciated. For example, any movement across two periods within a boundary of 5 percent on either side may be defined as stable.

4. **Conducting detailed information systems audit of selected areas:** The information systems auditor will conduct substantive testing for all high-risk areas. The auditor should note the details of the findings in each area of audit and maintain working papers describing the tests conducted and results observed.

5. **Reporting:** The risk-based information systems audit report will generally contain auditor's findings and observations regarding deviations from standard guidelines. The highlight of the report of risk-based information systems audit will be an assessment of the impact of the audit findings on risk exposure of the auditee. The auditor, in addition to bringing to the fore the errors and deviations observed, will comment on the impact of those findings on the risk matrix. For example, an auditee might estimate the control risk associated with a data backup plan as "medium" while the auditor may suggest that it should be classified as "high" based on the number of control failures observed during the audit.

RISK ASSESSMENT

The information systems auditor should identify and consider the following internal and external factors while conducting the risk assessment exercise:

1. Internal factors
   a. Complexity of the organization structure that will have direct bearing on the efficiency of the control function.
   b. Nature of activities that the organization indulges in as it will influence the inherent risk exposures.
   c. Personnel skill requirements and availability thereof, which will act as a limiting factor to efficient functioning of the control mechanism.
   d. Organizational changes and whether they bring about a change in the business and control risk profile.
   e. Employee turnover, which will have an impact on the skill inventory of the auditee and is likely to affect the control risk.
2. External factors
   a. Economic conditions and stability, which will contribute to the nature and potential impact of inherent risk faced by the auditee.
   b. Industry structure and stability, which influences the sustainability of the business and adds a dimension to the inherent risk.
   c. Technological trends, which have a dual impact on business and control risk as new technology brings about changes in functional profiles as well as in the design of control tools.

These internal and external factors could adversely affect the achievement of the goals of the auditee. In order to achieve a complete view of the auditee, the risk assessment needs to be conducted at various levels of the business, cutting across product lines, market segments, functional divisions, and so forth. Both measurable and non-measurable aspects of risks need to be addressed. While evaluating the control design, it must be ensured that the cost of controls does not outweigh the benefits they provide, unless such control is a statutory requirement.

The risk assessment process would also determine which of the identified risks are avoidable or can be mitigated. For risks identified as controllable, the auditor must review the decision of the auditee to accept or mitigate those risks. Control procedures are one of the most common tools adopted for mitigation of risk and the auditor needs to review the design and functioning of these control measures. For example, an auditee may decide to set up an alternative power source to supply power for two hours. This means that the auditee seeks to mitigate the risk of power outage continuing for up to two hours. This also means that the auditee is willing to accept the risk of power outage continuing beyond two hours. In addition, the auditor will evaluate the ability and performance of the alternative power source to supply power for two hours. The decisions of the auditee on the acceptance of risks that cannot be mitigated or avoided are to be reviewed. It may be noted that the auditee may sometimes seek to limit its exposure to activities associated with the identified risks. For example, the auditee may decide not to install critical system resources in areas susceptible to power outage for long durations. The right of the auditee to decide on the risk exposure to be accepted must be respected. The duty of the information systems auditor will be to comment on the readiness of the auditee to reduce the adverse impact that may arise from the exposure the auditee has decided to accept.

The auditee must have a system of continuous evaluation of risk factors that can significantly influence achievement of goals of the information systems. The system of evaluation should include review of the system of internal control to keep it effective in the face of changed inherent risk profile and internal competence. Further, significant alteration in operating environment must be followed up by an exercise of risk assessment.

In addition to reviewing the adequacy of risk management system, the information systems auditor should also be assured of integrity of data emerging from the risk management system. The information systems auditor needs to be updated on all major business developments, including new product introduction, new technology introduction, changes in organization structure, changes in security policies, and so forth. Unless the information systems auditor considers these developments while designing the audit plan, it will be improper to compare information systems audit reports of two different periods where there were two different operating environments.

An information systems auditor, in addition to using the internal risk assessment methodology adopted by the auditee, needs to conduct an independent risk assessment exercise in order to decide on the extent of reliance that can be placed upon the internal system of risk assessment. Both of these risk assessment processes will help the information systems auditor to focus on the material risk areas and prioritize the audit work accordingly. The methodology adopted for prioritization may involve a simple process of identifying areas to be audited more frequently than others. It may also involve sophisticated assessment systems for complex business activities that may involve the use of a risk matrix comprising of probability of a loss event materializing and financial consequences thereof.

Both the auditor and the auditee will find it extremely helpful to design a risk matrix while assessing risk. The usage of a risk matrix is described in the following section.

RISK MATRIX

The risk matrix is a visual tool for risk classification based on the relationship between the magnitude of related inherent business and control risks.

Inherent business risks reflect the intrinsic risk existing in a particular area of operation or activity undertaken by the auditee. These are usually grouped into a minimum of three categories: low, medium, and high. One can also use greater levels of granularity depending on the severity of the risk and availability of information necessary for granulation at a higher order.

Control risks arise out of inadequacies, deficiencies, and gaps in existing control systems. These deficiencies contribute to likely failure of the existing control processes. The control risks can also be grouped into three classifications—low, medium, and high categories. A classification can also be made with a higher level of granularity.

Both inherent risks and control risks are represented in the risk matrix that is drawn as a deliverable of the risk assessment activity. The risk matrix may be prepared for each business activity and business location. Figure 6.1 explains the basic constitution of a risk matrix.

The overall risk characteristic for each cell of the risk matrix is stated as follows:

- **High risk:** Despite control risk being low, high inherent risk classifies this cell as a high risk zone. Combination of medium inherent risk and medium control risk also have a high risk zone classification. Similarly a low inherent risk complemented by a high control risk will attract high risk classification.
- **Very high risk:** Combination of high inherent risk and medium control risk makes this cell a very high risk area. Not only do the risk factors here have potentially significant adverse impact, but there is also the likelihood of control being compromised. A combination of medium inherent risk and high control risk also merits a risk classification of "Very High."
- **Extremely high risk:** High degree of inherent risk as well as high degree of control risk classifies these activities as extremely high risk. In addition to immediate audit attention and frequent review, such areas are primary candidates for maximum allocation of audit resources.
- **Medium risk:** This is a medium risk zone since the control risk is low although the inherent risk is of medium severity. The same classification is awarded to a combination of low inherent risk and medium control risk.
- **Low risk:** In view of both inherent risk and control risk being low, this combination is classified as a low risk area. This classification attracts the least amount of audit resources and has the lowest frequency of review.

Inherent Risks		Control Risks		
		Low	Medium	High
	High	A High Risk	B Very High Risk	C Extremely High Risk
	Medium	D Medium Risk	E High Risk	F Very High Risk
	Low	G Low Risk	H Medium Risk	I High Risk

FIGURE 6.1   Risk Matrix

The information systems auditor needs to continuously review the inherent business and control risks to assess whether they demonstrate a stable, increasing, or decreasing trend. An increasing trend in a high risk classification will invoke immediate audit attention with allocation of commensurate resources.

RISK AND AUDIT SAMPLE DETERMINATION

The information systems auditor would not generally be in a position to examine all information system assets present in the auditee unit. For example, in a unit where there are a few hundred workstations, to assess whether physical access control is working adequately, the auditor may not go to all those workstations. The auditor would select a sample that would represent the general characteristics of the auditee unit.

The auditor faces two major issues of deciding on sample size and ensuring proper representation while selecting a sample. They are described in the following paragraphs:

1. **Sample size:** The information systems auditor needs to decide on the number of units to be examined closely. This is known as the sample size. Continuing with the earlier example, the decision required to be taken is on how many computers should be examined that can be reasonably expected to demonstrate the characteristics of the entire unit. The characteristics that the auditor needs to focus on are the following:
   a. **Mission criticality:** In the case of information systems assets, which are mission critical, the size of the sample will have to be larger. Mission criticality needs to be determined not only from the viewpoint of the auditee as an entity but also for individual functions. Ideally, when the number of such assets in a functional area is not very high, 100 percent of such assets should be verified. Usually, the number of assets that are mission critical is not very high in every functional area. The examples here would include the central server, fall-back server, centralized alternative power supply system, captive power unit, central mail server, network router, and so forth. In some cases, for example, in a bank, even the front office terminals may be mission critical since their failure would hamper the business function of the bank. A guideline can be developed around following four themes:
      i. Where the number of mission-critical assets in each functional area is less than 5: 100 percent.
      ii. Where the number of mission-critical assets in each functional area exceeds 5 but is less than 10: 75 percent.
      iii. Where the number of mission-critical assets in each functional area exceeds 10 but is less than 20: 50 percent.
      iv. Where the number of mission-critical assets in each functional area exceeds 20: 25 percent, subject to minimum of 10.
   b. **Investment:** Another criterion for deciding on the sample size would be the investment involved. It may be noted that mission criticality is not influenced only by the financial investment. In addition, there may be some assets that are individually not highly valuable but collectively involve significant

investment. This results in the sample size being dependent not only on the total investment in the specific group of assets but also on the number of assets in the group. A guideline can be developed around the following four themes:

 i. Where the investment in the specific group of assets exceeds 25 percent of total investment made in information systems assets: between 50 and 100 percent.

 ii. Where the investment in the specific group of assets exceeds 15 percent but is less than 25 percent of total investment made in information systems assets: between 30 and 50 percent.

 iii. Where the investment in the specific group of assets exceeds 5 percent but is less than 15 percent of total investment made in information system assets: between 15 and 25 percent.

 iv. Where the investment in the specific group of assets is less than 5 percent of total investment made in information systems assets: between 5 and 15 percent.

2. **Representation:** The auditor would attempt to ensure that no part of the activities at the auditee unit goes unaudited. The sample must adequately represent the characteristics of the population. The sample size must accommodate representation from all functional units, preferably in the same proportion in which they are present in the auditee organization. For example, if in an auditee unit 500 workstations are present in the front office and 250 in the back office, the sample size selected for the back office and front office should reflect the same ratio.

Sample Selection

Having decided on the sample size, the information systems auditor would decide on the process of identifying the specific audit objects from the population. Continuing with our example, if it is decided to check 100 computers, the next decision to be made is which 100 computers should be examined. The auditor may use various methods available for selecting samples. One of the popular methods of selection is called random selection. Under this method, the auditor decides on a number on a random basis, for example, by generating random numbers in a computer program or even by opening a page in a book. If the value chosen is 5, it would mean that the auditor would start with the fifth workstation on the list and examine every fifth item found there, for example, the 5th item, 10th item, 15th item, and so forth. This cycle would continue till the number of items observed reaches the sample size of 100. Any standard textbook in statistics will provide useful information on the topic.

The information systems auditor must recognize that the lower the sample size, the greater is the possibility of an error, including a material error, going unobserved by the auditor. This is known as audit risk, and one way to reduce it is to increase the sample size. The information systems auditor needs to decide on the extent of audit risk while deciding on the sample size. It must be recognized that an element of audit risk will always be present.

AUDIT RISK ASSESSMENT

An information systems auditor collects evidence to form an opinion on whether the auditee entity achieves its objective, which may include safeguarding assets, maintaining an efficient and effective system, and ensuring data integrity. Due to the fact that the opinion is based on observing a sample, there is always a chance that some control failures or potential threats may escape notice and the auditor may erroneously conclude that the system is controlled, secured, and well managed.

Audit risk has two major components:

1. The risk of the unchecked portion containing a material error.
2. The risk that the auditor has failed to detect an error that has occurred, which is known as detection risk.

The primary focus of risk-based information systems audit is to provide reasonable assurance about adequacy of design and effectiveness of performance of the control framework. During the process of ascertaining the effectiveness of a control framework under a risk-based information systems audit, the auditor should review and report whether major exceptions and excesses are properly recorded and reported. The extent of substantive testing necessary is determined on the basis of risk assessment. The auditor may find it prudent to conduct 100 percent substantive testing of an audit area that is classified as extremely high risk in the risk matrix. The auditor may not consider employing 100 percent testing for the very high risk classifications, but may resort to the same if the constituents of the classification demonstrate an increasing trend across different time periods. In case of audit areas with a low risk classification, the auditor may choose between surprise tests and conducting a scheduled audit at longer intervals.

No matter how successful the auditor is in reducing the exposure to audit risk, there will always be a residual audit risk since it is integrally associated with an audit process.

Audit Process and Audit Risk

Audit risk (AR) is the product of combined risk assessment (CRA) and detection risk (DR). Combined risk assessment itself is a product of inherent risk (IR) and control risk (CR). The framework operates in the following manner.

An information systems auditor needs to understand the system and its vulnerabilities to be able to recognize the inherent risks of the system. Controls are designed, wherever possible, as a tool to mitigate the inherent risk. Once an understanding of inherent business risk and control risk is achieved, a risk matrix can be designed. This risk matrix is used to decide on the type of audit process to be carried out, including test checks, walkthroughs, and compliance testing. The intensity of these processes will range from minimal to high depending on the risk classification in the risk matrix. The auditors then decide on the nature, timing, and extent of substantive tests to be carried out. The framework of understanding and usage of audit risk is shown in Figure 6.2.

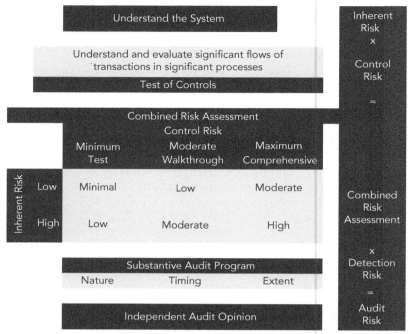

FIGURE 6.2 Audit Risk Framework

Some of the major terms used in audit risk assessment are described next.

Inherent risk: It is the propensity of information system assets or resources controlled by information systems to materially compromise information security, in absence of internal controls. It must be noted that internal controls are used to mitigate risk and there may be instances where no mitigation tool is available or the cost of deployment of the mitigation tool outweighs the benefit from it. Examples of inherent risk include the possibility of virus infection during e-mail communication. This assessment is to be made without considering the potential impact of the control mitigation.

Control risk: This is the risk whether the controls implemented to mitigate the inherent risk are adequately designed and function efficiently. Examples of adequate design of internal control include the existence of antivirus software to prevent a virus outbreak, but instances of the software not being kept up to date is an example of inefficient functioning of the internal control.

Combined risk assessment: This is the overall impact of the inherent risk and the control risk. It may be recalled that these are the two components of the risk matrix. This assessment goes on to define the risk classification.

Detection risk: This is the possibility that an error, in particular, a material error, may go unobserved by the auditor during the information systems audit.

Audit risk: This is the overall impact of combined risk assessment and detection risk leading to the auditor forming an erroneous opinion and making a misstatement. To reduce audit risk, the information systems auditor has to try to reduce the detection risk and identify the control risk that the auditee should try to reduce.

Populating a Risk Matrix

The critical aspect of any risk is its origin and adverse impact. Arguably, there can be another dimension—detectability, which we consider under the audit risk. One of the biggest challenges that an information systems auditor faces is to quantify the net impact of risk factors and to express them on a common scale to ensure comparability between one risk factor and another. The most common solution to this problem is designing a risk matrix. How to populate a risk matrix is discussed next.

The most common form of a risk matrix uses two metrics—severity and frequency. Severity refers to the potential adverse impact of a risk event materializing while frequency determines the likelihood of such materialization. Using both, one can develop a scale that can be used to describe the severity of risk events and the frequency of their occurrence. The scale can be numeric, descriptive, or qualitative, as shown in Table 6.1.

After defining the measure on the risk scale using numeric values, the next phase will be to design a matrix that will define the risk zones by multiplying the numeric values on both axes. The risk measurement matrix is shown in Table 6.2.

The auditee may decide on the level of acceptable risk, depending on the level of risk aggression. For example, all values above 15 may be considered as highly risky while all values below 4 may be considered low risk. The high risk zone may be defined as an unacceptable risk zone while the low risk zone may be defined as the preferred risk zone. The rest of the cells between 5 and 14 are the areas of executive decision where the organization will employ risk mitigation techniques to bring down the composite score to within the acceptable zone. Even if the mitigation strategy does not work, the auditee

TABLE 6.1 Severity and Frequency Scale

Risk Event			Damage to Data Storage Media		
Severity			Frequency		
Numeric	Descriptive	Remarks	Numeric	Descriptive	Remarks
5	Critical	Loss of all data of entire entity	5	Frequent	Weekly occurrence
4	High	Loss of all data of a division	4	Probable	Monthly occurrence
3	Moderate	Partial loss of data of entire entity	3	Common	Biannual occurrence
2	Minor	Partial loss of data of a division	2	Remote	Annual occurrence
1	Immaterial	Minor loss of data	1	Unlikely	Once in five years

TABLE 6.2   Risk Measurement Matrixes

		Severity				
		1	2	3	4	5
	5	5	10	15	20	25
	4	4	8	12	16	20
Frequency	3	3	6	9	12	15
	2	2	4	6	8	10
	1	1	2	3	4	5

may still operate processes in the acceptable zone provided the risk–return trade off is beneficial to the organization. In case mitigation is a regulatory requirement, the organization has to implement mitigation tools irrespective of the costs involved.

 ## RISK MANAGEMENT STRATEGY

The risk management strategy focuses on understanding the inherent risks as they are the major obstacles to achievement of goals and objectives of the information system. Inherent risk is often defined as the risk of failing to achieve operational efficiency and effectiveness—a definition that is particularly useful in the context of information system assets. Thus inherent risk may be considered as the threats to achievement of the performance objectives of the information systems assets. Organizations create strategies to respond to these threats, which are operationalized by various designed processes. The controls are designed at this stage. As the threats and operational objectives change, inherent risk profile changes. Failure to change controls to adapt to changes in the operating environment is likely to make the control ineffective and even dysfunctional.

Every organization and process has to accept risk to some extent, as the efficiency it achieves is determined by the ability of the organization or process to ensure that the risks do not interfere in the achievement of objectives. The management has to decide the extent of exposure to a risk that it is willing to accept. The success of risk management lies in striking a balance between accepted risks and controls designed to manage those risks. Thus if the management fails to recognize the risk factors, it is unlikely that a control will be designed for managing those risks.

An effective risk management system will provide an environment wherein the business executives can take informed decisions on matters that are linked with inherent risk. The major alternatives that a business executive has in terms of managing inherent risk are the following four:

1. **Accept:** These are the risks the business decides to accept. No mitigation tools are designed for these risks, either because there are none or the cost of deploying such controls outweighs the benefits. For example, a car manufacturer may not build a nuclear-attack-proof bunker to save their main server while the treasury of a country may find it prudent to make such an investment.

2. **Transfer:** This involves transferring the adverse exposure of the risk to a third party, which buys it for a price. A common example of this is buying a fire insurance policy.

3. **Avoid:** Essentially the only way a system can avoid an inherent risk is to stay away from the activity. This may often entail changes in the business goal. For example, an organization may decide not to use any open source software, apprehending that there may not be adequate support available.

4. **Reduce:** This strategy will involve either reducing the magnitude of loss arising out of a risk event or reducing the frequency of occurrence. Impact of data loss arising out of complete failure of the storage system can be reduced either by increasing the number of backups kept or by storing a lower volume of data in each storage medium. Whereas the first approach will reduce the magnitude of loss as there are backups available, the second approach will reduce the frequency of complete failure of the storage system as the data are stored across a number of storage media.

The control environment plays a significant role in setting up the discipline in the organization and may even contribute to setting systems objectives. For example, an extensive data backup system will allow the adoption of a control target of least systems disruption arising out of data loss.

In order to have an effective risk management system, organizations often classify their processes into the following two categories:

1. **Core processes:** These are the processes that are linked with activities that an organization uses to design, develop, produce, and deliver goods and services.

2. **Internal service processes:** These are processes that link various other business processes and provide resources for optimal performance.

The management needs to identify the process owners in order to have the necessary skill set for the functions and also to design an effective control system. The objectives for the process owners should be clearly defined so that the process performance can be measured. Unless a performance measurement system is working, the internal control system cannot be made effective. Often, the identification of inherent risks and monitoring control performance are the responsibilities of the process owner.

An information systems auditor needs to have a complete understanding of the entire process in the auditee organization to be able to develop an appropriate audit plan for conducting a risk-based information systems audit.

CHAPTER SEVEN

Business Continuity and Disaster Recovery Plan

THIS CHAPTER INTRODUCES THE concept of business continuity and disaster recovery and its importance in an organization. It provides various checklists that the information systems auditor may use while conducting an audit to review the effectiveness of business continuity and disaster recovery plans. At the end of the chapter, we will be able to recognize various aspects of testing of the business continuity and disaster recovery process that should be included in an audit plan.

BUSINESS CONTINUITY AND DISASTER RECOVERY PROCESS

The business continuity and disaster recovery process comprises distinct activities that are to be undertaken by the implementing organization. It is a common error on the part of many organizations to look at the process as a business continuity exercise without recognizing the criticality of independent components. This view often leads to design and implementation of an inefficient business continuity and disaster recovery process. The business continuity and disaster recovery process usually comprises the following four components:

1. Business impact analysis
2. Incident response plan
3. Disaster recovery plan
4. Business continuity plan

BUSINESS IMPACT ANALYSIS

Business impact analysis (BIA) is the process of identifying functions that are critical for the information system as a whole or a component thereof, and assessing possible losses and adverse impact in the event such functions are not available. The concept of availability includes maintenance of integrity and confidentiality of the information system resources. For example, if the backed-up data are compromised, they may be technically available but practically unusable. The information systems auditor may employ appropriate audit techniques, including interviews and observation, to assess the effectiveness of an impact analysis exercise carried out by the auditee.

Impact Analysis

The process of an impact analysis review will include the following seven steps:

1. Ascertainment of criticality of the function being audited for achievement of the information systems objective and overall enterprise strategy.
2. Determination of the maximum limit for which the function may remain unavailable without any adverse impact or loss. Determination of this limit will be useful in deciding on the risk tolerance level for each function and consequent design of mitigation strategies.
3. Identification of contagion impact on other functions if the function under study becomes unavailable. This analysis will lead to an assessment of overall loss caused by nonavailability of one system. Often a function may trigger more indirect losses than direct losses. For example, failure of the main server in a bank may have a limited direct loss at the data center but a larger loss arises out of disruption of service at the bank's branches. In order to prevent such losses, banks invest heavily in the setting up of a backup server. The impact of such analysis may be viewed from two perspectives:
   a. Overall operational impact of unavailability of the audit object.
   b. Overall financial impact of unavailability of the audit object.
4. Assessment of possibility of any damage and penalty arising out of breach of legal or commercial obligations. Such obligations include breaches of regulatory requirements, service level agreements (SLA), or any other contractual liabilities that may arise out of such unavailability.
5. Assessment of the probable impact of such service outage on reputation and customer confidence. This assumes criticality if the failure occurs at the point of service delivery.

6. Assessment of the strategy for reduction of adverse impacts on long-term sustainability, if any, including those on future sales or industry perception that may gradually convert themselves into financial loss. Some events may have a limited short-term adverse impact, but repetition of such events may seriously compromise long-term sustainability of the business.

7. Determination of level of tolerance defined in terms of maximum, acceptable, and permissible extent of service outage or corresponding financial loss.

Contagion Impact

Contagion impact refers to a situation where an attack that initially affected a localized function spreads over related functions and potentially affects the entire system. The term is widely used in the medical community to indicate the spreading of a disease from one person to another through close contact. In the context of information systems, a common example is the spread of a virus across the entire network that originated from a single computer that downloaded a virus-affected attachment from an e-mail.

Service Level Agreement

A service level agreement refers to an agreement between a service provider and its client, specifying the minimum quality criteria of service. The defined deliverables often include minimum performance level, recovery time in case of disruptions, key skill availability, and so forth. A client may include specific provisions in the service level agreement to ensure that the service provider is compliant with the internal security and quality requirements of the client.

Requirements for Recovery

The recovery requirements definition procedure may include the following 10 areas:

1. Requirements of resources necessary to restart the function, including specifications of minimum-level and standard-level requirements. This analysis should include the lead time necessary to procure the specified resource.

2. Point of origin of resources in terms of whether they are sourced internally within the organization or externally from an outside vendor. Sourcing from an outside vendor may involve a formal process that may be time-consuming. In such cases, the system should provide measures for expediting the process, which may include the automatic escalation of financial authority of an executive in the event of an emergency.

3. Dependency on other business functions for successful recovery and the cost thereof. It may also involve establishing a single point of command during the recovery phase, with authority across concerned divisions.

4. Impact of the recovery effort on the service level maintained at other business functions. There may be a requirement of temporary shutdown of other business functions during the restarting of the disrupted function. Such cases involve a forced service discontinuation as a part of the recovery process.

5. Dependency on external businesses, suppliers, and vendors for successful recovery and the cost thereof. This assumes criticality if the affected resources are proprietary assets of the third party and cannot be substituted by any other assets.

6. Scope of service level agreement requirements and commitments from external agencies that are related to the recovery activities. This procedure will also highlight potential weaknesses associated with the recovery process.

7. Resources and procedures for backup and recovery from backup for the disrupted activities. The recovery process often involves a relaxed control mechanism to expedite recovery. This relaxation may be a source of potential compromise of integrity of data and access process.

8. Backup requirement to be observed during recovery effort so that in case of a failed recovery effort the status quo can be restored. This assumes criticality when the recovery process is combined with technology upgrades.

9. Recovery time objectives in terms of time and resource requirements to achieve complete recovery from disruption. In the event of a complete recovery process being spread over time, the time schedule of periodic achievement should be reviewed.

10. Additional precaution or verification measures to be adopted if the recovery is being done without a test run. Though not advisable, such practices are not uncommon, especially in emergency conditions and when appropriate test facilities are not available.

INCIDENT RESPONSE PLAN

An incident is an attack against the information systems as a whole or a constituent asset that poses a clear threat to continuation of activity of the information systems. Such discontinuation may eventually lead to disruption of business activity. Incident recognition is based on existence of a threat irrespective of the magnitude of loss suffered. There is often a tendency to recognize an event based on adverse financial impact. Incident analysis clearly requires recognition of the incident irrespective of the amount of adverse financial impact essentially because such incidents can potentially lead to larger losses though the immediate impact may be limited. For example, the ability to secure unauthorized access to a website server may eventually be used to compromise the e-commerce website and commit fraudulent transactions.

Incidents are recognized by presence of specific indicators, though this is not a necessary requirement. The indicators can be classified based on associated certainty of occurrence of an incident. An illustrative list of four such classifications with inclusive examples is provided here:

1. Possible indicators of incidents:
   a. Existence of files that are unfamiliar or uncommon.
   b. Presence of unknown programs or running processes.
   c. Consumption of resources not commensurate with the perceived level of activity.
   d. Unusual and unexplained disruptions in systems service and utilities.

2. Probable indicators of incidents:
   a. Evidence of activities at inappropriate or unscheduled times.
   b. Presence of a new account, especially with administrative privileges.
   c. Reported attacks on information systems assets.
   d. Repeated failure of communication or power line.
3. Definite indicators of incidents:
   a. Unauthorized reactivation or use of dormant user accounts.
   b. Changes to system logs using external access.
   c. Presence of tools and utilities that potentially can be used to compromise security.
   d. Physical signs of instability, like cracks appearing in the floor or wall.
4. Predefined situations that signal an automatic incident:
   a. Loss of confidentiality, integrity, or availability of system assets.
   b. Violation of information systems policy that appears to be a deliberate act.
   c. Violation of any requirement under any statute.

DISASTER RECOVERY PLAN

A disaster could be defined as a situation characterized by any of the following five events:

1. Complete loss of each single physical site with information technology assets.
2. Complete failure of any single internal or external information technology systems infrastructure service provider.
3. Power outage and/or disruptions of internal and/or external network connections to locations having information technology production facilities.
4. Any single point of technology failure with significant impact and/or disruptions and outage of services related to information technology infrastructure.
5. Nonaccessibility of critical location.

Disaster recovery process enhances the ability of an entity to swiftly and readily respond to interruptions in services. These efforts are driven by a formal plan of restoration of critical business functions. Information systems auditors should verify whether the auditee has an appropriate disaster recovery plan in place and in practice. An information systems auditor may test the adequacy of the disaster recovery plan by ensuring that the plan covers, at the least, the following 24 areas:

1. Detailed description of the purpose and scope of the plan.
2. Specification of conditions under which disaster recovery plans will be activated.
3. Processes to be followed for activation of disaster recovery plan.
4. Identification and description of actions to be taken on a priority basis whenever an incident threatens the continuity of systems or business operations or human life.
5. Short-term procedures describing necessary actions to be taken, including moving specified activities to alternative temporary locations, to facilitate restoration of disrupted business process within a specified timeframe.

6. Detailed description of resumption procedures specifying actions to be taken subsequent to a disruption to restore normal business operations.
7. Procedures for maintaining an updated and relevant business continuity plan.
8. Procedures for periodic testing of the business continuity plan to ensure efficiency and performance of the plan.
9. Steps adopted to promote organization-wide awareness, including training, and to create an understanding of the business continuity process to ensure effectiveness of the designed plan.
10. Responsibility assignment procedures identifying persons responsible for performing various functions and activities under the business continuity plan.
11. Systems to ensure that the business continuity plan document is made available to all executives on the distribution list. One of the common methods used to achieve this is to maintain a copy on an intranet and notify authorized recipients about any updated version.
12. System to ensure that the document distribution list is updated. This may involve working in close coordination with the human resources department.
13. Procedures for testing the contingency plan and recovery procedure.
14. Lists containing name of contact person, contact numbers, and address of third-party suppliers that need to be alerted to the disruption.
15. Lists of phone numbers and alternative contact channels of employees, in particular those who have been assigned roles during an emergency.
16. Phone lists and alternative contact details of emergency services like fire, police, hardware vendor, software vendor, suppliers, customers, backup location, and so forth.
17. Contact details of medical professionals, including employees trained for emergency interventions such as administration of first aid and life-saving techniques.
18. Details of logistics providers such as airlines, hotels, and transport agencies.
19. Standard procedures for medical intervention, including for transfer to hospitals.
20. Insurance papers and claim forms.
21. List of information systems assets in all locations including software and hardware configuration.
22. A list specifying the location of data dictionary, data and program files, source and object codes, user manuals, backup media, and the like.
23. Description of alternative manual procedures to be followed if automated controls don't work. For example, if the fire sprinklers do not start automatically, manual intervention will be necessary.
24. Checklist for inventory taking and updating the contingency plan on a regular basis.

TYPES OF DISASTER RECOVERY PLANS

Disaster recovery plans may be categorized into the following four types:

1. **Emergency plan:** The emergency plan document specifies actions to be performed immediately after a disaster event. It covers four main aspects:

a. The plan must identify the notification chain to be observed immediately in the event of a disaster. The list will identify the persons and agencies to be notified, including management, police, fire department, medicos, and others, and wherever applicable the sequence and method of such notification.

b. The plan should identify immediate actions to be undertaken, such as shutdown of equipment, removal of files, termination of power, isolation of affected units, and so forth, that will prevent the disaster from spreading and contain the adverse impact.

c. Evacuation procedures, including the assembly point, must be specified in the plan. The plan should identify the person, and substitutes, who will be responsible for evacuation operation. This procedure needs to be reviewed whenever there is a change in office layout or office location.

d. Subsequent to evacuation, the return procedures are to be described in the plan document. In addition to specifying the reoccupation procedure, the minimum conditions that must be met before the site is considered safe should be defined. The plan should clearly identify the personnel responsible for specific actions and protocols to be followed.

2. **Backup plan:** The backup plan is an important component of the comprehensive disaster readiness activity of any organization. The backup plan will specify the type of backup necessary, the frequency and procedures for making the backup, the backup storage location and facilities, the personnel responsible for backup and restoration, and so forth. The plan will also specify an alternative venue where resources can be assembled and operations restarted along with assigned priority for recovering various systems.

3. **Recovery plan:** An information systems auditor needs to check whether the plan is optimized to restore operations quickly so that the information system function continues to service the organization. Recovery plans will set out procedures for restoration of full capabilities of information systems. The recovery time target also needs to be specified.

4. **Test plan:** This is the final component of a disaster recovery plan that is designed to identify deficiencies in critical aspects of the system, including emergency, backup, and recovery plans. The test plan lays out the processes to be followed to test the planned activities by way of simulation and mock drills. These drills would identify the critical deficiencies in the plan and examine the preparedness of the auditee organization and its personnel to face a disaster.

EMERGENCY PREPAREDNESS AUDIT CHECKLIST

When testing the emergency plan, the information systems auditor may use the following 10-point checklist to ensure that the auditee is prepared to face disasters.

1. Determine whether instructions are available for emergency shutdown of computer system and other components.

2. Inspect visibility of emergency exits, fire extinguishers, power switches, and other equipment for emergency intervention.
3. Determine whether clear instructions for operation of emergency intervention devices are available and understood by the designated users.
4. Examine building evacuation procedures for reasonableness and conditions of use and inquire about the last time they were tested.
5. Inquire about the availability of emergency telephone numbers for local police, ambulance, fire departments, help desk, building maintenance desk, and backup recovery people.
6. Ascertain whether components used in equipment are vendor recommended. This assumes criticality in equipment such as humidifiers, air-conditioning, air purifiers, and others where the use of nonspecified filters will allow damaging particles to drift into sensitive information systems assets.
7. Compare the frequency of maintenance of such equipment with the manufacturer's recommended schedule.
8. Determine whether information systems assets are maintained using materials and processes approved either by the manufacturer or the auditee.
9. Verify whether an uninterruptible power system is optimized to activate immediately on failure of commercial power supply.
10. Check the availability of private power generators to meet prolonged power supply problems. The availability of an adequate supply of backup fuel for the power generator is also to be verified.

BUSINESS CONTINUITY STRATEGIES

Business continuity planning should encompass various strategies, including the following five:

1. **Prevention strategy:** This strategy aims at reducing the probability of the disaster happening. Such reduction is achieved by balancing facilities and putting in place mitigation tools against probable causes of disaster. It may be noted that rolling out a prevention strategy involves cost and requires a careful cost-benefit analysis before being implemented.
2. **Response strategy:** This strategy seeks to ensure planned reaction to specific events. The strategy focuses on preventing further damage, assessing the extent of damage, and establishing a recovery time objective. The strategy also provides for an appropriate communication method to the external world to protect the reputation of the business entity.
3. **Resumption strategy:** This segment prioritizes the resumption of time-sensitive business processes at the earliest, preferably immediately after the interruption or at least within a stipulated period thereafter. It must be noted that all operations may not be fully recoverable immediately and, in extreme cases, where it involves a specialized technology or skill, may not be fully recoverable at all. Further, the resumption strategy should focus on the critical activities that can resume delivery of the bare minimum services necessary.

4. **Recovery strategy:** This strategy focuses on resumption of processes that were not addressed during the resumption phase. These are usually less time-sensitive processes. The recovery time objective for these activities is greatly influenced by the time taken for resumption of the time-sensitive functions. The strategy may also provide for the recovery occurring at an alternative location.

5. **Restoration strategy:** Restoration is the process of repairing and restoring the primary site or system to the level of operating capacity available before the disaster. Restoration strategy specifies processes that will ensure total resumption of business operations either from the original site or, in the case of a catastrophic disaster, from a new site.

■ BUSINESS RESUMPTION PLAN AUDIT CHECKLIST

The information systems auditor will review the business resumption plan of the auditee to form an opinion on adequacy and effectiveness of the plan. In order to be able to form an opinion, the information systems auditor may critically examine the plan using the following methodology:

1. Determine whether a business resumption plan exists and includes, at a minimum, the following elements:
   a. Identifies activities and processes that are essential for business continuation.
   b. Prioritizes activities based on how critical and essential they are for business continuation.
   c. Precedence of a business impact analysis over the plan development to assess and recognize the operational and financial impacts of loss of essential functions.
   d. Was developed with active participation from operations managers and key employees of processes that are covered by the plan.
   e. Conducts an assessment exercise to identify resources whose availability is critical for recovery activity, along with the location of their availability. The plan should also define the process to be followed to secure the supply of such resources and escalation of authority, wherever necessary.
   f. Is simple, understandable, effective, and easy to implement.
   g. Critical assumptions behind the plan are explicitly mentioned and are realistic.
2. Assess sufficiency of information backup procedures to facilitate recovery of critical data within the stipulated recovery time objective.
3. Confirm existence of a process for testing the business resumption plan.
4. Review extent to which the business resumption plan has been tested.
5. Review existing business impact analysis plan and reports to understand appropriateness and adequacy of the planning and reporting mechanism.
6. Be aware of the assumptions, background information, and recovery objectives to fairly assess the preparation and effectiveness of business resumption plans. It is to be noted that the extent of preparedness will be greatly influenced by the recovery objectives.

7. Review the process, methodology used, and skill set involved in development of the existing business resumption plan. If these elements are not contemporary to the business process, there is a distinct possibility that the business resumption plan will be suboptimally drafted.

8. Review and analyze the methodology used and assumptions considered while performing business impact analysis. The more realistic the assumptions are, the more implementable the business resumption plan will be.

9. Examine the adequacy and appropriateness of resources allotted to ensure the business resumption plan remains pragmatic, contemporary, and effective.

10. Review the version management system observed during the revision of the plan to ensure that in case of need, the most current version will be accessed and used.

11. Determine whether the plan was reviewed and updated at least once within the past 12 months. If there has been a technology or environmental change, the revision should be made at the instance of such a change being incorporated. Unless continuous examination for relevance and applicability is made, there is a possibility that the business resumption plan will be outdated or suboptimal.

12. Confirm whether copies of the business resumption plan are stored in several locations that are designed to survive disasters and will be available to authorized users on a need basis.

13. Conduct a general review of the information backup procedure followed by the auditee. Assess coverage of the information backup procedure and storage of backup media to form an opinion on the dependability of the same.

14. Confirm whether the business resumption plan includes provisions for the following resources:

    a. Personnel
        i. Awareness of and familiarity with the plan by key employees.
        ii. Awareness of employees about their roles and responsibilities as and when the business resumption plan is activated.
        iii. Availability of contact information of key employees, especially after working hours and on holidays.
        iv. Identification and availability of substitute staff if primary staffs accorded with a specific responsibility are unavailable for some reason, including as an impact of the disaster.

    b. Building, utilities, and transportation
        i. Provision for compulsory inspection of the building and facilities by a qualified civil engineer or equivalent expert soon after the disaster to identify the requirements of repairing any damage before declaring the premises safe for reoccupation.
        ii. Specification of situations that may call for arranging alternative shelter and the procedure of acquiring such an alternative shelter. It may be noted that alternative accommodation in the vicinity is likely to be similarly affected by the same disaster.
        iii. Review all third-party agreements concerning the use of backup facilities.

    iv. Confirm that backup facilities, including telecommunications and utilities, have adequate capacity in light of current and projected needs.

    v. Assess whether the backup site meets the security requirements of the processes activated. It is often found that security requirements observed in the primary location are relaxed at the alternative location enhancing chances of a security compromise. The information systems auditor needs to look out for such relaxation.

    vi. Review the impact of failures of third-party supplies, such as electrical power, natural gas, and others on the business resumption plan. In the event that such supplies are critical to the resumption plan, the recovery time objective will be greatly influenced by the time needed to restore such supply chain.

    vii. Confirm regular inspection and testing of safety features in the premises and system and review test reports to identify any observed deficiency.

    viii. Assess whether the impact of disruption of transportation systems was considered in the business resumption plan. Further assess the impact of the lack of transportation service on availability of employees and ability of vendors to provide goods necessary for the recovery activity.

c. Information technology assets

    i. Verify if the business resumption plan is contemporary and is based on the current information technology and facilities environment. In the event there has been a major change in technology, the resumption process may be affected because of nonavailability of support for assets using an earlier technology.

    ii. Review the principles and process of prioritization of resumption of critical applications and systems. The basis of prioritization is sensitivity of attainment of business objectives to availability of resources.

    iii. Confirm whether the plan specifies reasonable recovery time objectives for recovery and availability of the critical system.

    iv. Ensure that the business resumption plan considers urgent resumption of telecommunications and network facilities while maintaining the security requirement.

    v. Confirm existence of a testing schedule and whether the schedule is adequate in view of criticality of function and probability of disruption.

    vi. Obtain the date of the last test of the business resumption plan and determine if the weaknesses identified in the tests were addressed.

d. Administrative procedures

    i. Identify an alternative plan to be enacted by management to maintain operations if the building is inaccessible for an extended period of time owing to severity of damage.

    ii. Provision of a designated emergency operations center to be used by disaster management teams for coordinating response and recovery operation.

    iii. Confirm whether the business resumption plan provides for procedures for declaration of disaster, general shutdown, and migration of operations to backup facility.

    iv. Confirm identification of essential records and maintenance of a duplicate set of such records in a remote secured location.

      v. Confirm separation of essential records that are urgently required from other records to facilitate quick retrieval during a disaster or immediately thereafter.

   e. Ensure that the business resumption plan requires the maintenance of records of names and contact numbers of primary and alternative suppliers of equipment and other materials that are essential for recovery operation.

   f. Ensure that the business resumption plan identifies the critical materials needed along with their substitutes in case the identified primary material is unavailable.

   g. Ensure provisions for accelerated or automated approval for out-of-budget expenses required during the business resumption phase.

   h. Ensure the involvement of management in the following activities:

      i. Providing resource support for plan development.

      ii. Identification and prioritization of essential activities for recovery.

      iii. Defining backup process and setting up the backup system.

      iv. Defining the procedure to activate the business resumption plan.

RECOVERY PROCEDURES TESTING CHECKLIST

The real test of the business continuity plan is during recovery from a disaster. The closest thing to a real recovery is a simulated disaster. The following audit procedures are suggested for determining adequacy of testing of recovery procedures:

1. Determine whether there is organization-wide participation in periodic test plans and programs.
2. Observe the project team in action during testing and note audit concerns.
3. Prepare or obtain a checklist of time-driven actions and deliverables defined by the business resumption plan.
4. Ensure that functional users have reviewed the test results for critical application systems and have removed the observed deficiencies both at primary and backup facilities.
5. Ensure that someone in the recovery team is taking notes on the basis of time taken and action performed. These notes should include both positive and negative results, and later become part of the test report. These notes play a critical role in optimizing recovery time objectives.
6. Identify executives with knowledge of critical physical access enablers, such as master keys, combination numbers, special codes, and others necessary to activate physical security devices. Ensure that security administrator is authorized to access such information during recovery from a local disaster.

PLAN MAINTENANCE CHECKLIST

Business continuity and disaster recovery plan maintenance procedures are as important as, if not more than, the plan development process. A plan that is out of date cannot be used at the time of need. An information systems auditor may conduct the following five checks to determine the adequacy of the plan maintenance procedures:

1. Understand how the plan is updated, and what the conditions and criteria are that necessitate compulsory updates of the plan.
2. Determine the adequacy of plan update frequency. Ideally, the plan should be updated prior to the next testing and at every instance involving a change in technology or operating environment.
3. Inquire how plan changes are communicated, and to whom, how, and where.
4. Ensure that one central location or person is assigned the responsibility of updating the plan document. Decentralized responsibility does not work in many cases and often creates a problem of version management.
5. Determine the frequency of updating hardware and software inventory lists with input from all end-users and locations. A periodic questionnaire should be sent to confirm the additions and changes to the original inventory list.

VITAL RECORDS RETENTION CHECKLIST

The information systems auditor should conduct the following seven audit procedures to assess the extent of control over the record retention program adopted by the auditee:

1. Read the vital records retention guidelines of the auditee to understand the specific requirements of the auditee for records archiving.
2. Inquire how records are stored and whether maintained as hard copies or digitized. Verify how the organization minimizes duplication of records and establishes procedures for handling, storing, and retrieving records.
3. Confirm how the authenticity of digital records is verified and whether digital signatures or encryption tools are used for the process.
4. Inquire whether the legal staff reviews and updates the records retention schedule to ensure compliance with statutory and regulatory requirements for records retention.
5. Ensure that a manual log for paper-based and physical magnetic media is maintained that shows retention label number, name of the section/department, name of contact person, short description of the records, form or record number, and date. The auditor should take a sample of record entries from the log and trace them to the storage place indicated, to confirm existence and functioning of the system.
6. Ensure that an automated log for electronic magnetic media is maintained that shows file name and number, file owner's name and details, brief description of the records, transaction details, if any, and transaction beginning and ending dates. The auditor should take a sample of entries from the log, trace them to the storage place indicated, and confirm their existence.
7. Confirm that all unwanted paper materials were destroyed or recycled, and sensitive magnetic materials degaussed before being destroyed. Verify whether necessary technical safeguards are taken to prevent reading of file contents during handing over magnetic media for reuse or replacement.

Digitizing

Digitization, in the context of documents, refers either to scanned images of hard copies of documents or documents created in an electronic form like word processor, spreadsheet, and so forth. Authenticity of such documents is usually ensured by way of either physical or password-based access control, or digital signatures. Technically speaking, digitizing involves converting text, image, sound, and so forth into a binary format.

Binary Format

Binary format is a system where the expression is based on two values: one and zero. Each of the values (1 or 0) in a binary number is multiplied by an exponent of 2. Binary system is a base-2 system where each digit represents an exponential power of 2, with the exponential value being computed with reference to position from extreme right. The rightmost digit represents 2^0, the next digit represents 2^1, followed by 2^2, till the left most digit, which will represent 2^n. Thus the value 110101 will be converted into decimal system by $[(1) \times 2^5] + [(1) \times 2^4] + [(0) \times 2^3] + [(1) \times 2^2] + [(0) \times 2^1] + [(1) \times 2^0] = 32 + 16 + 0 + 4 + 0 + 1 = 53$. The original concept of binary was described in ancient India by Pingala, arguably sometime between 800 BCE and 2 CE. The binary system is the language all modern computers understand and work on.

Digital Signature

Digital signature is a mathematical methodology to ensure authenticity of a digital message or document. Digital signatures serve two purposes—they establish the authenticity of the sender of a message or the creator of a document, and validate whether the message or document was changed after the author had signed it. Digital signatures come in the form of software that allows affixing them on electronic messages or documents. If any change is made in the message or the document, the digital signature is removed, signifying loss of integrity. The recipient of the message or document may examine the digital signature to find out to whom it was issued. Digital signatures are issued by a certifying authority that maintains a record of all digital signatures issued by it. The signatures remain valid for a specific period and after expiration they are to be renewed. Digital signatures are also used to encrypt a document or message that prevents unauthorized users from reading it. Many countries have appropriate legislation in place permitting the use of digital signatures and admitting them as evidence in courts of law.

FORMS AND DOCUMENTS

The information systems auditor needs to be satisfied that the auditee uses documents necessary for a smooth roll out of the business resumption plan. Some of the forms that the auditee organization must have are listed here, along with a standard template for those forms. These documents (Exhibits 7.1 to 7.13) are also available for download. Please refer to About the Website at the end of the book for more information.

Alternative Site Procedure

This document describes the physical dimensions of the alternative sites along with facilities available there. A sample format is provided in Exhibit 7.1.

EXHIBIT 7.1 Alternative Site Procedure Sample Format

Name of Office:

Address:

Phone No./E-mail ID: Page __ of ___

Alternative Site Team		
Responsibility	**Name of Employee**	**Alternative**

First Alternative Site	
Name of Location	
Address	
Person to Contact	
Alternative Person(s)	
How to Reach	
Time to Reach	

Facilities	Available	Required	To Be Procured
Floor Space			
Computers			
Power Points			
Software			
Network			
Peripheral Devices			
Customer Service Area			
Services Offered			

Facility Provider	Name, Address, and Contact Number	Lead Time
Computers		
Software		
Network		
Peripheral Devices		

Restoration Target	Time to Shift	Time to Setup	Time to Restart
Hours			

Alternative Site Layout

(Continued)

EXHIBIT 7.1 *(Continued)*

Second Alternative Site			
Name of Location			
Address			
Person to Contact			
Alternative Person(s)			
How to Reach			
Time to Reach			

Facilities	Available	Required	To Be Procured
Floor Space			
Computers			
Power Points			
Software			
Network			
Peripheral Devices			
Customer Service Area			
Services Offered			

Facility Provider	Name, Address, and Contact Number		Lead Time
Computers			
Software			
Network			
Peripheral Devices			

Restoration Target	Time to Shift	Time to Setup	Time to Restart
Hours			

Alternative Site Layout

Communication Resources

This list provides details of the communication infrastructure available at the site of disaster and is useful for resource planning during the resumption phase. A sample format is provided in Exhibit 7.2.

EXHIBIT 7.2 Communication Resources Sample Format

Name of Office:

Address:

Phone No. /E-mail ID: Page __ of ___

Equipment	Supplier	Service Provider	Technical Specifications	Drawing	Support Contact
Voice Services					
Data					
LAN					
WAN					
	Last Update	Verification	Sent to Head Office	Sent to Branch	Sent to Off-Site
Date					
Verified by					

Contingency Log

This document is the register of all contingencies. Contingencies are noted in this register and serve as a guide to decide on replacement needs as well as to get data on the frequency and impact of such events. A sample format is provided in Exhibit 7.3.

EXHIBIT 7.3 Contingency Log Sample Format

Name of Office:

Address:

Phone No. /E-mail ID: Page __ of ___

Date	Asset Involved	Nature of Contingency	Resolution Procedure	Time Taken

	Last Update	Verification	Sent to Head Office	Sent to Branch	Sent to Off-Site
Date					
Verified by					

Contingency Plan Contact Information

This document contains contact information of all internal and stakeholder participants in a resumption plan. A sample format is provided in Exhibit 7.4.

EXHIBIT 7.4 Contingency Plan Contact Information Sample Format

Name of Office:

Address:

Phone No./E-mail ID: Page __ of ___

Keyword	Name, Address, Description	Office	Phone Numbers	
			Mobile	Residence
Internal				
Manager Database Administrator				
Regional Office				
Regional Manager				
Head Office				
Head-IT Senior Manager				
Backup Locations				
Nearby Branches				
Hardware				
Software				
Network				
Virus				
UPS				
Generator				
Telephone				

(Continued)

EXHIBIT 7.4 Continued

Mobile				
Fire				
Police				
Power				
Ambulance				
Doctor				
Hospital				
Insurance				
Transport Provider				

	Last Update	Verification	Sent to Head Office	Sent to Branch	Sent to Off-Site
Date					
Verified by					

Documentation List

This document is the master inventory of all documents that are identified as an integral part of business resumption process. A sample format is provided in Exhibit 7.5.

Emergency Procedures

This document describes various procedures adopted during an emergency procedure. The text in the format provided in Exhibit 7.6 will help in developing an idea about the content.

EXHIBIT 7.5 Documentation List Sample Format

Name of Office:

Address:

Phone No. /E-mail ID: Page __ of ___

Name of Document	Date of Receipt	Author	Custodian	On-Site Location	Off-Site Location
Manuals					
Plans					
Agreements					
Documents					
Procedures					
Guidelines					

	Last Update	Verification	Sent to Head Office	Sent to Branch	Sent to Off-Site
Date Verified by					

EXHIBIT 7.6 Emergency Procedures Sample Format

Name of Office:

Address:

Phone No. /E-mail ID:

Nonsystem Emergency

Keyword	Action	Evacuation Procedure
Fire	At each stage, assess whether it is possible to carry out the suggested action. If not, move on to the next action. If there is no time, evacuate immediately. ___ (Name of auditee) recognizes human resources as his or her most valuable resource.	Follow instructions of the civil authorities whenever applicable.
	Identify any injured personnel for immediate evacuation.	Assess approach from the main and emergency exits.
	Shut down computers.	First evacuate injured personnel followed by others along with IT resources.
	Shut down power system, including connection from uninterruptible power supply (UPS).	Form a queue for evacuation. If possible, take headcount to ensure safe evacuation of all.
	Remove server and data backup from the affected location.	Separated evacuees must establish contact with office head to confirm evacuation.
	Remove other IT resources from the affected location.	
	Alert the designated person from the Contingency Plan Contact List.	
	Alert the functional head of the defined alternative site for possible relocation.	
Power	Confirm power failure by checking with neighborhood and main power connectors to ensure that a fuse has not blown.	In case of fire hazards, follow the evacuation procedure suggested in case of fire.
	If a fuse has blown, check for possible fire hazards and any injury to person(s) requiring immediate evacuation.	
	For power outage exceeding ___ minutes, check with substation/power office.	
	Confirm availability of fuel for generator.	
	Inspect all UPSs for battery outage warning.	
	Assess alternative lighting arrangement, whenever required.	
	Instruct the guard to enforce restricted entry.	
	Inform the appropriate person from the Contingency Plan Contact List.	
	Assess if power outage could cause business disruption.	

Civil Disorder, Vandalism	At each stage, assess whether it is possible to carry out the suggested action. If not, move on to the next action. Evacuate only after assessing the scenario and preferably after getting the go-ahead from concerned authorities. _____ (Name of auditee) recognizes human resources as his or her most valuable resource. Inform the appropriate person from the Contingency Plan Contact List. When evacuation is ordered, shut down power system, including UPS. Shut down computers. If time does not permit, disconnect the power line. Remove server and data backup from the affected location. Remove other IT resources from the affected location, to the extent possible. Lock the location as per evacuation guide. Reenter the premises after the appropriate authorities give the go-ahead.	Follow instructions of the civil authorities whenever applicable. Assess approach from the main and emergency exits. First evacuate injured personnel followed by others along with IT resources Form a queue for evacuation. If possible, take headcount to ensure safe evacuation of all.
Evolving Natural Calamity (Flood, Isolation, etc.)	At each stage, assess whether it is possible to carry out the suggested action. If not, move on to the next action. Evacuate only after assessing the scenario and preferably after getting go-ahead from concerned authorities. _____ (Name of auditee) recognizes human resource as his or her most valuable resource. Inform the appropriate person from the Contingency Plan Contact List. Initiate action to procure necessary supply to face prolonged isolated stay at the facility. Recharge battery-based communication devices, such as mobile phones. When evacuation is ordered, shut down power systems, including connection from UPS. Shut down computers. If time does not permit, disconnect the power line. Remove server and data backup from the location. Remove other IT resources from the location, to the extent possible. If removal is not possible, relocate to reduce chances of loss, for example, locate on a high location in case of flood. Lock the location as per evacuation guide. Reenter the premises after the appropriate authorities give the go-ahead.	Evacuees who were separated from the group must establish contact with office head to confirm evacuation. Lock the location, if complete evacuation is established.

(Continued)

EXHIBIT 7.6 (Continued)

Sudden Natural Calamity (Lightning, Earthquake)	At each stage, assess whether it is possible to carry out suggested action. If not, move on to the next action. If there is no time at all, move on to evacuation procedure. _____ (Name of auditee) recognizes human resources as his or her most valuable resource.	Follow the instructions of the civil authorities whenever applicable.
	Identify any injured personnel and proceed for immediate evacuation.	Assess approach from the main and emergency exits.
	Shut down power systems, including connection from UPS.	First evacuate injured personnel followed by others along with IT resources
	Shut down computers. If time does not permit, disconnect the power line.	Form a line for evacuation. If possible, take a headcount to ensure the safe evacuation of all.
	Remove server and data backup from the affected location.	Evacuees who were separated from the group must establish contact with office head to confirm evacuation.
	Remove other IT resources from the affected location.	
	Lock the location as per evacuation guide.	Lock the location, if complete evacuation is established.
	Inform the appropriate person from the Contingency Plan Contact List.	

System Emergency Keyword	Action
Malfunction	Contact contingency plan designate for support and log in the problem.
	Ensure availability of last data backup.
Virus	Notify Virus Alert Team.
	De-link affected machine(s) from network and other shared resources.
	Take custody of last data backup.

External Support Agreement

This list summarizes the various arrangements that the auditee has with external suppliers. In addition to providing a summary of terms, this list also states the location of the agreement for its fast retrieval. A sample format is provided in Exhibit 7.7.

EXHIBIT 7.7 External Support Agreements Sample Format

Name of Office:

Address:

Phone No. /E-mail ID: Page ___ of ___

Name of Vendor	Terms of Agreement	Location of Agreement	Point of Contact		

	Last Update	Verification	Sent to Head Office	Sent to Branch	Sent to Off-Site
Date Verified by					

Hardware Inventory

This is the list of hardware available at each site and is useful for maintenance. This record is also necessary for rebuilding the facility during the resumption phase. A sample format is provided in Exhibit 7.8.

EXHIBIT 7.8   Hardware Inventory Sample Format

Name of Office:

Address:

Phone No. /E-mail ID: Page ___ of ___

Name of Hardware	Installed on	Make	ID No.	Warranty	AMC	Support Contact

	Last Update	Verification	Sent to Head Office	Sent to Branch	Sent to Off-Site	
Date Verified by						

Information Asset Usage Procedure

This document describes the physical processes to be observed for the use of information assets. Often these procedures are provided in the hardware or software user manual and may be available in soft copy. A sample format is provided in Exhibit 7.9.

EXHIBIT 7.9 Information Asset Usage Procedure Sample Format

Name of Office:

Address:

Phone No. /E-mail ID: Page ___ of ___

Action	Normal Procedure	Emergency Procedure		
Power On				
Power Down				
System On				
System Shutdown				
System Login				
System Logoff				
Application Login				
Application Logoff				
Data Backup				
Data Restoration				
	Last Update	Verification	Sent to Head Office	Sent to Branch	Sent to Off-Site
Date Verified by					

Layout Inventory

Information on layout is necessary for restoration and also to secure entrance during emergency. Layout designs form a critical component of business resumption plan. A sample format is provided in Exhibit 7.10.

EXHIBIT 7.10 Layout Inventory Sample Format

Name of Office:

Address:

Phone No. /E-mail ID: Page ___ of ___

Layout	Description and Salient Features	Drawing	Location
Building			
Physical Layout Electrical Layout Data Cable Layout Water Line Layout			
Office			
Physical Layout Electrical Layout Data Cable Layout			
Manager's Chamber			
Physical Layout Electrical Layout Data Cable Layout			
Server Room			
Physical Layout Electrical Layout Data Cable Layout			
Other			
Physical Layout Electrical Layout Data Cable Layout			

	Last Update	Verification	Sent to Head Office	Sent to Branch	Sent to Off-Site
Date Verified by					

Software Inventory

This list provides an inventory of software available in the auditee's organization. It may be necessary to reinstall some of the software during the business resumption process. A sample format is provided in Exhibit 7.11.

EXHIBIT 7.11   Software Inventory Sample Format

Name of Office:

Address:

Phone No. /E-mail ID: Page ___ of ___

Name of Software	Licensee	No. of User	Media Location	License Number	License Location	Support Contact

	Last Update	Verification	Sent to Head Office	Sent to Branch	Sent to Off-Site
Date Verified by					

Team Staffing and Tasks

This document describes the roles and functions of the participants in the business resumption plan. A sample format is provided in Exhibit 7.12.

EXHIBIT 7.12 Team Staffing and Task Sample Format

Name of Office:

Address:

Phone No. /E-mail ID: Page __ of ___

Contingency Plan Coordinator

Name	Roles and Functions	Contact

System Contingency Coordinator

Name	Roles and Functions	Contact

Damage Assessment Team

Name	Roles and Functions	Contact

Operations Team

Name	Roles and Functions	Contact

Communications Team

Name	Roles and Functions	Contact

Administrative and Facilities Management Team

Name	Roles and Functions	Contact

Internal Audit Team

Name	Roles and Functions	Contact

Facility Representative

Name	Roles and Functions	Contact

Vendor Contact List

This list maintains the contact details of vendors that need to be contacted during the disaster and resumption phase. A sample format is provided in Exhibit 7.13.

EXHIBIT 7.13 Vendor Contact List Sample Format

Name of Office:

Address:

Phone No. /E-mail ID: Page __ of ___

		Point of Contact		
Name of Vendor	Nature of Requirements	Normal	Escalate	Urgent

	Last Update	Verification	Sent to Head Office	Sent to Branch	Sent to Off-Site
Date					
Verified by					

Auditing in the E-Commerce Environment

THIS CHAPTER INTRODUCES THE reader to the world of auditing in an e-commerce environment and identifies additional security concerns that an information systems auditor should address while auditing such systems. E-commerce includes e-banking applications. Upon completing this chapter, the reader will be able to design a strategy and plan for conducting an information systems audit of an e-commerce application and its related environment.

▦ INTRODUCTION

Electronic commerce includes activities of promoting and selling a product or service and obtaining payment for the same. This may also include the payment of bills and government revenue services. The purchase of products and services may be made using the Internet, such as in the cases of movie tickets, airline tickets, and downloadable software, or physically, as in the cases of electronic gadgets, books, fashion accessories, and so forth. The payment may be online using a credit card or integrated with a banking application for transfer of funds from a bank account. In some cases, the payment is also accepted upon physical delivery of the product. In case of banking applications, the activities include accessing financial information, making payments, and transferring funds from one account to another, opening new accounts, using an electronic bill payment service, and so forth. The scope of e-commerce covers such applications available on smartphones and similar handheld devices. One of the major developments in this front is the increasing use of mobile phones for funds transfer.

E-commerce also covers "electronic money," which refers to "stored value" or prepaid payment mechanisms that are used to make payments at point-of-sale terminals, or by way of direct transfers between two devices, or across computer networks, including the Internet. This is implemented by way of the user buying a prepaid card that acts as virtual money for making payments. All payments made using the prepaid card reduce the balance amount of funds available on the card unless the user recharges the same. Major credit card service providers are now developing prepaid cards that are essentially a similar product with additional features, such as the withdrawal of money from a bank ATM.

OBJECTIVES OF AN INFORMATION SYSTEMS AUDIT IN THE E-COMMERCE ENVIRONMENT

Major objectives of conducting an information systems audit of any e-commerce installation include the following six:

1. To gain an understanding of the product line available for purchase over the e-commerce platform, the related system of inventory management, the data flow necessary to complete a transaction, payment settlement processes, including interface with banks and credit card companies, and with other related applications, such as customer loyalty programs.
2. To ensure that adequate internal controls are in place along with audit trails necessary to recreate a transaction, keeping in mind that many of the buyers will be one-time customers without any repeat purchase.
3. To determine whether the top management of the auditee recognizes additional business and control risks involved with e-commerce-based applications and adopts specific policies for e-commerce and enforces observance of the same.
4. To determine the adequacy of existing contingency and disaster plans to effectively address risks arising out of e-commerce applications.
5. To determine whether legal compliance is being ensured, especially with regard to the verification of the customer's identity and evidence management.
6. To determine whether implemented controls are appropriate to the type and level of risks arising from e-commerce activities.

GENERAL OVERVIEW

During an audit of e-commerce applications and systems, the information systems auditor may observe the following six procedures:

1. Obtain a current list of the duties of employees and outsourced agencies that are involved in e-commerce functions.
2. Obtain, if available, or prepare a flowchart and/or narrative detailing various e-commerce processes and functions. Special attention should be given to processing logic flowchart to identify possible weaknesses in the process. (See the feature at the end of the chapter to learn how to read a flowchart.)
3. Obtain the following documentation prior to the audit:
   a. Summary of strategic plans relating to e-commerce activities with specific emphasis on the importance of e-commerce activities in the future scheme of business growth.
   b. Reports of reviews or assessments performed by external independent consultants or technology experts, wherever used.
   c. Information detailing e-commerce activities conducted by the auditee.
   d. Summary of fault logging and user complaints specific to e-commerce function.
   e. External information systems audit reports of e-commerce activities, if available.
   f. Summary of relevant operating policies and procedures governing e-commerce activities with equal importance given to internal and external processes.
4. Determine the extent of dependence on external vendors in general, and specifically for critical functions, and the exact role of such vendors, particularly during a disaster.
5. Review documents, observe practices, and interview people to determine:
   a. How security of e-commerce activity is addressed. This includes a wide range of activities starting from verification of customers, ensuring nonacceptance of compromised credit cards, permissive download by bona fide customers, and so forth.
   b. How e-commerce activities are monitored, especially the outsourced functions. This ranges across procurement by the customer to physical delivery of products.
   c. Policies, practices, personnel, or control systems that are unique to e-commerce activity.
   d. Internal or external factors critical to e-commerce activity.
6. Review the e-commerce site to obtain an understanding of its features and capabilities.

AUDITING E-COMMERCE FUNCTIONS

The information systems auditor should perform the following steps while auditing an e-commerce application and environment.

Preliminary Review

1. Obtain a description of the e-commerce system and its capabilities along with relevant diagrams, if any. This will include a review of the hardware and software environments along with points of connectivity to internal systems, as well as remote access points. It is often likely that the extent of user verification made for external connection is different than for internal connection, opening up a possible source of compromise. The information systems auditor should further evaluate:
   a. The links of the e-commerce system with other systems and network infrastructure. These links are potential points of compromise by internal users and deserve a special audit focus.
   b. The flow of transactions and data through the network to understand the control design and identify potential points of compromise.
   c. Potential areas of vulnerability arising out of technology, design, and practice. It may be noted that often, poor implementation exposes a system to vulnerabilities that could otherwise be technically mitigated. For example, since recording of audit trail slows down the system, a user may deactivate the feature at the cost of loss of audit trail.
2. Review and develop an overview of e-commerce payment services and service delivery flow. This would address the following issues:
   a. Responsibilities of the auditee being clearly defined.
   b. Whether there is a process by which the auditee addresses issues of failed payments and customer service.
   c. Whether there is a process of backup and contingency planning, and disaster recovery for delivery and payment on the e-commerce platform.
3. Review the control systems and opine whether they are adequate to ensure data integrity, access control, and confidentiality of the e-commerce systems.
4. Review policies of providing hyperlinks and relationships with affiliated and unaffiliated third parties. It is necessary that the auditee is expressly disassociated from unaffiliated third parties and disclaims any legal responsibility.
5. Ascertain overall information security and privacy policies of vendors and linked entities. It is important to note that the primary obligation of maintaining the privacy of all data collected by the auditee lies with the auditee, which remains responsible for any abuse by the vendor.
6. Ensure that formal contracts or agreements were entered into, defining the rights and responsibilities of the auditee and third parties.

Implementation

1. Determine whether top management approved of the e-commerce system after considering the relevant risks.
2. Determine whether adequate training was provided to all related to the e-commerce systems. This will include executives responsible for products, services, information systems, and compliance with internal and legal requirements. It may also be necessary to provide training to users.
3. Determine whether the auditee verifies the accuracy and content of various interfaces and information services before they are made available through the e-commerce system.

Policies and Procedures

1. Determine whether the auditee has policies to implement mechanisms that enable consumers to clearly distinguish between the websites, products, and services of the auditee and others. This assumes great importance in cases where the auditee acts in a consortium and promotes the products and services of all consortium members using the e-commerce platform of consortium members. For example, airlines, hotels, car rental companies, and tour operators often join hands to promote airline ticket, hotel reservation, car hiring, and holiday packages from a combined e-commerce site. It is important that the buyer identify the product seller and e-commerce vendors separately in the event of submitting a complaint.
2. Determine whether existing policies and procedures governing access to and disclosure of confidential information of the customer have been extended to the e-commerce platform. This gains importance since the information is made available to various suppliers of logistics, including banks for payments and courier services used to deliver the material.
3. Review how the identity of e-commerce customers is established and how fraudulent payments are identified.
4. Determine how the auditee monitors system performance, especially with regard to the following:
   a. Number of visitors to the website.
   b. User information.
   c. Number and volume of new e-commerce business over a specified period.
   d. Security threats or repeated unauthorized access attempts.
   e. Downtime of e-commerce site for longer than permissible period.

Administration

1. Ascertain whether an e-commerce security officer has been identified and properly briefed about his or her responsibilities.
2. Ascertain how the unique user ID is enforced for all customers and other users. One of the most common ways of ensuring unique user IDs for customers is to use their e-mail ID as the user ID in the e-commerce portal.

3. Ensure that the password for accessing the e-commerce portal is periodically changed by the user.
4. Determine adequacy of management of employee access and privileges on e-commerce server and review the corresponding policies.
5. Determine the adequacy of the customer service and support program. Special attention is to be given to outsourced services and to established service level agreements.
6. Review the process of generating exception reports, their content, and periodic review mechanisms.
7. Visit the server location to determine whether access to the console is controlled and business continuation issues have been adequately addressed.

Accounting and Processing

1. Determine whether there is a periodic reconcilement procedure covering all transactional capabilities of the e-commerce system.
2. Determine the scope and performance of reconciliation activity for incomplete transactions or for transactions where complete information is not available.
3. Confirm that adequate safeguards are in place to detect, prevent, and notify duplicate transactions. This control assumes criticality in cases of hotel or airline reservations where customer may be warned of an earlier purchase of a similar description. For example, in two different sessions, a user may reserve two rooms in the same hotel for the same date. The system may automatically verify that the user actually wishes to book two rooms.
4. Determine whether appropriate audit trails are compulsorily generated in each system.
5. Determine whether daily task log is reviewed regularly.
6. Determine whether the following minimum controls were implemented for opening new user accounts on the e-commerce portal:
   a. A credit review report, if applicable, to the satisfaction of the auditee.
   b. Ensuring that the customer meets the requirements of the "Know Your Customer" policy. This is a compulsory requirement in most banks and financial institutions.
   c. Customer identity is established through an appropriate manual or electronic process.
   d. The payment instrument used by the customer is verified for compromise.
7. Ascertain whether the auditee obtains and reviews annual financial statements from vendors that perform major services related to e-commerce. This is done to foresee any closure of business by the vendor so that the auditee can take preemptive steps to avoid any discontinuation of service.
8. Obtain reports from all vendors that process customer information and ensure that they observe all controls designed for maintaining confidentiality and integrity of customer information.
9. Ensure that all e-commerce customers have been made aware of the rights, responsibilities, and liabilities of each party and further ensure that the right of the auditee to monitor, store, and retrieve electronic transmissions between the auditee and its customers has been established.

10. Determine whether the auditee has an adequate process in place for resumption of e-commerce services, including those outsourced. Further, ascertain whether contingency and business resumption plans are tested and test results are reviewed on a regular basis.
11. Review the backup policy to ensure that the policy specifies an appropriate backup frequency along with retention periods for backup data. Further, obtain a list of all information assets and media that are to be stored off-site and confirm their availability.

Legal and Regulatory Matters

1. Review the e-commerce website to ensure that information regarding products and services, security features, hours of service access, names of contact persons, office locations, and working hours are correct.
2. Determine whether appropriate procedures exist to ensure compliance with regulatory circulars and guidelines, including verification of identity of a new customer. Special attention must be given to identify potential fraud and money-laundering activities.
3. Determine whether the e-commerce portal displays a notice for users, announcing that they are accessing a private information asset and that any unauthorized access or use or violation of the terms of use may constitute a crime punishable by law.

Internet Security Administration

1. Assess adequacy of password administration process for the e-commerce system. This would include allocation of password, stipulating criteria for compulsory periodic change, ensuring adherence to best practices, and so forth.
2. Review whether identity verification systems using multiple platforms can be or are implemented. For example, an access request after a long period of inactivity or a request for change of password can be confirmed by asking for a reconfirmation key that has been sent to the registered mobile phone of the customer.
3. Ascertain whether access to the Internet backbone password, master password, and server password is secured and appropriately restricted. It should also be ascertained whether these passwords have been changed periodically in conformance to the organizational policy. It has been observed that often supervisory passwords are not changed periodically because of poor working practices.
4. Ensure that automatic login lockout control is enforced whenever repeated failed attempts to gain access are made. The procedure to unlock the login should also be reviewed cautiously and evidence of the observance verified. This assumes criticality if the account in question have supervisory privileges.
5. Review the connectivity between the internal system and external electronic service and systems.
6. Review the procedures for monitoring unauthorized attempts to access the e-commerce system. The auditee must maintain a balance between not being intrusive and being cautious. The activities of an account holder must be tracked, but the information collected may not be used for any purpose that can be termed

as a breach of privacy of the user. For example, the e-commerce portal may definitely record the login IP address of the user but should not, without informing the user, analyze the purchase pattern for embarking on profile-based marketing.

7. Determine the adequacy of the virus detection and prevention process. It is also necessary to verify the frequency at which the virus definitions are updated and whether there is a mechanism to proactively obtain information about new virus threats.

8. Review physical and logical security for accessing computer hardware, software, communication equipment, and communication lines associated with the e-commerce application. This may also involve interacting with third-party service providers as various services of e-commerce platform are often outsourced.

9. Determine whether the auditee has entered into formal contracts with vendors and whether, where appropriate, the contract addresses, in addition to financial aspects, the following issues:

   a. Description of work to be performed by the vendor.
   b. Services to be provided by the vendor.
   c. Responsibilities regarding addition, modification, and deletion of records.
   d. Processing frequency and report generation.
   e. Processing priorities under both normal and emergency situations.
   f. Definition of emergency situation and procedure for appropriate notification.
   g. Rights, responsibilities, and liability for each party.
   h. Ownership of any special software developed for the auditee.
   i. Responsibility for security of communications network.
   j. Right of conducting audit of vendor facilities and responsibilities therein.
   k. Contingency plans for service continuation, backup, and security provisions.
   l. Backup arrangements of the vendor.
   m. Disaster recovery and contingency plan of the vendor.
   n. Access, ownership, and control of customer data and other confidential information lying with the vendor.
   o. Availability of financial information of the vendor.
   p. Reasonable penalty and cancellation provisions along with predefined events that will amount to a breach of contract.
   q. Prohibition of assignment of contract without consent of the auditee.
   r. Inclusion of "key person" clause requiring availability of an identified individual or a defined skill set at the vendor during the entire duration of the agreement.
   s. Security precautions on the part of the service provider.

10. If the auditee obtains software products from a vendor, ascertain whether the vendor supplies source code or maintains the same in a third-party escrow account for use by the auditee in the event of discontinuation of business of the vendor. Verify the process to ensure that the code maintained in the escrow account is the same code that has been used in the software.

E-COMMERCE POLICIES AND PROCEDURES REVIEW

The information systems auditor needs to review the policies and procedures relating to E-commerce activities to have a clear understanding of the strengths and weaknesses of the same. The process of this review will include the following four activities:

1. Determine whether the e-commerce security policies include:
   a. Clear allocation of responsibility for system security.
   b. Identification of duties of the security administrator and whether the corresponding authority is adequate to enforce policies.
   c. Control over network and data access preventing unauthorized access.
2. Determine whether e-commerce firewall policies and intruder detection systems include defined access rules and identify responsibility for firewall maintenance and monitoring.
3. Determine whether security requirements are adequately addressed by enforcing encryption technique. Confirm whether responsibility for enforcing encryption, scope of encryption, and encryption application process is clearly enunciated.
4. Identify whether security policies are periodically reviewed and updated.

 ## IMPACT OF E-COMMERCE ON INTERNAL CONTROL

E-commerce activities will require the internal control system to be calibrated to recognize the special needs of the system. The following five aspects of internal control are seriously affected by e-commerce activity:

1. **Security:** This involves additional security measures that are to be taken to mitigate the technology-based risks that come with remote access. These include protection against virus attack and unauthorized access, maintaining privacy of data (especially during transmission), establishment of identity by multiple means in addition to access passwords, and so forth.
2. **Transaction integrity:** The information systems auditor needs to verify the process that confirms completeness, timeliness, accuracy, and authenticity of information provided by the e-commerce system before it is integrated with the main information system of the auditee. A common example is Internet banking, wherein the transactions carried out at the Internet banking portal are ultimately integrated with the main banking software. Special attention must be given to the following processes:
   a. Input validation.
   b. Prevention of duplicate entries often caused by the use of the "back" button of the browser.
   c. Defining and confirming terms of trade before proceeding with the service request; for example, defining and agreeing on the delivery and return terms before any product is sold on an e-commerce portal.

3. **Process alignment:** Any e-commerce function will engage multiple components of information technology services. It is necessary that transactions at the e-commerce portal are reflected properly in all other components of the information technology systems of the auditee, including accounting system, inventory system, customer relation system, and so forth.

4. **International laws:** Often e-commerce portals involve transactions outside the political boundary of the country of the auditee. This requires adherence to different sets of laws and regulations. For example, many countries require additional security measures to be enforced in addition to normal validations for credit card transactions. Consequently, the e-commerce system must recognize the country originating the service request and decide to enforce additional controls. In addition, the object of trade itself may require adherence to different sets of law. For example, the legal age for selling alcoholic products varies in different countries.

5. **Audit evidence:** Another important impact of e-commerce is the use of third-party electronic records as audit evidence. The process of maintaining integrity of electronic records originating at the end of the audit can be evaluated whereas the same adopted by a third party involved in the e-commerce activity may not be accessible. The lack of consistent quality of audit evidence is a serious concern for the auditor of e-commerce activities.

HOW TO READ A FLOWCHART

Flowcharts are visual depictions of sequential steps in a process. This is an easy-to-understand tool widely used to communicate how processes work. In addition to making it easy to understand a process, the flowchart allows the identification of established control points. Flowcharts are great tools to examine existing possibilities for improving a process.

An information systems auditor can use a flowchart for the following three reasons:

1. Define and analyze processes.
2. Observe step-by-step workings of the process for analysis, discussion, and review.
3. Identify areas for improvement in a process.

Perhaps the greatest advantage of flowcharts is aiding in the understanding of a project in a simple step-by-step manner without being intimidated by the larger complex system.

To read a flowchart, it is necessary to be able to read its symbols. Table 8.1 gives a brief description of the common symbols used in a flowchart.

Some of the symbols shown in Table 8.1 are used in Figure 8.1. You can practice reading diagrams by studying the sample flowchart in Figure 8.1.

TABLE 8.1 Common Flowchart Symbols

Name	Symbol	Usage
Connector	◯	The connectors act as terminal nodes of a page with an alphabetic tag and connect with nodes with corresponding alphabets on the next page.

Decision		This symbol poses a question and the answer to that determines the subsequent step. Mostly the question is so framed that the answer is always either "Yes" or "No" (we are following the binary system) and is followed by lines with arrowheads leading to the next stage. One may have more than two options, and in those cases there is usually one line coming out of the diagram leading to various solutions.
Document		This symbol represents a document or a report. There may be a cascading series of these symbols to indicate multiple reports.
Extract data		The triangle denotes an extraction function wherein one or more specific sets of items are removed from a database.
Input/Output		The parallelograms show an input or output. For example, they may be used to denote the input of a value or generation of a command.
Internal storage		This denotes internal storage and suggests that the functions being described are carried out at the level of internal storage, which is usually the computer memory.
Lines with arrowhead		A line with an arrowhead denotes movement of the process from one function to another in the direction of the arrowhead.
Manual input		This symbol indicates that manual input is required at this stage.
Manual operation		This symbol signifies manual operation, which will automatically be demanded by the system to be conducted. For example, the user may be prompted for an input to continue the process.
Merge data		The inverted triangle signifies the merger of two or more data sets into one. This is usually used when there are multiple inputs to a database.
Process		The rectangle is perhaps the most widely used symbol in a flowchart. This shows a process, task, action, or operation. It defines what is to be done at that stage, and consequently the text description almost always will contain a verb.
Stored data		This symbol represents data stored on any media, such as a hard drive or memory card.
Terminal shapes		This is the symbol with which a flowchart begins and ends. One would usually have labels such as "Start" or "End" inside the symbol to signify its role. Text is usually inserted in all shapes used in a flowchart.

(Continued)

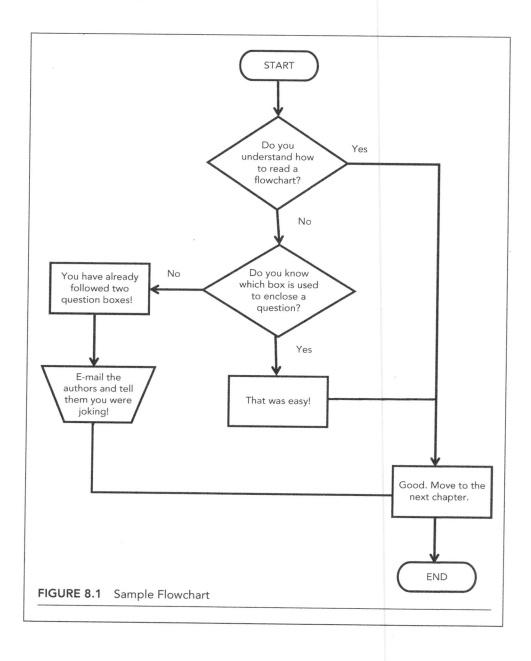

FIGURE 8.1 Sample Flowchart

CHAPTER NINE

Security Testing

THIS CHAPTER INTRODUCES US to the world of cybersecurity, testing, and evidence collection. Although security testing is usually an optional item in an information systems audit, it is imperative in cases like network audits and technical reviews. In order to act as a network auditor, one is required to go through specialized training on cybersecurity and cyberforensics, which are outside the scope of this book. As you complete this chapter, you should form a working idea about common security threats and a common tool-based approach to security testing.

CYBERSECURITY

Cybersecurity focuses on prevention of damage to, protection of, and restoration of information system assets, including information. The objective is to ensure availability, integrity, authentication, confidentiality, and nonrepudiation of information systems assets. Cybersecurity may include technology, policies, and training to achieve its goal of protecting and assuring information quality.

CYBERCRIMES

An information systems auditor must be aware of various types of cybercrimes being committed to judge the extent of exposure of the auditee. Cybercrimes are a genre of crimes that use computers and networks for unlawful activities. A computer can be used for crime either as a tool or as a target or both.

The first type of crime is basically an extension of "real-world" crimes, such as forgery, fraud, or copyright piracy, using computers. These types of computer-enabled crimes are usually prosecuted under relevant laws and not usually under laws relating to cybercrime.

The second type of crime is pure cybercrimes where criminals damage or modify computerized systems through illegal access of these systems and cause loss to the victims. These types of activities are usually prosecuted using specific cybercrime-related legislation.

The third type of crime is where computers are used both as a tool and as a target.

Broadly, cybercrimes include but are not limited to the following 10 types:

1. Financial crimes involving cheating, frauds, money laundering, and so forth.
2. Intellectual property crimes such as theft of computer source code, software piracy, copyright infringement, trademark violations, and so forth.
3. Impersonation.
4. Forgery of documents, including currency.
5. Cyberpornography involving production and distribution of pornographic material.
6. Sale of illegal articles such as narcotics, weapons, and wildlife.
7. Online gambling, subject to laws of the country.
8. Harassments such as cyberstalking, cyberdefamation, and indecent and abusive mails.
9. Deployment of viruses, trojans, and worms.
10. Cyberattacks and cyberterrorism aimed at compromising the security of information assets.

Nonrepudiation

Nonrepudiation is a feature that prevents the originator of a communication from denying the origin of the communication. This is enforced by a technology that allows only originators to affix their digital signature. Thus the recipient of a digitally signed document is at liberty of acting on the belief that the communication was sent by the entity whose digital signature is affixed.

Cyberstalking

Cyberstalking refers to use of the Internet or other electronic gateway to stalk or harass a person in cyberspace. The cyberstalker selectively communicates with the victim mostly either in a threatening tone or in a manner that violates the privacy of the victim. The cyberstalker takes advantage of the apparent anonymity provided by the Internet to commit the crime. Cyberstalking is a crime in almost all countries.

Spam Mails

One of the most unwanted burdens that electronic communication has brought in is "spam mail," which is essentially unsolicited bulk e-mail sent to users of e-mail. This is mostly used by marketers who find this an easy medium to reach a large number of people at virtually no cost. This brings down productive time for work as well as slowing down Internet traffic. This may even cost money whenever the recipient pays for network use by the volume of inbound and outbound data transmitted. There are many spam filters that seek to identify such spam e-mails and filter them out from useful e-mails. The name spam allegedly came from a comic sketch that presents a restaurant where almost all dishes contain a canned meat called Spam. A customer is determined to get a dish without the Spam and is served by an irritated waitress who mouths the word "spam" repeatedly.

If we look at the types of cybercrimes that generally occur in enterprises, the following nine activities are seen commonly:

1. E-mail abuses/spam mail
2. Cyberdefamation
3. Theft of source code
4. Disclosure of business secrets and documents
5. Insider attacks on personnel databases
6. Use of office information system assets for personal gain
7. Transmission and viewing of pornographic material
8. Cyberattack on entities from external source
9. Cybervandalism, wherein websites are compromised and defaced, mostly as a mark of protest against political or social issues

From the viewpoint of an information systems auditor, any compromise to the confidentiality, integrity, and availability of information assets is a security threat. The information systems auditor should also identify information assets that are vulnerable to cyberattack. Usually those in the first line of interface with the outside world or those that form the perimeter installations are popular targets for cyberattacks. For example, an Internet banking interface or e-mail log-in interface is likely to be the first target.

WHAT IS VULNERABLE TO ATTACK?

All information assets that are valuable, monetarily or otherwise, or are treated as confidential are potential attack targets. They include the following four types of assets:

1. **Personal information:** Birthplace, birthdate, mother's maiden name, citizenship card number, credit card numbers, bank account number, health records, and so forth.
2. **Business information:** Customer records, product and sales information, business plans, proprietary product designs, software code, materials and inventory data, financial statements, and so forth.
3. **Information systems assets:** Communication network, information processing capabilities, hardware, software, personnel, and so forth.
4. **Infrastructure:** Power, communication, support services, and so forth. The majority of these are operated by outsourced agencies.

 ## HOW CYBERATTACKS OCCUR

A cyberattack can take place in various ways. These include the following eight:

1. **Denial of service:** Attack on a network that floods it with traffic, preventing passage of normal traffic. This can halt network-based services. A variant of this attack is obtaining control over a website and defacing the same, leading to bonafide users being denied service from the website.
2. **Malware:** Malicious software, including spyware, virus, and worm.
3. **Phishing:** A scam to steal personal information over the Internet. The initial e-mail "fishes" by inviting victims to visit a fraudulent but official-looking site and asking them to correct their personal information. Collected information is then used to commit frauds, mostly of a financial nature. An example of a phishing attack is given later in the chapter.
4. **Spyware:** Software that surreptitiously records web surfing and application usage for abuse by digital peeping toms. Spyware can be very dangerous as it often logs passwords.
5. **Stupidity:** Displaying passwords on an adhesive memo stuck to a computer monitor, using passwords that are easy to figure out, such as "ABC," giving out passwords over the phone to cold callers pretending to be "verifying information," not using industry-standard security measures, and so forth.
6. **Trojan:** Ostensibly "good" software that fools users with a hidden virus, just like the hollow wooden horse with Greek soldiers hiding inside that fooled the citizens of Troy.
7. **Virus:** Software that exploits system vulnerabilities by copying itself to other computers over the network or through storage media. Usually requires a human trigger, such as opening an infected e-mail file attachment.

8. **Worm:** Similiar to a virus but requires no human trigger for infection and action. It automatically hits vulnerable systems.

An information systems auditor may conduct vulnerability analysis to identify which threats have an exploitation potential in the auditee's information system.

ANATOMY OF A PHISHING ATTACK

A phishing attack almost without fail starts with an e-mail informing the recipient about the deactivation of an online bank account or a similar platform. Sometimes it comes with information about a bank transfer that could not be completed because of technical problems. The common element of such attacks is that the recipient needs to provide the user ID and password of an online platform. The e-mail usually replicates the look and feel of the organization from which the communication is reportedly being sent. Figure 9.1 shows an example of a phishing e-mail.

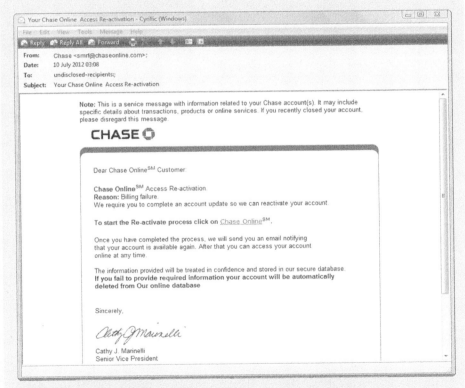

FIGURE 9.1   Example of a Phishing E-mail

(Continued)

An unsuspecting user is likely to follow the link provided in the e-mail and will reach a fake website that looks similar to the genuine website of the organization it is impersonating. Figure 9.2 shows an example of a phishing website.

FIGURE 9.2 Example of a Phishing Website

If you compare the image of the phishing website with the image of the genuine website shown in Figure 9.3, you will find that they are virtually the same.

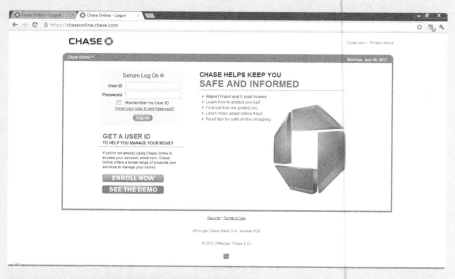

FIGURE 9.3 Image of the Genuine Website

However, if you look at both images intently, you will notice two differences. First, there is a small icon at the bottom of the genuine website, which presumably the cybercriminal overlooked. The second difference is the critical one. Look at the address bar of the browser. You will find that while the address bar of the genuine website carries the URL of the actual organization, the fake website shows some other URL. Cybercriminals keep changing fake URLs; once used, a fake URL is usually soon deactivated.

The best way of avoiding a phishing attack is to access a website directly using the URL known to the user and not through links provided in an e-mail. One should always look at the URL bar and verify the URL. Some browsers now come with a facility to mark suspect websites, and this feature should be enabled.

WHAT IS VULNERABILITY ANALYSIS?

Vulnerability analysis is a process that defines, identifies, and classifies the security weaknesses (vulnerabilities) in a computer, network, communications infrastructure, and in any information systems asset or associated system. This process is also known as vulnerability assessment. Vulnerability analysis results are useful to assess the effectiveness of proposed countermeasures to mitigate external threats and evaluate their functioning once they are put into use. Vulnerability analysis can be a tool-based exercise and can also be built into a process.

Steps of Vulnerability Analysis

Vulnerability analysis consists of five steps:

1. Defining and classifying an information systems asset like network or system resources.
2. Assigning relative levels of importance to assets from the viewpoint of the potential for compromise and the impact of such compromise.
3. Identifying potential threats to each resource.
4. Developing a strategy to prioritize problems so that the problems with the greatest potential are addressed ahead of others. The potential is measured in terms of the extent and impact of the compromise.
5. Defining and implementing ways to minimize the adverse consequences if the threat materializes and the attack successfully compromises the vulnerability.

An information systems auditor should verify whether the auditee conforms to the four following processes of vulnerability management.

1. At the first stage of vulnerability analysis, if security weaknesses are found during a vulnerability analysis, then a vulnerability disclosure must be made to inform

other users. In addition to the internal disclosure, a subscription to mail lists managed by various computer emergency readiness teams (CERTs) or the software and hardware vendors is a preferred practice. This subscription is an easy and effective way of keeping updated on new vulnerabilities that are discovered.

2. In the second stage of vulnerability analysis, identified vulnerabilities are to be classified from high-level to low-level threats. Generally, the vendor comes out with a patch to resolve the problem within a short period of time. An information systems auditor should review the auditee's process of updating the patches. The auditor should specifically observe any precautions taken during the period in which the system is exposed to known vulnerabilities that are not patched.

3. The third stage of vulnerability analysis involves identifying potential threats. This is often achieved by conducting ethical hacking on selected information system assets. This method of assessing vulnerability involves security experts attacking the information systems asset to identify its weaknesses. The results of this process provide guidelines for developing countermeasures to prevent a genuine attack. This phase is also known as penetration testing. The information systems auditor should verify the threat identification process followed by the auditee. Special attention should be given to precautions taken to safeguard assets targeted during ethical hacking. This has the utmost importance as a successful ethical hacking effort may lead to a service interruption.

4. The fourth and fifth stages of vulnerability analysis are essentially management functions. The information systems auditor should verify whether the auditee has in place a strategy to deal with serious potential problems. These issues must be reviewed with reference to business continuity and disaster recovery practices, and problem management procedures of the auditee. The process of identification of vulnerabilities is to be reviewed to keep the process capable of meeting contemporary challenges.

Types of Vulnerability

Vulnerabilities can be broadly classified into two kinds:

1. Practice based
2. Infrastructure based

Practice-based vulnerabilities refer to such vulnerabilities that arise out of bad security practices. Examples of practice-based vulnerabilities would include keeping an administrator password blank, not changing default passwords, and so forth. The auditee needs to have a system for implementing security-related policies that address these practice-based vulnerabilities. The information systems auditor should verify the existence of and adequacy of such policies.

A security audit also focuses on *infrastructure-based* issues. These refer to the vulnerability that is a part of the system being used by the auditee. These vulnerabilities are essentially weaknesses in a system that can be exploited to run an unauthorized function on the compromised system. Examples of infrastructure-based vulnerability include vulnerabilities in the web server or in the operating system.

Conducting a Vulnerability Analysis

In order to conduct a vulnerability analysis, one needs an understanding of the known vulnerabilities of the auditee system. This information is usually maintained and provided by the vendors and various information security agencies such as CERT. Armed with such information, the security auditor can test the system for known vulnerabilities.

With the number of vulnerabilities increasing rapidly, it is recommended to use software for conducting the analysis. There are various software applications available for this purpose. Further, there is open source–based software that is often free to use and modify. One of the most common tools that is usually embedded in an application is the upgrading option that searches for whether the software has all the latest updates installed. Under Microsoft Windows there is an option named "Windows Update" that performs this function. A screenshot of the application is shown in Figure 9.4.

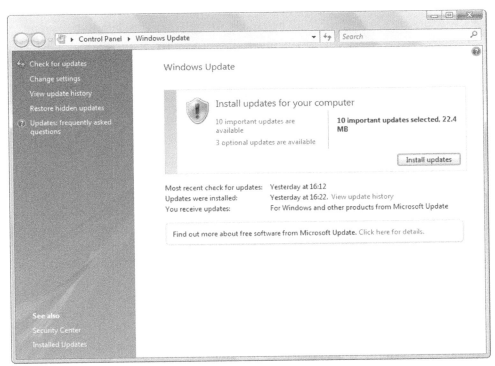

FIGURE 9.4 Screenshot of an Update Management Screen

Security auditors, in addition to observing and reporting the findings, may also be required to collect evidences as a proof of their findings or to substantiate claims of the existence of a vulnerability. This requires knowledge of cyberforensics and the use of forensic tools.

CYBERFORENSICS

Legal frameworks define offenses that are punishable under law. Most cybercrimes lack physical evidence to prove that the crime was committed unless there is involvement of forced physical entry. The evidence available in a cybercrime is digital in nature. Application of special techniques and tools is necessary to collect this evidence and present it in the courts of law. This digital evidence is highly volatile and prone to modification by others and often on its own. For example, the time stamp of the last access to the computer changes with subsequent access. Unless the history of access records is maintained, any efforts to ascertain when the computer was last accessed will automatically change the audit log of the last access date to the date of the current access and the evidence would become useless in the courts of law. Thus the challenge before any security auditor is to select techniques to preserve evidence of cybercrimes such that the evidence can be effectively presented before the court. This is the objective of cyberforensics.

Cyberforensics is the process of extracting information and data from computer storage media to establish an audit trail and guaranteeing accuracy and reliability of that audit trail. The real challenge is finding the relevant data and collecting, preserving, and presenting them in a manner that is acceptable in a court of law while ensuring that the evidence is not disturbed during the process.

There are two major applications of cyberforensics:

1. Computer forensics
2. Network forensics

The first one, computer forensics, involves the methodology and process of gathering evidence from computer media seized at the crime scene. Major activities involved with computer forensics include creating duplicate images of storage media, recovering deleted files, searching slack and free space for evidence of deleted activities, preserving collected information as evidence, and so forth. One aspect of computer forensics is the limited physical boundaries within which the investigation takes place.

Network forensics, on the other hand, involves greater technical expertise and is spread across networks that may or may not be owned by the victim. This involves gathering digital evidence from large-scale, complex networks, some of which may not be under territorial jurisdiction of the investigator or the governing law. The complexity increases as this evidence is often transient in nature and may not be preserved in permanent storage media.

To prevent the inadvertent loss of digital evidence, specific procedures are followed by cyberforensics experts. Though detailed discussion is outside the scope of this book, the information systems auditor must be aware of the following six procedures:

1. How to secure the crime scene
2. How to seize information system assets
3. How to acquire the evidence
4. How to preserve the evidence
5. How to analyze the evidence
6. How to present the evidence

Computer forensics is a technical process where computer media are first imaged by the examiner to maintain authenticity of the original evidence. In computer forensics, the analysis is done only on the image of the suspected media. This brings in the issue of ensuring authenticity of the evidence that is necessary to ensure admissibility in the courts of law. This invites the necessity to prove that the image exactly replicates the original. Various technologies are available to establish this. One commonly used technology is called hashing, wherein if the hash value of the original evidence is equal to the hash value of the image, then the image is considered as authentic. Hash value is computed by using a hashing algorithm that converts the contents of a storage medium into a value having regard to the contents and sequence thereof.

The analysis often involves identification and recovery of deleted files and folders that are critical to establish the crime and identify the criminal. The history of the use of files is one of the most important components of the forensic report. This timeline acts as a major audit trail and provides enough information to corroborate the cyberevidence with other evidence. The security auditor needs to create a detailed report and present it to the investigating authorities. On the other hand, the court and the investigating authorities need to understand the technology to appreciate the presented digital evidence.

Slack

Slack refers to portions of storage space that are not fully used by the currently allocated file and may contain data from another file. In computer storage, data are not necessarily stored in a contiguous space but are stored in a scattered manner. The file allocation table takes care of the addresses where the data belonging to a unique file name are stored. The space occurs because the data content does not necessarily match with the length of the file cluster. A cluster is the smallest unit of space that can be allocated to stored data. Thus a set of data may use space almost to the end of a file cluster and the vacant space may be used by data belonging to another file. A cluster may contain one to four sectors with each

(Continued)

sector having 512 bytes available for storage. It may also contain data from an earlier file that has since been deleted (see "Recovering Deleted Data" further on). The slack spaces are searched for such evidence.

Disk Image

Disk image is a single file that saves the entire content, including the structure of storage media like hard disk, CD, and so forth. This is created by replicating sector by sector images of the host medium so that once the image is copied into another medium, the target medium becomes functionally an exact replica of the host. Commercially this speeds up the process of replication while maintaining the functionality. In the work environment this technique is used to avoid the trouble of setting up parameters for each installation. In cyberforensics, this image is burned onto another medium and searched for digital evidence.

Recovering Deleted Data

When a file is deleted, the data contents are not immediately removed. Instead, the storage space where they were saved is marked as available for future storage. The new data that overwrite the earlier data are unlikely to have the same length as the old data. Thus the storage space would contain parts of old data that are "parentless," as the file has been technically deleted. Disk-level access to these spaces can help in the recovery of old data, and if all data pertaining to a file can be recovered, the whole file stands recovered.

 DIGITAL EVIDENCE

Digital evidence is necessary in a court of law to prove one's contention. However, some of the accepted practices in presenting physical evidence cannot be applied in the case of digital evidence. We have discussed some international best practices in the field of digital evidence.

Please note that this material is provided for informational purposes only and discusses best practices. It is not legal advice and should not be construed as such. If you are using the information contained within this material to help prepare for an investigation, please consult your legal counsel to find out the related status and procedure in the country of application.

Presenting Digital Evidence in a Court of Law

Though there are many tools for extracting and preserving digital evidence, the focus should be, instead of on the tool, on the following three aspects:

1. Whether the security auditor has technical background to support the results of the investigation

2. Whether the results have been properly authenticated
3. Whether a sound investigation was performed from start to finish

Tools are mechanisms to find evidence on an information system asset, and several different tools can replicate the process or perform identical functions. Use of a specific tool is not obligatory as the same evidence can be unearthed by a competent forensic analyst using a variety of tools or by adopting a different methodology. The major contribution of forensic experts comes in the form of proper interpretation of evidence collected to establish the crime and the crime path.

The information systems auditor must be careful in observing the manner of gathering evidence for the purpose of establishing the same in a court of law. Whether a cyberforensics expert is used or the information systems auditors act as forensic experts, the expert must be ready to face queries in the following eight areas:

1. **Manner of gathering and verifying evidence:** A detailed account of how the affected systems asset was handled and the processes adopted to extract data from the same. The methodology of creating an image, tests conducted to assure that the image is a verbatim copy of the original, and measures taken to ensure that the original is not manipulated should be documented by the expert.
2. **Chain of custody:** The chain of custody across the activities involved in the collection, analysis, and presentation of evidence must be maintained. This would include maintaining a detailed list of who had custody of the evidence and for how long. The data should also include the purpose for which custody was given to the concerned persons and how it was ensured that the original evidence was not tampered with.
3. **Ownership and licensing:** Any tool-based evidence is only as good as the tool used and the claim made by the developer. It is important to prove that the cyberforensics expert had the right to use the tool. The quality of the evidence may be doubted if the developer of the tool disclaims assurance on the quality of the output generated by a copy of the tool that was not licensed for use.
4. **Proper examination environment:** The quality of digital evidence is affected by the examination environment, including access system, storage system, protection from magnetic interference, and allied environmental objects. The process of extracting evidence and the environment should be documented to emphasize the quality of evidence extracted.
5. **Repeat technical analysis using other tools:** One of the confirmatory approaches that a cyberforensics expert may employ is to replicate the evidence extraction process using different sets of tools or approaches. When two different sets of tools generate similar results, the credibility of the evidence increases.
6. **Understanding of technical tools:** Interpretation of evidence is the main challenge of a cyberforensics expert. The expert must establish that interpretations made are final and no other interpretation is tenable in face of the evidence produced.
7. **Use of common techniques and methodologies:** It is always recommended that the tools and techniques used by the cyberforensics expert are well-established

ones. Use of a new technique that is not established may lead to questions regarding the quality of the tool and consequently discount the quality of the evidence. Thus, unless necessary, use of uncommon tools and techniques should be avoided. This does not mean that new tools and techniques will not be used. But in case these are used, the cyberforensics expert may be required to establish the credibility of the tools and techniques before defending the quality of the evidence.

8. **Technical capability of the analyst**: The cyberforensics experts may be required to prove their technical competence, which may come from professional qualifications, group affiliations, or industry endorsements.

Conventional information systems auditors need to undertake special training to be able to perform these activities.

Acceptability Tests

There are various tests that courts can apply to the methodology and testimony used by an expert to determine the admissibility, reliability, and relevancy of digital evidence. The specific test may vary even from court to court let alone from country to country.

One of the popular tests of reliability is the Daubert Reliability Test adopted in *Daubert v. Merrell Dow Pharmaceuticals* (1993) in the United States. Though the underlying principles therein would generally hold in many countries, the reader must confirm the applicability of these principles before using them in a court of law.

Essentially, the Daubert test insists that experts must use objective methodological principles in their work, and should have adequate technical qualifications to testify as an expert. The Daubert Reliability Test is built around a number of factors, including the following five:

1. Establishing the appropriateness of choice and application of technology and technique by way of objective evidence, including third-party expert opinion or theoretical justification. If the choice of technology and technique is based on a subjective and conclusive approach, it cannot be properly assessed for reliability.
2. Confirming whether the technique or theory has been subject to peer review and publication.
3. Assessing the known potential rate of error, including instances of a "false positive" arising out of application of the technique. False positives are instances where evidence suggests the occurrence of an event while in reality there was no such occurrence.
4. The availability of a protocol to ensure a standardized approach to the application of the technique.
5. Whether the theory or method has been generally accepted by the scientific community.

The security auditors should be satisfied that the evidence collected by them or by other experts would qualify as evidence in a court of law.

CHAPTER TEN

Case Study: Conducting an Information Systems Audit

N THIS CHAPTER, WE learn about the steps involved in conducting an information systems audit. We have selected a bank as a case study essentially because banks represent one of the most critical and sensitive applications of information systems assets. In addition, the multiple guidelines issued by the central banks of different countries on this matter provide a rich collection of best practices from which we have drawn. The chapter provides a step-by-step guide to conducting an information systems audit at the various levels of a bank, including its branches.

The lessons presented in this chapter are not restricted to applications in bank information systems alone. The methodology is applicable to all information systems, although the specific object of examination is likely to vary. At the end of this chapter we will be ready to conduct an information systems audit of any entities, including those with multilocation systems.

IMPORTANT SECURITY ISSUES IN BANKS

Important security issues involved in an information systems audit of a bank, as well as other organizations, include the following:

User Access Management

The auditor needs to verify the following two points:

1. The existence of formal procedures controlling the allocation of access rights for individual users.
2. The procedures must cover the entire life cycle of user access, from registration of new users to deregistration.

User Registration

The information systems auditor should confirm whether the user registration process and policy include the following 10 areas:

1. Use of unique user IDs so that a user can be identified from the user ID used to access information system resources.
2. Group IDs are to be allotted only when nature of work to be performed demands so. Group IDs are used by several individuals and are usually allotted when the user primarily retrieves information and does not input any. An example of such a profile is that of an auditor. Cost of individual licences may also motivate the auditee to allot group IDs so that instead of a single user accessing the resource, multiple users can access it with the same ID. Often system-defined user IDs force an organization to use them as group IDs. For example, if the system-defined system administrator ID is "admin," everyone who needs to use the administrative features of the application will be compelled to use the same ID.
3. The owner of the asset is required to authorize specific users to use the asset.
4. The level of access granted is in line with functional requirements of the user and is aligned with the information system security policy of the auditee.
5. Users have to sign a declaration containing their respective access rights and agree to the terms of usage.
6. No system resource is made accessible to anybody before the authorization procedure is complete.
7. All access permissions granted are documented.
8. Access rights are removed as soon as the user no longer needs such access and specifically when the user has left the organization.
9. Redundant user IDs and accounts are identified periodically and removed. Such redundant user IDs are not reissued to other users before lapse of a specific time. In cases of generic IDs, this may not be possible and additional care has to be taken to reset the password used by the earlier user.

10. Employment contracts and service provider contracts specify that violation of access rights will invoke penal procedures.

Authentication of Users

All users, irrespective of their functional profile, should have a unique identifier (user ID) so that the activities can subsequently be traced, documented, and used as legal evidence, if necessary. The only exception to this is the use of generic ID and group ID where additional controls are to be established to identify the individuals using the asset.

Identification of individual users of the information asset can be facilitated by adopting the following best practice–based procedure:

1. Assignment of unique user IDs to each individual user of the information systems asset.
2. Holding the assignee of a user ID responsible for all acts, or absence thereof, performed under the user ID unless identity theft has been reported and established.
3. Establishing an audit trail of all activities performed by any user ID.

Password Management System

The information systems auditor should verify whether the password management system has implemented, among others, the following 12 best practices:

1. Use of individual passwords to maintain accountability, unless group access is granted to some resources.
2. Users should be able to define and change their own password and the process should include a confirmation procedure to control input errors.
3. Definition and enforcement of a minimum strength for the passwords proposed by users, including the following:
   a. Use of a minimum number of characters.
   b. Enforcement of a combination of alphabet, numeric, and special characters.
   c. Prohibition of use of a user ID, user name, or similar information as a part of the password.
   d. Informing the users on the dangers of using a password that can be related to the user, such as date of birth or phone number.
   e. Discouraging the writing down of passwords and storing the same in a publicly accessible place.
4. Wherever a temporary password is granted, users should be compelled to change it at the first log-on.
5. Enforcing change of passwords upon expiration of a certain period, irrespective of whether the password was used.
6. A defined period of time or number of instances for maintaining the history of a password, which cannot be reused for a defined period.

7. Providing a distress password for sensitive operations, which can be used to alert system administrators, other members of staff, and law enforcement agencies when the access is under duress.
8. Passwords are masked on the screen when entered, irrespective of the devices being used.
9. Password files are not stored with the application system data.
10. Passwords are transmitted and stored in an encrypted form.
11. The default password provided by the vendor or implementing agency is changed immediately after installation of the hardware/software.
12. Sharing of passwords is defined as a breach of acceptable conduct invoking disciplinary and legal actions.

Limiting Sign-On Attempts

The information systems auditor should verify whether the following two best practices are considered for unauthorized sign-on attempts:

1. Suspension of user IDs after a defined number of unsuccessful log-in attempts. In the case of a sensitive system, the number of attempts may be cumulative across days and reset to zero only if a successful log-in takes place. A common application of this control is in the user access system for Internet banking. In some cases, the suspension is released automatically at the end of the day, for example, the PIN number for an ATM card.
2. Definition of a maximum time limit for inactivity and termination of the session if the specified time limit is exceeded. A common application is found at bank ATMs, which cancel the log-in if no activity is observed over a specified time. Most of the secured sites terminate the session after inactivity over a defined period.

Unattended Terminals

The auditor needs to review whether appropriate steps, including the following six, have been implemented to prevent unauthorized use of an unattended terminal that is connected to the system:

1. Forced log-out after a defined period of inactivity, which will require a fresh user authentication before work can recommence on the terminal.
2. Compulsory shut-off of the terminal after a certain time of the day or period of inactivity.
3. Educating all users, internal and external, on security requirements and procedures to be observed to protect unattended terminals. The users should also be made aware of their responsibilities for implementing such protection.
4. All active sessions should be terminated once the user indicates completion of their function. In cases of functions involving processing over a long period of time where the session cannot be terminated despite there being no user

interface, the system must be secured by an appropriate locking mechanism, including a password-protected screensaver.

5. When a terminal completes a session with the server, the session must be terminated even when the terminal is switched off without logging off.

6. Terminals in sensitive locations or involved in sensitive functions should shut down automatically after a defined period of inactivity. This feature must sequentially clear the terminal screen, close the application, and disconnect network sessions after the defined period of inactivity.

Information Access Restriction

Information access restrictions can be enforced by designing controls that address various issues, including the following four:

1. The applications used should provide menu-based access privileges to application users on a need basis and restrict access to limited menu items for a specific user.

2. User documentation may be tailored to suit different user group profiles, and it may include, on a need-to-know basis, information on how to access application system functions. Thus users would not be apprised of various functionalities that the application offers that are not relevant for them.

3. Access rights of the users may be categorized and controlled to ensure that the rights to read, write, delete, and execute are enjoyed by specified users or user groups.

4. The outputs from application systems containing sensitive information should contain information relevant for the specific use. Further, such information should also be sent only to authorized terminals and locations.

Use of System Utilities

System support staff use system utility programs that are generally capable of overriding various system and application controls. Though these utilities serve useful functions to maintain uninterrupted services, the intrusive nature of these tools can compromise system security and this capability can be abused. An information systems auditor must confirm that the use of system utilities is restricted and follows a strict authorization scheme. The following eight controls may prove useful in this regard:

1. Existence and strict observance of rigid authentication procedures for acquisition, installation, and use of system utilities.

2. Clear segregation of authorization and access to system utilities and application software.

3. Restriction on the use of system utilities to a closed group comprising the least possible number of trusted and competent users.

4. Requirement of restrictive and escalated authorization process for ad hoc use of such utilities.
5. Restricted availability in terms of access to and installation of system utilities.
6. Detailed logging of all activities performed using system utilities.
7. Compulsory backup requirement before usage of critical system utilities that may render the system resources unavailable.
8. Compulsory removal of all unnecessary utilities from the information systems, including immediate uninstallation after completion of service.

Limitation of Connection Time

The information systems auditor should evaluate the restrictions on connection time imposed to provide greater security for sensitive and high-risk applications. The time restriction can be imposed in two ways:

1. **Connection time restrictions:** This control restricts connection to a particular time of the day. For example, the server for an electronic funds transfer should refuse connection on banking holidays.
2. **Usage time restrictions:** This control forces the user to complete the function within a specified period of time. The system terminates the connection upon expiration of the time and the user needs to reinitiate the entire process, which may include a fresh log-in. A common use of this control is on e-commerce sites. It is also a good practice to warn the user about the time left to complete the transaction.

Enforcement of the control of limiting connections time reduces the window of opportunity for unauthorized access and also releases system resources for critical and other uses.

Warning

A warning notice serves a major role in educating a user to the consequences of his or her actions and reduces the opportunity of erroneous conduct by a bona fide user. This is achieved by displaying a warning screen, prior to completing sign-on as well as before committing an action, that makes the user aware of the unauthorized access or potentially harmful implications of his or her conduct. Once the user elects to act after having been adequately warned, such actions can be construed as mala fide and even illegal. This control, in addition to reducing innocent errors, also makes enforcement of internal or statutory provisions easier. The majority of such warnings are generated by the operating system or specific applications. For example, a web browser may warn the user when the user is moving from a secured site to an unsecured site that does not provide any encryption facility. If the user is not permitted to transmit any information using a nonencrypted network, the warning will make the user aware of such a violation.

In case of transaction processing, the warning screen reminds the user of the transaction he or she is about to perform. In addition, once the user reviews the warning and completes the transaction, the user cannot deny knowledge of the implication of the transaction.

External Users

The extent of control implemented for allowing access to an internal network by an external user should be more robust than the measures implemented for an internal user. All external access requests should be required to go through a firewall or an intrusion prevention and detection system before being allowed to commence the access verification process. There may even be a requirement for a secondary identity verification system for access to sensitive resources within the network. The information systems auditor needs to examine the access security framework to be able to judge the vulnerability of the system to unauthorized access from outside. For example, most Internet banking sites require the logged-in user to provide a "transaction password" to be able to perform any financial transaction. This is in addition to the initial log-in necessary to access the transaction menu.

Audit Trails

Audit trails are documented records of activity performed by a user. Such a record assists in restructuring an event and establishing accountability. The audit trails can be system-based as well as nonsystem-based. For example, user log-in information will provide a system-based audit trail while a gate pass will provide a physical audit trail of an access. The quality of an audit trail, especially in terms of integrity, is critical for its being admitted as evidence.

Fault Logging

The information systems auditor needs to be assured that all faults are reported and corresponding actions taken. The actions can be corrective or investigative in nature. All faults reported by users, whether arising out of system-based deficiencies or out of improper training, must be logged. The auditee must have an established policy for management of reported faults, which may include the following four procedures:

1. A defined service turnover time target within which specific faults need to be addressed and resolved.
2. Regular review of the fault logs to identify whether any fault report remains unresolved.
3. Formal, and preferably automated, system of escalation of unresolved faults after expiration of relevant service turnover time.
4. An audit of corrective measures to ensure that the solution has not been achieved by compromising controls and, whenever such compromise is observed, that the resolution process was appropriately authorized. For example, tripping of power

arising out of a faulty power stabilizer system can be solved by allowing direct connection with an external power source.

Logging and Reviewing of Events

Regular review of various system logs is essential to develop a better understanding of security threats faced by information systems. This should include instances of successful and failed compromise attempts. One major practical problem with the review of audit logs is the volume involved that makes searching difficult. This may be countered by creating a copy of the audit log and then using audit tools or even data-mining tools to scan for specific contents. It is important to create a copy to maintain integrity of the original log files.

The auditor should verify existence of a documented plan, which will define, among others, the following seven items:

1. Volumes of information to be logged
2. Encryption requirement of log files
3. Rotation of log files
4. Retention requirement of log files
5. Disposal norms of log files
6. Backup of log files
7. Security of log files to deter possible tampering, including modification and fabrication

It is critical to ensure segregation of duties while assigning responsibility for the log review so that those responsible for the log review are different from those whose activities are being monitored and logged.

IMPLEMENTING AN INFORMATION SYSTEMS AUDIT AT A BANK BRANCH

The following procedure details the flow of the information systems audit in a bank branch. It may be observed that the essence of the process is also applicable in an audit of a nonbanking institution. The overall audit workflow described in Chapter 11 of the book and the checklists provided in Chapter 12 could be used while following the audit process.

1. **Commencement of audit:**
    a. The information systems audit team introduces themselves to the branch manager or the functional head in case of nonbanking organizations.
    b. The auditor may be required to provide identification.
    c. The auditor undertakes a preliminary discussion about computerization at the branch and awareness of personnel about computers and their usage.

    d. The auditor should specifically enquire about the existence of a mixed process wherein a part of the process is performed manually and the rest uses information systems.

2. **Review of start-up operations:**

    a. The auditor observes start-up procedures. If any error messages, such as a checksum error, or system errors occur, a note of the same is made for reporting.

    b. The auditor then observes the process of initiating head-cashier application and distribution of cash on the system to other cashiers.

    c. The auditor makes a preliminary overview of the server room. The environment, presence of unrelated information systems assets, evidence of use of server room for various purposes, wiring and cabling, and so forth, are observed.

3. **General overview:**

    a. The auditor would make a business overview of the branch to identify the core areas of focus. This would include the following:

        i. Size of the branch in terms of information systems assets, branch details, and identification code.

        ii. Business position—amount of deposits and advances. In case of nonbanking organizations, this will include information on turnover, profit, and so forth.

        iii. Number of personnel, computer literate and otherwise.

    b. The auditor subsequently observes various operations, the number of computers, availability of necessary skilled personnel, maintenance of the computer assets, and so forth.

    c. The auditor visually determines whether there are any excess or unused information system assets. Often there are cases where information system assets have been delivered to the branch but not commissioned for work. Details of such occurrence must be recorded as they represent underutilized investment.

4. **Overview of records:** The information systems auditor makes an overview of the following:

    a. List of all books, registers, and logs maintained at the branch

    b. Fixed asset register relating to information technology assets

    c. Day-end reports of prior day

    d. Previous audit report

    e. Report of inspection by independent and regulatory agencies

    f. Register evidencing records of maintenance activities

    g. Register containing emergency contact numbers

5. **Physical environment:** The environmental factors that the information systems auditor needs to review and report on include the following:

    a. Air-conditioning system

    b. Power supply system, uninterruptible power supply system, generators, record of testing of electrical lines

    c. Physical security to prevent unauthorized access

    d. Controls specific to access to server room

    e. Quality of environment—humidity, dust, and so forth

    f. Presence of food items, smoke, water, and so forth in work area

    g. Presence and working condition of fire protection system and fire extinguishers

    h. Overall space and working environment present

6. **Hardware audit:** The information systems auditor needs to look into the details of hardware installations at the auditee site. The activities that the auditor would perform include the following:

    a. Hardware audit commences with an overview of the hardware present at the branch and its corresponding entry in the fixed asset register for information system assets.

    b. The satisfaction of users, promptness of vendor service, and adherence of the vendor to terms of maintenance contracts are verified.

    c. An overview of the hardware configuration will be made to identify age and obsolescence status of hardware. Conversation with users also provides corroborative evidence on whether systems asset performs efficiently.

    d. The information systems auditor would review details of repair and maintenance records to identify recurring and unresolved problems.

    e. An assessment of utilities present should be made to evaluate their appropriateness.

    f. Adherence to terms of insurance contract will be verified and adequacy of the insurance coverage will be ascertained.

    g. Presence, usage, and authorization procedure for access to hardware manuals is reviewed.

    h. The reporting on hardware audit would address the following aspects:

        i. Physical environment

        ii. Peripheral devices and storage media

        iii. Client-server

        iv. Authentication devices

        v. Maintenance

        vi. Problem management

        vii. Change management

        viii. Security management

        ix. Asset classification and control

7. **Software audit:** Various aspects that an information systems auditor needs to cover include the following:

    a. Satisfaction of users, promptness of vendor service, and adherence of the vendor to terms of software maintenance contracts are to be reviewed.

    b. Application of latest updates to all software at the branch needs to be verified.

    c. Procedures of preventive, detective, and corrective maintenance of software are to be verified.

    d. Security of, use of, and authorization for software manuals are to be verified.

    e. Verify whether all software is licensed.

   f. Ascertain whether antivirus software is regularly updated and whether reports of virus attacks are reviewed.

   g. Access privileges of users and their limitations are to be reviewed.

   h. The reporting on software audit may include the following aspects:
- i. Antivirus
- ii. Asset classification and control
- iii. Change management
- iv. Communication software
- v. File and directory protection
- vi. Maintenance
- vii. Operating system
- viii. Package software implementation
- ix. Parameter setting
- x. Problem management
- xi. Security management
- xii. Software license
- xiii. System conversion and reconciliation
- xiv. System software control
- xv. Transaction processing
- xvi. Utility program

8. **Network and communication audit:** The objective of a network audit is to ensure that network integrity is maintained, only authorized users have access to system resources, network performs efficiently and effectively, network security is ensured, and network remains available to authorized users. The following areas are reviewed in terms of their impact on overall confidentiality, integrity, and availability of network assets while performing the network audit:

   a. Communication software

   b. Data communication

   c. Electronic funds transfer

   d. Internet security

   e. Local area network

   f. Maintenance

   g. Change management

   h. Problem management

   i. Security management

   j. Wireless network

9. **Personnel awareness:** Personnel form an integral part of computerized systems. The information systems auditor should comment on the following areas:

   a. Adequacy of training

   b. Awareness of security issues, especially the following:
- i. Secrecy of passwords
- ii. Responsibility during contingency
- iii. Authentication of reports
- iv. Prevention against network threats

     c. Awareness about applicable legal issues with specific attention to criminal violation of law

10. **Password maintenance:** Password maintenance lies at the heart of access security. The information systems auditor should address the following issues while reporting on password management:

     a. Minimum length of passwords

     b. Secrecy of passwords

     c. Enforced periodic change of passwords

     d. Active passwords of personnel no longer present

11. **Logical environment:** Parameters set in the system need to be reviewed by the information systems auditor to ensure correct functioning of application programs. The auditor should verify their update process, and whether the maker-checker methodology of authorization is followed while updating parameters.

     a. The auditor may test whether directions of circulars and internal guidelines have been updated into the system on a timely and correct basis.

     b. The auditor may conduct a test of parameters, such as deposit interest rates, advance interest rates, and penal interest rates.

     c. Parameters such as authorization levels, privilege levels, and system-related parameters must be verified.

12. **Access to server:** The information systems auditor needs to be assured that access to servers is appropriately protected. The auditor may examine the following to verify the same:

     a. The auditor should review the list of persons authorized to access the server room. The methodology of control of access to the server room is to be ascertained. This may include a limited number of personnel accessing the server room, the key being maintained by two persons, and so on.

     b. Use of structured query language (SQL) or similar tools for direct access to the database bypassing the application software should be limited and controlled. The information systems auditor should verify the records for such direct access, including use of SQL and other techniques to ascertain the level of control over direct access to the database.

     c. The auditor may verify the record of all activities carried out in the server and whether written authorization for each of those activities was obtained.

     d. A record of occurrence of database errors is to be reviewed by the auditor with a specific focus on analysis of the causes and effects of the errors.

13. **Repair and maintenance:** The information systems auditor should verify the records and documents, and ascertain the process for the following:

     a. Identification of maintenance personnel

     b. Vendor declaration of fidelity and secrecy

     c. Diagnostic access allowed to maintenance personnel

     d. Declaration by vendor of activities performed by the vendor

     e. Record of removal of information assets

14. **Unauthorized programs and folders:** The information systems auditor should verify whether there are folders (directories) present on the system that

are not authorized. The auditor should also look for whether any of the following are installed in the system and, if they are, whether authorization has been obtained.

a. Password-cracking tools
b. Utility programs
c. Games
d. Personal folders
e. Other programs or data apart from those belonging to authorized operating and application systems

15. **Day-end reports:** The information systems auditor should provide a special focus on reports generated at the day-end. The auditor should specifically obtain and examine the following:

a. List of reports required to be generated
b. Whether there is any error in report generation
c. Error messages during the day-end process
d. Reports for
   i. Audit trails
   ii. Activity logs
   iii. Exceptions
   iv. Failed log-in attempts

16. **Backup:** During the course of audit, the information systems auditor should review the backup procedure in practice with special reference to the following:

a. Procedure of backup
b. Periodic testing of the media
c. Periodic testing of recovery from backup
d. Storage of backup
e. Areas selected for backup

17. **Contingency plan:** This critical control requires a thorough review by the information systems auditor. The review will include the following:

a. Presence of the plan
b. Awareness about the plan
c. Testing of the plan and results
d. Corrective tests taken in view of results of testing the plan
e. Ready availability of emergency numbers
f. Personnel list to be contacted in case of emergency
g. Record of breakdowns, downtime, and maintenance
h. Presence of adequate fallback arrangements for critical assets

SPECIAL CONSIDERATIONS IN A CORE BANKING SYSTEM

The core banking system is an environment that uses client-server architecture, with a remote server and client branches. The remote server is often referred to as a data center, while the clients are located at various service outlets including branches.

Similar architecture is found in most nonbanking organizations with multi location operations. The information systems auditor may focus on the following areas.

Migration Controls

If the branch has migrated to a core banking system, it is critical to establish consistency and integrity of data that have been migrated. Various validation checks may be conducted for this purpose, including verification of system and application-related parameters, verification of master-data, mapping of customer accounts, particularly linking thereof with appropriate tables, scheme codes, general ledger subheads, and so forth.

Day-End Controls

Day-end processing is a crucial process in the core banking system environment. The day-end processes involve various operational issues such as interest calculation, execution of standing instructions, interbranch transactions, interbranch reconciliation, and so forth. The process, among other activities, identifies critical issues, such as incomplete transactions with one leg posted, cash not balanced, ATM withdrawals not reconciled with account holder of a different bank, and similar problems. The day-end process will not be completed unless all defined processes set by the bank have been completed correctly.

Under the core banking system, the day-end procedure is essentially managed centrally at the data center. During the day-end process, the bank can identify whether any transactions have remained unauthorized. Various control reports are generated at the day-end to ensure integrity of transactions and provide information of contravention of specified controls such as log-on, system of authorizations, exceptions, and anomalies. Some of the reports generated that need to be reviewed by the information systems auditor include the following four:

1. Exceptional report containing:
   a. Accounts where balance has changed from debit to credit and vice-versa
   b. Deletion of maturity records
   c. Reactivation of inactive accounts
   d. Withdrawal permitted in excess of limit
   e. Debit posting to income-related accounts
   f. Overdue bills and bills returned
   g. Withdrawal permitted against collection under clearing
   h. Debit balance in deposit accounts
   i. Credit balance in loan accounts
   j. Temporary overdraft beyond sanction limit
   k. Standing instruction not executed or not honored in the day
2. List of users
3. Access logs
4. List of rejected or canceled entries

Control over Periodical/Mass-Runs (System Generated Transactions)

Under the core banking system, often the data center executes various transactions relating to a customer group. Branches or other service channels verify the reports on such transactions to ensure their completeness and correctness. Examples of such transactions include the following five:

1. Interest application
2. Service charge application
3. Changes in global parameters such as interest rate
4. Balancing and reconciliations of general and subsidiary accounts
5. Identification of loan accounts that are not servicing interest or repaying principal and classifying them under the internal or statutory norm.

Centralized processing is mostly an automated process, but during a processing cycle, some of the processes remain unexecuted or are erroneously executed. For example, there may be an incorrect application or nonapplication of interest during an interest application processing because of following five reasons:

1. Interest rate is not mapped correctly to the product. For example, the interest rate of a personal loan is wrongly linked to the interest rate of a housing loan.
2. Interest collection flag is kept as "N" instead of "Y," causing a nonapplication of interest.
3. Next interest demand date is kept the same as the date of application of interest.
4. Account has remained unconfirmed though a transaction has commenced on the same.
5. Account has been wrongly marked as past due or nonperforming, causing nonapplication of interest.

Control over Inter-SOL Transactions

In a core banking system environment each accounting entity, which is usually a branch office, is designated by a service outlet (SOL) or frame. Automated transactions are initiated by the auditee SOL for another SOL and also by another SOL for the auditee SOL. These transactions have to be reconciled centrally at the data center during the day-end process. Entries that are not reconciled automatically are matters of concern and need to be looked into to identify whether the error was caused by an input error or was a system design error or a processing error.

Control over Proxy/Parking Transactions

In the normal course of banking business and in observance of maker-checker protocol, some transactions might not be verified and authorized for posting and remain unposted though they have been entered. At the same time, banks need to run the day-end process, which is not permissible in presence of such outstanding entries. As a workaround, these transactions are posted in an account called the proxy account or parking account. If the information systems auditor finds that a large number of such outstanding entries are posted in the parking account, he or she should investigate the matter to ascertain the reason.

These transactions are generally of two types:

1. **System generated:** This includes transactions that are executed during various system runs. Execution of standing instructions at the data center on the last day of the month to close the SOL is a common example of such transactions. If the account number of the account holder has changed for any reason, this transaction may not be posted to the relevant account and will remain in "entered" status and get posted in the proxy account.

2. **User generated:** These transactions are initiated by the user, but because of erroneous input or incomplete processing they are not posted to the designated account. These transactions are also kept in a proxy or parking account. For example, if a check has been deposited in favor of an account and a wrong account number has been provided, the transaction will be parked in the parking account.

Mapping of Accounts

Mapping refers to linking of accounts with various scheme codes, tables, general ledger subheads, and so forth. It determines how the system executes parameter-driven transactions for those accounts. For instance, a car loan account needs to be linked with the car loan master for application of the relevant interest rate. Incorrect mapping would compromise data integrity, cause misleading reports, and may lead to serious legal complications. The information systems auditor needs to check such transactions on customer accounts selected on a test basis to ensure that mapping is done correctly. The auditors will also need to verify that global parameters for the linked files are correctly entered.

Application Control Review

The areas that an information systems auditor needs to verify include the following seven:

1. **User-profile maintenance:** The user-profile maintenance module is used to create, modify, and delete users. The information systems auditor should verify that only authorized users are active. Users who have left the branch or have been terminated should not have any user ID in the system. The archived data should verify that these user IDs were deleted. If any user is temporarily absent, the user ID should be marked as inactive. The information systems auditor needs to review whether user access to menus and their permissions are commensurate to the job assigned to the users. The authority and responsibility settings in the system should also be verified.

2. **User-ID maintenance:** Each user ID should be assigned a standard user profile that defines the data-access rights and privileges of the user. The profile may define access to menus, grant power to override exceptions, authorize transactions for posting, and so forth. Various standard user profiles, also called work classes, may be defined in the system for various operating functions, such as systems operator, teller, supervisor, vault-in-charge, branch-in-charge, database administrator, financial auditor, information systems auditor, administrator, and so forth. The information systems auditor needs to verify the adequacy of design and implementation of the user-ID maintenance system.

3. **Password management:** The password should have a minimum length as per prescribed standards and be changed periodically. The information systems auditor may carry out test checks and review the history of password changes to establish whether the policy is being followed.

4. **Log-on attempts:** Usually after a specified number of sign-on attempts in which the user fails to provide the correct password, the system locks the person out. The user ID has to be released or unlocked by the administrator. This process of locking and release should leave an audit trail, which should be reviewed by the information systems auditor.

5. **Access logs and reviews:** The access logs generated by the system should be reviewed on a daily basis by an authorized person at the branch to ensure that no unauthorized access has been made. The information systems auditor should verify that the review is carried out only by the authorized person.

6. **Virus detection and protection:** The antivirus program on each machine should be activated and updated. The information systems auditor should verify the last date of the update and the archived report on virus containment present in the antivirus archives.

7. **Module interfacing:** A core banking system is often interfaced with various third-party applications modules, for example, a government business module, customer relationship module, loan presanction and postsanction module, antimoney-laundering module, know-your-customer module, electronic funds transfer module, mobile banking module, Internet banking module, point-of-sale management module, and so forth. The information systems auditor should verify these interfaces and assess their security implementation to ensure that they do not compromise the security framework of the host system.

Database and System Administration

The aspects of database and system administration that an information systems auditor needs to verify include the following 10:

1. **Database administrator and system administrator:** The system administrator should not have any data access. Hence, in a core banking system, the system administration and the database administration function should be carried out by two separate individuals. The system administrator and the database

administrator should be changed at periodical intervals. The information systems auditor needs to review the arrangement and comment on any violation.

2. **Segregation of duties:** In a computerized system, it is generally inappropriate to have a single person performing multiple steps leading to completion of a single function, including that of creation and control. Usually such functions are performed by different persons in a manual system and are commonly known as "noncompatible functions." The possibility of a single person being able to execute all the steps of a function often leads to serious compromise of the basic principle of the segregation of duties. Principle of segregation of duties assures nonperformance of incompatible functions by a single individual. It is required to ensure that no user of a sensitive system be able to perform all parts of a transaction. The information systems auditor needs to verify that "noncompatible functions" are not being performed by one individual.

3. **Access to super-user accounts:** These accounts have higher privileges. They usually have authorization privileges, privileges to perform exceptional transactions, and so forth. The access to such user profiles should be restricted and audit trails of their usage should be maintained in detail. The information systems auditor needs to confirm that there were no exceptions to this critical control.

4. **Usage of passwords:** The passwords ideally should be stored in an encrypted form, though often this is not the case because of the level of technology being used. Passwords should be compulsory for all operating and application systems apart from the core banking application. Passwords of the system software should be regularly changed. The information systems auditor should verify whether the password maintenance procedure complies with the accepted password policy.

5. **Change in privilege levels:** The information systems auditor should verify the process of making changes to privilege levels. A user with a lower privilege level should not be allowed to alter the privilege level of a user with a higher privilege level.

6. **Problem management:** The information systems auditor should refer to the problem register to understand recurring system-related problems. Database problems that have occurred may be a harbinger of data integrity compromises.

7. **Change management:** The information systems auditor should verify security measures adopted when migrating from one system to another along with data integrity and consistency issues arising out of such migration. In case of inadequacy or ineffectiveness of procedures being observed, an independent migration audit may be recommended by the information systems auditor.

8. **Access to database logs:** Access to database logs should be restricted. The user should not be able to modify any entries in the database logs. Usage of direct database access programs such as SQL should be restricted. Direct access made to the database should be logged with reasons for use and details of the commands used.

The information systems auditor needs to verify the effectiveness of these controls and comment on the same in the audit report.

9. **Encryption of data:** The information systems auditor should verify whether standard encryption methodologies are used. The usage may be at two levels:

   a. **VPN level:** The data should be encrypted while being transferred over the network.

   b. **Storage level:** The data stored in the database should be encrypted.

10. **Test of backup and periodic recovery:** The system and database should be periodically backed up. The auditor should verify the process of backup, storage of backup, and whether the storage media are periodically tested for recovery.

Firewalls

Major aspects of firewalls that an information systems auditor needs to verify include the following 13:

1. **Bandwidth-level estimation:** The system may become very slow unless bandwidth availability is computed considering installation of a firewall. If the information systems auditor observes such a situation, a comment should be included in the audit report.

2. **Location of firewalls:** The information systems auditor should verify the location of firewalls by reviewing the network diagram. The presence of a firewall is a must for all points of interaction of the internal system with the external environment.

3. **Presence of proxy server:** To safeguard the main database from attacks, banks may use a proxy server. Ideally, the user should first be authenticated at the proxy server before being permitted access to the database. The proxy server should also have a firewall installed. The information systems auditor should verify the procedure in place and comment on any deviations.

4. **Restriction of network services:** The information systems auditor should verify whether permissions provided for network services comply with the network policy. These restrictions, among others, may include the following:

   a. The server may not be permitted to initiate a network connection but only receive and respond to connection requests.

   b. Port 80 (and/or port 443 for SSL) connection from outside with a specific attribute may be permitted access, with all other requests denied.

5. **Port restrictions:** The information systems auditor may ask for a printout of permissions set in the firewall and verify port restrictions and their compliance to permitted authorizations in the network policy.

6. **Internet connection:** The information systems auditor should verify that there are no machines connected directly to a dial-up USB modem. All Internet connections should be routed through the firewall.

7. **Domain name system:** The information systems auditor should verify that separate internal and external domain name system (DNS) servers are utilized and configured to "mask" internal host names before they are transmitted over the network. The auditor should also verify additional controls enforced in cases where such masking is not done.

8. **IP address:** The information systems auditor should verify that all internal IP addresses are hidden from the Internet user through techniques such as network address translation (NAT), which replaces the internal IP address with a substitute IP address.

9. **Router password management:** The router passwords should be changed at periodic intervals. The information systems auditor should verify the router password management system and evidences of periodic change.

10. **Logging and review of logs:** The information systems auditor should verify whether the firewall logs are maintained and reviewed on a regular basis.

11. **Demilitarized zone:** The information systems auditor should verify if application and database servers are kept separated from the web server in the demilitarized zone. A firewall should be placed before the DMZ.

12. **Updating of patches for the firewall:** The firewall program should be updated with the latest patches and the information systems auditor should examine the latest patch implemented and verify whether it is the latest patch released.

13. **Firewall operation in backup site:** Firewalls should be present not only at the main server but also at the disaster recovery server. The information systems auditor should verify the presence and configuration of the firewall at the disaster recovery server.

Bandwidth

Bandwidth essentially represents the rate of data transfer. It is a measure of data that can be carried from one point to another in a given time, usually expressed in seconds. The base unit of measure of bandwidth is bits per second (bps). However, the more common expression used now is megabits per second, or mbps. Across the network, when data are transmitted they can have different bandwidths in different network segments.

Virtual Private Network

When establishing a connection between two computers across a large network, the same network is simultaneously shared by other computers. A virtual private network (VPN) provides security to ensure that the network traffic between the two computers stays isolated from other computers using the same network. Connection through VPN emulates a direct connection with the server, as would be the case in a point-to-point link. Essentially, VPN is a private network that uses a public network to establish connectivity. The security is ensured by encrypting the data being transmitted.

Proxy Server

A proxy server is positioned between a client computer and the main server. The proxy server handles the requests from the client and forwards them to the main server after evaluating the requests in terms of security and functionality. Proxy servers can be used to filter requests, for example, preventing employees from accessing a specific website. It can also be used for improving performance; for example, if a client requests the same information that has just been handled by the proxy server, the proxy server, instead of forwarding it to the main server, will respond to the request by itself.

Domain Name Server

The resources of a network are identified through the IP address. However, since IP addresses are difficult to remember, often they are given an alphabetic name, which is easier to remember. For example, wiley.com is easier to remember than a set of 12 digits. A domain name server (DNS) is essentially a service that translates these domain names into IP addresses. The DNS system is a large network in itself. If a particular DNS is not aware of the IP address equivalent of a domain name, it asks another DNS on the network. This process continues till the IP address is found. If DNS service is stopped, all access based on the domain name will cease to function.

Network Address Translation

Network address translation (NAT) is a system wherein resources residing on a local private network use a single IP address for connecting to the public network. The translation of the IP addresses of various resources of the local network is done by the router. Consequently, only one IP address is required to represent a group of resources on a local private network. Upon receipt of an inbound communication, the router sends it to the individual resources residing inside the private network. VPN works much like a telephone switchboard where all internal users access the same external line from multiple internal extensions. Thus, NAT reduces the demand for individual public IP addresses for every resource used in the private network.

Demilitarized Zone

Demilitarized zone (DMZ) is a small network working as a neutral zone between a private and a public network. DMZ prevents direct access to the private network from the outside world. Most commonly, this network receives requests both from the private network and from computers on the public network. Subsequently, the DMZ host initiates sessions for the requests on the public network. Usually a the DMZ host does not initiate a session in the private network but forwards data packets that have been requested. A DMZ can be a physical or a logical network.

Help Desk

Banks manage and operate a help desk on a 24/7 basis either by themselves or through outsourced agencies. These help desks are a single point of contact for users of system resources for all their operational queries. The help desks are usually connected with the networks of all of the branches, using a combination of voice support, a dedicated help desk web page, and a help desk problem logging application.

The majority of problems arising in a core banking system related to hardware, software, network, and so on, are resolved through the help desk. The situation is similar in nonbanking organizations. The help desk software analyzes the problem profiles and automatically generates a list of commonly encountered problems and resolution history. Review of these responses by the information systems auditor would allow them to identify recurring problems and the efficiency of the resolution process. Analysis of the help desk log is extremely useful to define the vulnerability profile of the auditee.

Information Security

In a core banking system environment, the information systems auditor should verify the following four procedures:

1. Adherence to the security policy of the auditee.
2. Whether all programs used are updated with the latest security patches.
3. Whether the bank branch adheres to the privacy policy of the bank and ensures confidentiality of customer information.
4. In case of outsourced services, whether the vendor complies with the information security policy of the bank. It may also be necessary to conduct an information systems audit of the outsourcing agency to verify this fact.

Logs of Activity

The information systems auditor should overview the procedure of verification and periodicity of verification of logs by the bank. It should be ensured that the logs contain adequate details, such as access time, activities performed, and user IDs. These logs may include, among other items, the following five:

1. Operating system logs
2. Firewall logs
3. Application system logs
4. SQL logs
5. ATM terminal access log

Departure from Normal Patterns

The information systems auditor should verify the following seven items in the system to detect any abnormal patterns:

1. Synchronization of terminal and server clock.
2. Failure and success of log-on and log-off events.
3. Record of restart, shutdown, and system access.
4. Record of changing security profile of the system.
5. Changes in user and group management profile.
6. Success and failure of obtaining access to file and other information assets.
7. Deviation from "normal" usage patterns, including the following:
   a. Unusual system load at specific points of time.
   b. Number of consecutively running processes.
   c. Utilization of processing power and network.
   d. Unusual ratio of failed connections to connection requests.
   e. Unusual frequency of requests handled by firewall, including number of successes and denials.
   f. Multiple access attempts from the same user account or multiple user accounts from a terminal.
   g. Access request or activity on unusual ports, which may also indicate virus attacks.

Management Practices

The information systems auditor should verify the process of governance of information systems. Important areas that warrant attention of management and auditors include the following six:

1. System to measure usage of physical resources and utilization of communications bandwidth.
2. Arrangement to acquire information on new security vulnerabilities.
3. Event logging and reporting methodology for change procedures.
4. Evaluation of impact of changes on security of the system.
5. Where software is procured from outside, whether the source code is held in an escrow account or appropriate steps have been taken to ensure continuity of business in the event of the external agency discontinuing business or support.
6. Whether adequate summary-level reports are available to management to allow monitoring of the following:
   a. Transaction volume
   b. System problem logs

    c. Exceptions

    d. Unreconciled transactions

    e. Other customer or operational issues

Operational Activities

Operational areas that the information systems auditor would focus on include the following 13:

1. Whether a single user has multiple user IDs.
2. Whether the command prompt is available to users.
3. The procedure for issuing new password to customers who report having forgotten their password.
4. The norms of restrictions on the use of individual laptops or other mobile computing devices in the system.
5. Presence of operations manuals/desk cards for operators.
6. System of authorization for batch processing.
7. List of files that are authorized to be present at the user end.
8. Presence of a list of permitted server tables.
9. Presence of a network diagram.
10. Presence of extra access points—static and dynamic IPs.
11. Whether guest accounts have been disabled.
12. Whether the server space is adequate.
13. Whether a robust disaster recovery center is present.

PART TWO

Information Systems Auditing Checklists

CHAPTER ELEVEN

ISecGrade Auditing Framework

I N THIS CHAPTER, WE learn about the ISecGrade framework for conducting an information systems audit and according a risk score to the audit object. At the end of this chapter we will be in a position to use the ISecGrade framework while conducting an information systems audit.

INTRODUCTION

The ISecGrade framework is an open source project undertaken by South Asian Management Technologies Foundation. The design process involved consulting various open source and proprietary tools and processes. The designed draft framework was implemented in various organizations with the help of a practicing information systems audit firm. The project has been enriched by practical experience gained from putting the framework to use.

The framework has two components:

1. Checklists to ascertain adherence to the information systems management best practices.
2. Grading methodology to award ISecGrade certification to the auditee.

The information systems audit community is free to use the checklists and conduct information systems audits under the ISecGrade framework.

LICENSING AND LIMITATIONS

The approach and sample checklists compiled and designed under the ISecGrade framework are available for use by the purchasers of this book. The grading methodology and compilation is made by South Asian Management Technologies Foundation. Information systems auditors or other auditing entities may award the ISecGrade certificate according a risk grading to their clients.

METHODOLOGY

ISecGrade methodology is based around checklists. The information systems auditor is required to use the checklist provided in Chapter 12 of this book to conduct an information systems audit and verify the auditee responses by conducting substantive testing.

The methodology is built around identification of the controls necessary to manage a majority of risks faced by information system assets and processes. The objective of the auditee entity is to protect itself from the risks by building controls. The checklists are designed to identify the existence of such controls and to test the performance of such controls. Upon being satisfied of the existence and performance of each control, the information systems auditor may consider the control to be effective and respond accordingly to the question in the checklist.

Questions in the checklists are designed to obtain an objective answer: Yes or No. Existence of a control merits a "Yes" response and awards a 0 (zero) risk score to the auditee, while a "No" response awards a minimum of 1 (one) risk score to the auditee. Higher risk scores are awarded in specific cases. The higher the score, the riskier are the information systems of the auditee.

DOMAINS

Presently, the following domains and special application areas are covered under the ISecGrade methodology. These checklists are based on various best practice controls relevant to the domains or applications. ISecGrade audit checklists primarily focus on six critical aspects of information systems and help the auditor to form an opinion on the risk classification—which is the seventh step. These seven steps are as follows:

1. **Planning:** This covers the top-level controls that the auditee should put in place to ensure a proper governance framework for the information systems assets.

2. **General control testing:** These are the "hygiene" factors. These controls are applicable on information systems of the auditee, irrespective of the nature and type of hardware and application controls used by them.
3. **Hardware audit:** These controls focus on management, effectiveness, and efficiency of hardware.
4. **Software audit:** These are essentially application controls that should generally be present in any software.
5. **Network and communication audit:** This comprises checklists for the connectivity backbone of the auditee.
6. **Legal compliance review:** These controls ensure that the auditee is observing relevant legal provisions.
7. **IT risk assessment:** In this section we arrive at a composite risk score through a test of controls identified in the checklists. It may be noted that not all controls may be applicable to every entity. The auditor needs to use only those control questions that are relevant for the auditee.

The domains that are covered by ISecGrade include the following:

- Access control
- Antivirus
- Application development
- Asset classification and control
- Audit plan
- Authentication devices
- Business strategy
- Change management
- Client-server
- Communication software/devices
- Data communication
- Disaster recovery plan
- Electronic funds transfer
- File and directory protection
- Human resources, job definition, resourcing and training
- Implementation of information systems security policy
- Internet security
- Information systems security policy
- Legal compliance
- Local area network
- Long-term IT strategy
- Maintenance
- Management control system
- Operating system
- Packaged software implementation

- Parameter settings
- Peripheral devices and storage media
- Physical access control audit
- Physical environment
- Problem management
- Security management
- Segregation of duties
- Short-range IT plans
- Software license
- System conversion and reconciliation
- System software controls
- Third-party and vendor services review
- Transaction processing
- Utility program
- Wireless network

The information systems audit must commence with completion of the audit plan checklist. The audit plan checklist is an important document that will be necessary for substantiating the quality of work and for awarding an ISecGrade certificate.

ISecGrade recommends reporting in a prescribed format, which is discussed later in this chapter.

GRADING STRUCTURE

Every checklist under ISecGrade has three possible answers—Not Applicable, Yes, or No. As described earlier, in the case of the control being "Not Applicable," the ISecGrade auditor will exclude the question from the scope of the audit. "Yes" answers are recognized by awarding a 0 risk score, while "No" answers cause awarding of at least a risk score of 1.

The ISecGrade adoptee may assign different higher risk scores reflecting the relative importance of the control in the auditee entity. As recognized earlier, all controls listed in a checklist as well as all checklists may not be applicable to all auditees.

Once the ISecGrade audit is complete, the ISecGrade compliance auditor will compute the total risk score obtained by the auditee against each checklist and compare the total risk score obtained against the possible maximum score, which excludes the "Not Applicable" controls. The auditor will express the total risk score obtained as a percentage of total possible maximum score. This step will be repeated for all checklists. The auditor should note that nonapplicability of a control is to be ascertained, keeping in view the application being used and the processes adopted by the auditee. Proper justification must be documented before classifying a control as "Not Applicable."

Finally, the auditor will make a summary of all checklists and arrive at the grand total of risk scores awarded to the auditee against the grand total of possible maximum score. The total score will be expressed as a percentage of the total maximum possible score. This final percentage is the ISecGrade score obtained by the auditee.

TABLE 11.1 ISecGrade Score Summary

ISecGrade Summary	Maximum Possible Score	Auditee Score	Percentage Score	Risk Grade
Audit Areas				
Access Control—Logical				
Antivirus Audit				
Application Development				
Asset Classification and Control				
Authentication Devices				
…… checklist				
…… checklist				
Utility Programs				
Wireless Network				
Combined ISecGrade Score				

The standard risk grading of the auditee may be done using a differential of 20 percent in the following manner:

- Risk score up to 20 percent: Highly secured
- Risk score above 20 percent and up to 40 percent: Secured
- Risk score above 40 percent and up to 60 percent: Safe
- Risk score above 60 percent and up to 80 percent: Risky
- Risk score above 80 percent: Highly risky

During the formal awarding of the ISecGrade, the grade classification slabs may be altered and differential weights may be provided on each control to reflect the risk tolerance of the auditee. Risk tolerance refers to the extent of risk that the auditee is willing to be exposed to. This in turn is primarily defined by the ability of the auditee to withstand any losses that the risk exposure may present. For example, if the auditee observes a zero-tolerance policy for computer viruses, the scores obtained against the checklist may be multiplied by a factor to increase their impact on the overall risk grade.

The ISecGrade auditors should provide a summary sheet in their report. This summary would contain the risk score obtained by the auditee against each checklist and may be presented in the manner shown in Table 11.1.

SELECTION OF CHECKLIST

The checklists that are used under the ISecGrade framework can be classified according to the audit domain that the checklist relates to. In case the information systems auditor performs a review with a limited scope, the referencer shown in the Table 11.2 can be used to select appropriate checklists that will be relevant for forming an audit opinion.

TABLE 11.2 ISecGrade Checklist Master Referencer

Audit Program Selection Referencer

Checklists to Be Used	Planning	Evaluation and Testing of General Controls	Hardware Audit	Software Audit	Network and Communications Audit	IT Risk Assessment	Legal Compliance Review
Access Control— Logical Access		√					
Antivirus Audit Program				√			
Application Development		√					
Asset Classification and Control			√	√			
Authentication Device			√				
Business Strategy	√						
Change Management			√	√	√		
Client-Server			√				
Communication Software				√	√		
Data Communication					√		
Disaster Recovery Plan		√					
Electronic Funds Transfer					√		
File and Directory Protection				√			
Human Resources, Job Definition, Resourcing and Training	√					√	√
Implementation of IS Security Policy	√						
Internet Security					√		
IS Security Policy	√						
Local Area Network					√		

TABLE 11.2 ISecGrade Checklist Master Referencer

Audit Program Selection Referencer

Checklists to Be Used	Planning	Evaluation and Testing of General Controls	Hardware Audit	Software Audit	Network and Communications Audit	IT Risk Assessment	Legal Compliance Review
Legal Compliance							√
Long-Term IT Strategy	√						
Maintenance			√	√	√		
Management Control System	√						
Operating System				√			
Packaged Software Implementation				√			
Parameter Settings		√		√			
Peripheral Devices and Storage Media			√				
Physical Access Control		√					
Physical Environment		√	√				
Problem Management			√	√	√		
Security Management			√	√	√		
Segregation of Duties		√					
Short-Range IT Plans	√						
Software Licence				√			
System Conversion and Reconciliation				√			
System Software Controls		√		√			
Transaction Processing				√			
Third-Party and Vendor Services Review		√					
Utility Program		√		√			
Wireless Network		√			√		

It may be noted that some checklists feature in more than one domain. These checklists need not be used more than once during a full-scope ISecGrade audit, but are an integral component for domain-specific, limited-scope ISecGrade audits.

 ## FORMAT OF AUDIT REPORT

The recommended structure of an ISecGrade audit report is provided in this section. This format can be freely used by ISecGrade auditors and suitably modified to reflect the audit scope.

SAMPLE AUDIT REPORT

Letterhead of the Information Systems Auditor

Date

Client Contact Person
Client Name
Client Address

Dear Mr./Ms.,

Sub: ISecGrade Information Systems Audit Report

1. We have conducted an Information Systems Audit of ___[Audit object]___ of ___[Client]___ following the ISecGrade methodology.

2. We have obtained all information and explanations that to the best of our knowledge and belief were necessary for the purposes of our audit.

3. Our observations during the ISecGrade audit have been detailed in the appendix to the report and form a part of the audit report.

4. In our opinion, based on the information provided, explanation given, and evidence found and evaluated by us, the information system and its related environment adequately safeguards assets, maintains data and system integrity, provides relevant and reliable information, consumes resources efficiently, achieves information system goals effectively, and provides a reasonable assurance that its operational and control objectives will be met.

   OR

5. In our opinion, based on the information provided, explanation given, and evidence found and evaluated by us and subject to paragraph number 3 of our audit report, the information system and its related environment adequately safeguards assets, maintains data and system integrity, provides relevant and reliable information, consumes resources efficiently, achieves information

systems goals effectively, and provides a reasonable assurance that its operational and control objectives will be met.

OR

6. In our opinion, based on the information provided, explanation given, and evidence found and evaluated by us and reported in paragraph 3 of our audit report, the information system and its related environment does not adequately safeguard assets, maintain data and system integrity, provide relevant and reliable information, consume resources efficiently, or achieve information system goals effectively, and does not provide a reasonable assurance that its operational and control objectives will be met.

OR

7. Based on the information provided, explanation given, and evidence found and evaluated by us, we are not in a position to opine whether the information system and its related environment adequately safeguards assets, maintains data and system integrity, provides relevant and reliable information, consumes resources efficiently, achieves information system goals effectively, and provides a reasonable assurance that its operational and control objectives will be met.

The ISecGrade score awarded to the auditee is _____, signifying that the auditee is highly secured/secured/safe/risky/highly risky.

Signed in terms of our audit report and appendix on this date,

Signature of Auditor

Date:
Name of Signatory:
Place:
Designation:

USING THE AUDIT REPORT FORMAT

The auditor should draft the audit report using the format provided earlier and following these three guidelines:

1. In the first paragraph, the auditor should mention the object of the audit. For example, if the audit is of a bank branch, the auditor should write the branch name as *Audit object* and the bank name as *Client*. If the audit is of the data center of a manufacturing company, the auditor should write "data center" as *Audit object* and name of the manufacturing company as *Client*.
2. The auditor then asserts his or her satisfaction on the adequacy of information and explanation received from the auditee to form the audit opinion.

3. The standard format may be maintained by the auditors when they provide their observations. In most cases, there will be one or more observations. In rare cases where such observations have not been made, this paragraph will have to be deleted.

4. The auditors will express their opinion in one of the suggested four formats:

    a. If the auditor is fully satisfied and the referred paragraph 3 is deleted, the first option is applicable.

    b. The second option will be used when the auditors have enclosed their observations but the ISecGrade score is not greater than 60 percent, that is, below the "Risky" category. The auditors are free to adjust the 60 percent level depending on how strongly they wish to calibrate their opinion or how risk averse the auditee is.

    c. The third option will be used when the ISecGrade score is more than 60 percent, that is, in or above the "Risky" category.

    d. The fourth option should be used if the auditor is unable to form any opinion. Paragraph 3 may not be enclosed in such cases.

5. The ISecGrade score and corresponding grade should be mentioned in the final paragraph.

CHAPTER TWELVE

ISecGrade Checklists

THIS CHAPTER PROVIDES A series of checklists for use by information systems auditors. These checklists follow the ISecGrade methodology described in Chapter 11. Readers may consult this chapter and select appropriate checklists for their use during the audit.

CHECKLIST STRUCTURE

Checklists provided in this book use the pattern shown in Table 12.1.

The top heading is the name of the checklist. The query column describes the control to be tested. "Used" is marked as selected if the control is applicable. "Y" and "N" each signify the response of the auditee. "Value," unless grayed, contains the value for the control, which is otherwise 0 for "Y" and 1 for "N." "Score" is the value obtained by the auditee. A soft copy of the checklist is available at the companion website.

TABLE 12.1 Checklist Structure

Access Control Checklist—Logical Access					
			Response		
Query	Used	Y	N	Value	Score

INFORMATION SYSTEMS AUDIT CHECKLISTS

Exhibits 12.1 to 12.40 contain checklists to be used under the ISecGrade methodology. These checklists are also available for download. Please refer to About the Website at the end of the book for more information.

EXHIBIT 12.1 Audit Plan Checklist

Auditee:	Date:
Address:	
Name of Auditor:	
Action	**Observation**

A.	*Understanding the IT Environment and the Business*	
1.	Overview the organization's business objective.	
2.	Assess the organizational structures and the role of IT.	
3.	Identify the critical areas in the organization and their related IT service support model.	
4.	Identify the significant applications that sustain the business operations.	
5.	Identify the critical infrastructure for the significant applications.	
6.	Identify the supporting technologies.	
7.	Identify new developments in the information system since the time of the last audit.	
8.	Understand the objective and scope of the audit.	
9.	Update self about new threats and exposures in above IT environment, new viruses, new program patches, and so forth.	
10.	Review the organization's IT policies, including the audit policy, security policy, business continuity policy, and other related policies.	
11.	Review the previous audit's permanent and working paper files, where available.	
12.	Note important and critical observations made during the previous information systems audit.	
13.	Identify major projects and initiatives that are in progress and to be implemented in future.	
14.	Communicate with the earlier auditor wherever necessary and possible.	
B.	*Overview of the IT Systems*	
15.	Ascertain the various locations of the IT implementations of the auditee.	
16.	Get an overview of the hardware present at these locations.	
17.	Identify the servers under review and their related applications.	

(Continued)

18. Identify the operating system, communication software, and antivirus program being used.

19. Identify the network infrastructures and their locations.

20. Identify the number and location of firewall/IDS/IPS, and so forth.

21. Identify the telecommunications equipment, switches, routers, modems, and so forth (type and speed).

22. Identify IT equipment, and applications that are present but not in use.

23. Identify the IT infrastructure covered by annual maintenance contracts. Note the areas not so covered.

24. Identify applications that are not computerized yet or are in a process of computerization.

25. Identify applications that are computerized but not being used.

C.   *IT Risk Assessment*

26. Review the previous year's IT risk assessment.

27. Establish the audit cycle and frequency.

D.   *Audit Team Selection*

28. Communicate with all who need to know about the audit.

29. Check availability of the person who will be assigned to accompany the auditor at the auditee's site.

30. Ascertain the number of days the audit is expected to take.

31. Determine the audit schedule and the commencement date.

32. Identify the specific skill requirements, and the person(s) equipped to perform them.

33. Identify the audit team and their time schedules.

34. Confirm the above action plan with the management.

E.   *Audit Program Selection*

35. Use the ISecGrade checklist master referencer provided in Table 11.2 in Chapter 11.

EXHIBIT 12.2 Access Control Checklist—Logical Access

| | | | Response | | |
Query	Used	Y	N	Value	Score
1. Business requirements for access:					
a. Are the business requirements for access control defined and documented?					
b. Is there an access control policy?					
c. Does the access control policy reflect the business and security requirements?					
d. Does the access control policy address the rules and rights for each user or group of users?					
e. Have the users been given a clear statement of the business requirements to be met by access control?					

(Continued)

EXHIBIT 12.2 *(Continued)*

Query	Used	Y	N	Value	Score
			Response		
2. Account management:					
a. Are standards for user profile and privilege management defined?					
b. Has user registration and de-registration process been defined?					
c. Is process for allocation of privileges and changes therein restricted and controlled?					
d. Are all privileges allocated on a need-to-use basis?					
e. Are new user accounts created only through a duly laid-out process requiring dual authorization?					
f. Are user accounts created using a specified naming convention?					
g. Does the system record the date of creation and date of joining of the user?					
h. Is creation of all user IDs documented and signed by the creator and the user?					
i. Do modifications of existing accounts require dual authorization from persons at the same privilege level as the person authorized to create user IDs?					
j. Is a user profile register maintained? Does it contain user details such as Employee Name, Designation, Date of Joining the Office, User ID Allotted, Date of Creation of User ID, Date of Deletion of User ID, Signature of the User, and Initials of the Creator?					
k. Are audit trails maintained for creation, modification, and deletion of user IDs?					
l. Can a user ID be created only with simultaneous creation of a password?					
m. Are user IDs of terminated, retired, or transferred users inactivated and removed from the system? Is a record of all such user IDs maintained?					
n. Are all user accounts periodically reviewed to locate inactive user IDs?					
o. Is a review of all users with special privileges done on a periodic basis?					
p. Does reactivation of an inactive user ID require dual authorization similar to that required for other modifications?					
q. Are system access capabilities duly changed with functional changes in the individual user's activities?					

	Query	Used	Y	N	Value	Score
			Response			
r.	Does the software prevent the creation of two accounts with the same user ID?					
3.	Password management:					
a.	Does the system require passwords to be immediately changed on receipt of a new user ID and password by the user?					
b.	Does the password expire after a time period specified by the auditee?					
c.	Does the system prevent the use of passwords of a length shorter than eight alphanumeric characters or that specified by the auditee's policy?					
d.	Have users been advised on procedure for password maintenance?					
e.	Have users been advised that passwords cannot be shared and cannot be authorized to be used by others?					
f.	Are there satisfactory procedures for resetting and reissuing passwords to users who have forgotten them?					
g.	Does the system require a dual authorization for overriding and changing a password?					
h.	Does the system disallow use of the latest password again when the user is changing the password?					
i.	Are passwords stored in encrypted form?					
4.	User-profile management:					
a.	Does the access control policy address the rules and rights for each user or group of users?					
b.	Does the system prevent users from getting simultaneous log-ins from two terminals using the same user ID?					
c.	Do terminals automatically log out if inactive for a specified time?					
d.	Are time restrictions imposed on use of accounts and user IDs that have a fixed time of service delivery?					
e.	Are terminal restrictions imposed for sensitive applications and used only by certain designated users?					
f.	Do systems get inactivated/locked after a maximum of three unsuccessful log-in attempts?					
g.	Are invalid log-in attempts being logged and are these logs reviewed and signed on a daily basis?					
h.	Are access logs reviewed?					

(Continued)

EXHIBIT 12.2 (Continued)

Query		Used	Y	N	Value	Score
				Response		
i.	Is there a procedure for documentation of date and order for escalation of privileges?					
j.	Are privilege escalations authorized by a functional head or other authorized person?					
5.	Group-profile configuration:					
a.	Has group profile access to various menus and applications been duly planned and authorized?					
b.	Are group profiles configured to use restricted applications and menus?					
c.	Are the use of and access to default vendor-supplied group profiles (e.g., admin, root) controlled?					
d.	Are default vendor-supplied group profiles restricted from using transaction menus?					
e.	Have the passwords for vendor-supplied generic user IDs been changed from the password supplied by the vendor?					
f.	Are logs of access to these generic user IDs being maintained and reviewed on a periodic basis?					
g.	Are access rights and privileges provided to the user by the group profile commensurate with each user's job responsibilities?					
h.	Are there no discrepancies between the group profiles and present employee profiles?					
6.	Network access control:					
a.	Is there a documented and authorized network access policy?					
b.	Is there a network access policy that at minimum addresses the following areas:					
i.	Parts of network to be accessed					
ii.	Authorization for use of various network services					
iii.	Security issues relating to access to network connections and network services					
c.	Does the system allow remote access in a secured manner?					
d.	Does the policy restrict use of telnet and ftp commands without documentation authorizations?					
e.	Is there an authentication mechanism for challenging external connections? Examples: cryptography-based technique, hardware tokens, software tokens, and challenge–response protocol.					

Query	Used	Y	N	Value	Score
			Response		
f. Are all connections to remote computer systems, outside the security management of the auditee, authenticated?					
g. Are accesses to diagnostic ports securely controlled, especially for third-party access?					
h. Are perimeter security mechanisms, such as firewalls, in place where the networks are accessed by third parties?					
i. Are network connection controls implemented for shared networks that extend beyond the physical boundary?					
j. Are no applications used that allow direct network access, circumventing the perimeter security mechanisms?					
k. Is there a system in place that monitors all network connections?					
l. Is there a clear description of security requirements for public and private network services?					
m. Do contracts with the external service provider for use of public networks contain clauses for safeguarding confidentiality and integrity of data and restricting access to the data packets?					
n. Are unique identifiers (IDs) provided to every user?					
o. Is use of built-in system utilities that may override normal access protection systems and application controls limited to use by select personnel for authorized purposes only?					
p. Is an emergency alarm available to users who might be targets of coercion?					
q. Are connection time restrictions in place for critical and high-risk applications?					
7. Application access control:					
a. Have sensitive systems been provided with an isolated computing environment?					
b. Are audit logs, recording exceptions, and other security-relevant events maintained, periodically reviewed, and archived for an agreed period of time?					
c. Have access requirements to various applications been defined and users been given access on a need basis only?					
d. Are the real-time clocks of all computers and communication devices in the organization synchronized?					

(Continued)

EXHIBIT 12.2 *(Continued)*

Query	Used	Y	N	Value	Score
8. Third-party access:					
a. Does the network access policy contain specific security and access requirements for third-party access?					
b. Are types of accesses identified and classified and reasons for access justified?					
c. Are security risks with third-party contractors working onsite and offsite identified and appropriate controls implemented?					
d. Is there a formal contract with third parties addressing security requirements they need to adhere to, including compliance with the organization's IT policies, IT security policies, business continuity policies, and other policies?					
e. Is the identity of the software personnel and vendor established before allowing them access to the system?					
9. Privileged accounts maintenance:					
a. Is there an inventory of privileged accounts, including administrative accounts, hard-coded and embedded application accounts, administrator accounts on laptops, and so forth?					
b. Does the number of privileged accounts not exceed the authorized number of accounts?					
c. Does documentation exist to support the authorization of each account assigned to the "privileged" level?					
d. Are privileged accounts that are at a super-user level restricted to authorized persons?					
e. Are the passwords for super-user accounts (e.g., root—UNIX, Administrator—Windows/NT, and so forth) unique to each server?					
f. Is there an audit trail for the use of privileged accounts?					
g. Are privileged user access rights reviewed on a regular basis?					
h. Are there no privileged-level accounts associated with a terminated employee?					
i. Is the database administrator prevented from accessing transaction menus?					
j. Are only designated persons authorized to perform security systems maintenance jobs?					

Query		Used	Y	N	Value	Score
				Response		
k.	Are permissions for creation or changing of parameters available only to the designated persons?					
l.	Are the back-end database and operating system command prompts available only to high-level users?					
m.	Is access to back-end database and operating system command prompts logged with reason thereof and signed by the person making such access?					
n.	Have privileged accounts that were assigned to vendor been inactivated in the live system?					
o.	Is access to the source code restricted and awarded only after obtaining specific written permission that states the reason for such access?					
p.	Is the record of access to systems by personnel of the data center/centralized processing facility available in the auditee's location with reasons for their access?					
10.	Other general access controls:					
a.	Are storage media removed from the auditee premises only after due authorization?					
b.	Are system documentations protected from unauthorized access?					
c.	Do users log off their computers whenever they leave the workplace for a break?					
d.	Is there a formal authorization process in place for information to be made publicly available?					
e.	Are any controls in place to protect the integrity of publicly available information from unauthorized access?					
f.	Are there any policies, procedures, and controls in place to protect the exchange of information through the use of data file, voice, facsimile, and video communication facilities?					
g.	Are staffs reminded to maintain the confidentiality of sensitive information while using it on any information exchange facility?					
h.	Are strict controls in place over access to program source libraries?					
Applicable Score				**Total Score**		

Prepared by:

Date:

Reviewed by:

Place :

EXHIBIT 12.3 Antivirus Audit Checklist

				Response		
	Query	Used	Y	N	Value	Score
1.	Is the auditee aware of the antivirus policy?					
2.	Is a copy of the antivirus policy available to the auditee?					
3.	Is there Internet connectivity at the auditee's site?					
4.	Are removable media from untrusted sources prevented from being used?					
5.	Does the auditee know how to identify a virus attack?					
6.	Does the auditee know how to respond to a virus attack?					
7.	Is there an information dissemination process in place to ensure that all users of the system are alerted about the attack?					
8.	Is there any antivirus software in use?					
a.	Is antivirus available for all operating systems?					
b.	Are the latest antivirus definitions downloaded and installed automatically?					
c.	At what frequency are virus definitions updated? (1) Every week, (2) Every month, (3) More than 30 days, (4) Never					
d.	Are users prevented from disabling the antivirus?					
e.	Is there a schedule in the organization for a periodical scan of the entire system?					
f.	Is the antivirus program set to scan every file accessed?					
g.	Are all files relating to the operating system and applications scanned regularly?					
h.	Are all compressed files scanned on a periodic basis?					
i.	Is all inbound traffic originating from untrusted networks into the organization checked for viruses?					
j.	Are e-mails scanned by the antivirus package?					
9.	Is information about virus attacks maintained?					
10.	Are the backups verified to be virus-free?					
11.	Where laptops are used in the LAN, does each one have an antivirus installed?					
12.	Is the antivirus on the laptops updated and not disabled?					
13.	Does the antivirus cover remote access?					
14.	Is there any protection for preventing SPAM?					
Applicable Score				**Total Score**		

Prepared by: Reviewed by:

Date: Place:

EXHIBIT 12.4 Application Development Checklist

	Query	Used	Y	N	Value	Score
				Response		
1.	Is there a management authorization process in place for setting up new information processing facilities?					
2.	Have the client/users and service provider agreed on all development activities, milestones, and deliverables and documented the same?					
3.	Have the client/users signed off on technical and functional specification documents prior to the application's development?					
4.	System development life cycle (SDLC):					
a.	Has an SDLC methodology been implemented?					
b.	Is the SDLC sufficiently documented to provide guidance to staff with varying levels of skill and experience?					
c.	Is there an appropriate system development methodology that provides for periodic milestone events?					
d.	Does the SDLC provide a means of controlling changes in foreseeable requirements that occur over the system's life?					
e.	Does the corporate policy require sign-off at milestones by appropriate authority before proceeding?					
f.	Have the programming staff and staff involved in developing and testing software been trained to become familiar with the use of the SDLC methodology?					
g.	Have access control and segregation been maintained during the development, testing, and migration of codes or programs?					
h.	Is authorization required at various stages of development: feasibility study, system specification, testing, parallel running, post implementation review, and so forth?					
i.	Do auditee policies provide a framework for the development of controlled applications?					
j.	Are policies regularly reviewed and updated?					
k.	Does adequate documentation exist for:					

(Continued)

EXHIBIT 12.4   *(Continued)*

	Query	Used	Y	N	Value	Score
				Response		
i.	Programmers to maintain and modify programs?					
ii.	Users to satisfactorily operate the system?					
iii.	Administrators to manage the system?					
l.	Has the internal audit department been involved in the design stage to ensure that adequate controls exist?					
m.	Has an independent review been carried out at each stage of the SDLC process, and the review process documented?					
n.	Is system implementation properly planned and implemented by either parallel run or pilot run?					
o.	Are problems and deficiencies during the implementation phase noted and properly resolved?					
p.	Are there adequate controls over the setting up of the standing data and opening balances in financial applications?					
q.	Are security requirements incorporated as part of a business requirement statement for new systems or for enhancement to existing systems?					
r.	Are risk assessments completed prior to commencement of system development?					
s.	Is a postimplementation review carried out?					
t.	Are user manuals prepared for all new systems developed and revised for subsequent changes?					
u.	Is there a quality assurance function to verify the integrity and acceptance of applications developed?					
5.	Are copies of the application code updated with the changes applied to the latest production version of code?					
6.	Is the code modified/developed in an area separate from testing/quality assurance and production?					
7.	Are records maintained of code check-ins/check-outs and deletions that are made to the production library?					

	Query	Used	Y	N	Value	Score
			Response			
8.	Is use of personal and public domain software restricted?					
9.	Is antivirus software present?					
10.	If yes, is the antivirus software updated?					
11.	Testing:					
a.	Have test plan standards been developed for testing?					
b.	Do the testing standards define the responsibilities for each party, for example, system analyst, users, quality assurance, auditors, and so forth?					
c.	Are software changes documented so that they can be traced from authorization to the final approved code?					
d.	Does software change documentation facilitate "trace-back" of code to design specifications and functional requirements by system testers?					
e.	Is a comprehensive set of test transactions and data developed that represents the various activities and conditions that will be encountered in processing?					
f.	Are live data not used in testing of program changes, except to build test data files?					
g.	Are system test data protected and controlled?					
h.	Do logs record problems encountered during the unit or integration testing phase, as well as issues notified by the client after the user testing phase?					
i.	Are the problems followed up and resolved?					
12.	Is the documentation updated for software, hardware, operating personnel, and system users when a new or modified system is implemented?					
13.	Do procedures exist to ensure the approved code from the test environment is the version moved into production?					
14.	Does a process exist to reconcile changes scheduled for implementation with changes actually implemented?					
15.	Emergency changes during system development life cycle:					

(Continued)

EXHIBIT 12.4 *(Continued)*

	Query	Used	Y	N	Value	Score
				Response		
a.	Does a process exist to control and supervise emergency changes?					
b.	Are all emergency changes approved by appropriate levels of management prior to implementation?					
c.	Is the number of emergency changes during the period of audit within reasonable limits?					
d.	Are all emergency changes supported by appropriate documentation within the prescribed time after the emergency is resolved, if not done earlier?					
e.	Is the procedure for recovery when a new version of a tested program fails to work in production sufficient?					
f.	Does the version of the executable program correspond to the version maintained in the source control?					
16.	Are standardized procedures used to distribute and implement new software?					
17.	Are audit trails maintained for all program changes?					
18.	Are copies of previous versions of programs maintained?					
19.	Are separate libraries maintained for program development and maintenance, testing, and production programs?					
20.	Do operations manuals provide instructions on operating specific applications?					
21.	Are there controls in place to ensure that the covert channels and Trojan codes are not introduced into a new or upgraded system?					
22.	Are the intellectual property rights defined?					
23.	Are SDLC controls in place over outsourced software?					
Applicable Score				**Total Score**		

Prepared by: Reviewed by:

Date: Place:

EXHIBIT 12.5   Asset Classification and Control Checklist

Query	Used	Y	N	Value	Score
			Response		
1. Is an inventory or register maintained for assets associated with each information system?					
2. Does each asset have an owner, the security classification, and the location identified?					
3. Is there an information classification scheme in place that will assist in determining how the information is to be handled and protected?					
4. Is there an appropriate set of procedures defined for information labeling and handling in accordance with the classification scheme adopted by the organization?					

Applicable Score	Total Score
Prepared by:	Reviewed by:
Date:	Place:

EXHIBIT 12.6   Authentication Devices Checklist

Query	Used	Y	N	Value	Score
			Response		
1. Is there any list of authentication devices used?					
2. Do these devices carry a unique identification signature?					
3. Is there any record of use of the devices?					
4. Can individual devices be identified with individual users?					
5. Is there an issue register identifying to whom such devices have been issued?					
6. Is there a system of reporting the loss of such device?					
7. Is there any system of deactivating individual devices?					
8. In case of hierarchical access, are separate devices used to access separate sections?					
9. In case of failure of such devices, is there any override system to grant access?					
10. Is the power to grant such access restricted?					
11. Does the authentication system deny access in the event of any hardware or power failure?					
12. In the case of such failures, is there an alternative device or manual process defined that would replace the original authentication device?					

(Continued)

EXHIBIT 12.6 *(Continued)*

	Query	Used	Y	N	Value	Score
				Response		
13.	Does the authentication system have a power backup?					
14.	Where such devices control access to sensitive systems:					
a.	Is there a requirement of dual authentication before providing access?					
b.	In the case of a system having restricted access, is there any record of such access being granted?					
c.	Is there any log of use of such device?					
d.	Does the log identify the authentication device used?					
e.	In the case of failure of such devices, is there any override system to grant access?					
f.	Is the power to grant such access restricted?					
g.	Is there any log of such interventionist access?					
h.	Can the user exercising the override privilege be identified?					

Applicable Score   **Total Score**

Prepared by: Reviewed by:

Date: Place:

EXHIBIT 12.7 Business Strategy Checklist

	Query	Used	Y	N	Value	Score
				Response		
1.	Is the business strategy documented?					
2.	Are business objectives defined?					
3.	Is the role of IT clearly spelled out in the business strategy?					
4.	Are IT issues and opportunities assessed and reflected in the auditee's strategy and long- and short-term plans?					
5.	Are assessments made periodically to ensure that IT initiatives are supporting the organization's mission and goals?					
6.	Are major developments in technology assessed for their impact on the business strategy and are necessary steps taken?					

Applicable Score   **Total Score**

Prepared by: Reviewed by:

Date: Place:

EXHIBIT 12.8 Change Management (Hardware and Software) Checklist

	Query	Used	Y	N	Value	Score
				Response		
1.	Are capacity demands monitored and projections of future capacity requirements made?					
2.	Are all changes planned and advance information given to users?					
3.	Do the change schedules allow time for adequate installation and testing of new hardware/software?					
4.	Are user acceptance tests performed for all hardware and software?					
5.	Does the person signing acceptance know how to evaluate an installation?					
6.	Are changes documented with date and items of change?					
7.	Are the computer asset records appropriately updated to reflect changes in hardware/software?					
8.	Are there any problem logs in the problem register just after a change in hardware/software?					
9.	Is there a cross-reference between the change and its cause, that is, the problem, the trigger, the solution, or the escalation for unresolved problems?					
10.	Does the change management procedures include at least:					
a.	Accountability for managing and coordinating changes					
b.	The change management flow(s) within the organization					
c.	The change management responsibilities of each function					
d.	The deliverables from each organizational function					
e.	Specific timetables for reviewing and scheduling planned changes					
f.	Specific duration for retention of historical records					
g.	Handling of all changes, including change rollback					
h.	Circumstances when normal change management controls can be waived, and the procedures to be followed in those emergency situations					

(Continued)

EXHIBIT 12.8 *(Continued)*

	Query	Used	Y	N	Value	Score
				Response		
i.	User/system documentation being updated after a change is made?					
11.	Change initiation and approval:					
a.	Is there a formal approved procedure for initiation and approval of changes?					
b.	Is a written approval available for all changes with expected completion time frame and costs and with proper authorization of user and management?					
c.	Is there a written request available for all changes that include (at a minimum) all the following information? • Name of requester • Phone/extension number and department • Requester's signature • Reason for change • List of modules that need to be changed • Supervisor's approval (changes must be approved by someone other than the requester)					
d.	Are priorities assigned to the change requests?					
e.	Is an impact analysis performed for every change request to determine the effect on the integrity and availability of the affected system?					
f.	Are estimated completion target time and cost communicated to all concerned?					
g.	Is there a process used to control and monitor change requests?					
h.	Is a sequence number assigned to change requests and approval documents for tracking and monitoring purpose?					
12.	Modification or development:					
a.	Is code modification and development performed in a controlled environment separate from quality assurance (QA) and production?					
b.	Are all changes applied to a copy of the latest production version of code?					
c.	Is there a procedure whereby a programmer is made aware of all modules that are to be changed?					
d.	Are history records kept of code changes and deletions that are made to the production library?					

	Query	Used	Y	N	Value	Score
				Response		
e.	Does a process exist that requires programming management to review the source code to ensure that changes are appropriate and meet the programming and documentation standards?					
13.	Testing and acceptance:					
a.	Is code tested in a controlled environment separate from development and production?					
b.	Is there a procedure for moving code into testing environment?					
c.	Is there a process to "lock" code once migrated into the testing/quality assurance environment?					
d.	Are users involved in the testing process (e.g., preparation of tests and data)?					
e.	Are test results reviewed and approved by the user?					
f.	Are there rollback procedures in the event the user does not approve of the changes and requires additional functions or modifications?					
g.	Does a process exist to document problems encountered during this phase of the change methodology?					
14.	Implementation:					
a.	If an independent group updates the program changes in production environment, do procedures exist to ensure possession of the change request form before the update?					
b.	Is there a procedure to ensure that the right version is moved into production?					
c.	Is the code to be implemented in the production environment duly authorized?					
d.	Does a process exist to reconcile changes?					
15.	Nonemergency changes:					
a.	Have all changes been formally initiated, documented, and approved by someone other than the requester?					
b.	Are all change documents stating that code can be moved from development to testing/quality assurance endorsed by authorized signatory?					
c.	Are all change documents reviewed by a QA function approved by users prior to installation into production?					

(Continued)

EXHIBIT 12.8 *(Continued)*

	Query	Used	Y	N	Value	Score
				Response		
d.	Does documentation exist showing a source comparison was performed prior to installation into production?					
e.	Is there evidence of the review and reconciliation of changes?					
f.	Are audit logs maintained for any change made to the production programs?					
16.	Emergency changes:					
a.	Does a process exist to control and supervise emergency changes?					
b.	Is there a backup system of emergency user IDs?					
c.	If emergency changes are made through the use of emergency IDs, does a process exist to enable and disable them either automatically or with a minimum of two people being involved in the process?					
d.	Does an audit trail exist of all emergency ID usage and is it independently reviewed?					
e.	Are emergency changes approved by appropriate levels of management prior to implementation into production?					
f.	Do procedures require that emergency changes be supported by documentation (e.g., evidence of management approval, code review) immediately after the emergency is resolved?					
g.	Are there no programmers who are able to initiate emergency changes?					
h.	Is prior approval of business or operation required to implement emergency change?					
i.	Do rollback procedures exist?					
17.	Where an outside vendor provides a patch or executable program for implementing any change, has this patch or executable program been tested before implementation into production environment?					
18.	Where service level agreements are in use, do the changes made attain the requirements of the service level agreement?					
Applicable Score				**Total Score**		

Prepared by:

Date:

Reviewed by:

Place:

EXHIBIT 12.9 Client-Server Checklist

Query	Used	Y	N	Value	Score
			Response		
1. Server:					
a. Is there any record of the types and versions of operating systems of the client and the server?					
b. Does the record match with the existing installation?					
c. Is there a list of personnel having the highest authorization?					
d. Does the list agree with the record maintained by the system?					
e. Does the password policy agree with the organization's policy?					
f. Is there any system of protecting the password file?					
g. How often is server backup undertaken? (1) Weekly, (2) Every two weeks, (3) Monthly, (4) Never					
h. Are batch jobs not executed on the server?					
i. Is there any system of authenticating the batch jobs?					
j. Are log records maintained?					
k. Are these logs reviewed?					
l. Is there an individual responsible for reviewing any violation?					
m. Are other file servers (excluding fall-back/mirror server) prevented from connecting to the primary file server?					
n. Does such a connection require a formal authorization?					
o. Are dial-up capabilities of the server inactive or protected by an authorization procedure?					
2. Database management system:					
a. Is there an identified database administrator?					
b. Are client-server tables listed?					
c. Is there any list of users with authority to select, insert, update, and delete entries in the client-server tables?					
d. Is there any procedure preventing other users from selecting, inserting, updating, and deleting entries in the client-server tables?					
e. Is there any list of programs that can select, insert, update, and delete entries in client-server tables?					

(Continued)

EXHIBIT 12.9 *(Continued)*

	Query	Used	Y	N	Value	Score
				Response		
f.	Is there a list of users authorized to use such a program?					
g.	Are there procedures preventing other programs from selecting, inserting, updating, and deleting entries in the client-server tables?					
3.	Network components:					
a.	Is there a diagram of the network of the client-server environment?					
b.	Is there a list of various network components that connect to the client-server environment?					
c.	Is there any authorization process to ensure that only the Network Administration Group has access to the components?					
4.	Others: Program library:					
a.	Is there a separate test and production library?					
b.	Is there a list of users who can access the test and production library?					
c.	Is there any process that prevents nonauthorized users from accessing the test and production library?					

Applicable Score **Total Score**

Prepared by: Reviewed by:
Date: Place:

EXHIBIT 12.10 Communication Software/Devices Checklist

	Query	Used	Y	N	Value	Score
				Response		
1.	Is there a procedure for installing a communication device?					
2.	Is there a procedure for installing communication software?					
3.	Is there a list of purposes for which such devices are used?					
4.	Is there a list of installed communication devices?					
5.	Are infrared, wireless LAN, Bluetooth, and so forth generally disabled?					
6.	Are USB ports enabled after assessing the user requirements?					

	Query	Used	Y	N	Value	Score
				Response		
7.	Are there no drivers for infrared, wireless, Bluetooth, USB port, and so forth installed on the computer, except those that come with the operating system?					
8.	Is the system free from any installed software for such communication devices?					
9.	Does the system prevent the use of "plug-and-play" devices by nonauthorized users?					
10.	Is LAN card disabled on computers not authorized to be on LAN?					
11.	Is access to the computer on which communication devices are installed restricted?					
12.	Is the computer on which the communication devices are installed protected from unauthorized access?					
Applicable Score				**Total Score**		

Prepared by: Reviewed by:

Date: Place:

EXHIBIT 12.11   Data Communication (Router) Checklist

	Query	Used	Y	N	Value	Score
				Response		
1.	Has a router policy been defined?					
2.	Is a router configuration file available for each router?					
3.	Have individuals been identified as responsible for the management of routers?					
4.	Is there any inventory of routers?					
5.	Are there select users who have access to privileged accounts?					
6.	Are unused interfaces disabled?					
7.	Have the DNS hookups for routers been turned off?					
8.	Has the link layer discovery protocol been disabled when it is not used by any application?					
9.	Has the Bootp server been disabled on the routers?					
10.	Has source routing been disabled on the router?					
11.	Has proxy ARP been disabled on the router?					

(Continued)

EXHIBIT 12.11   *(Continued)*

	Query	Used	Y	N	Value	Score
				Response		
12.	Have ICMP redirects been disabled on the router?					
13.	Do all accounts have passwords following the password policy of the organization?					
14.	Is there any system for changing passwords periodically?					
15.	Are passwords appearing in encrypted form when configuration files are viewed?					
16.	Is "enable secret" used for the enable mode?					
17.	Is the enable secret password unique and not similar to that used for another router?					
18.	Is the "exec timeout" and password defined in the console port?					
19.	Is the aux port disabled?					
20.	Are the exec timeout and password defined on the vty lines?					
21.	Are the vty lines restricted to certain IP addresses only?					
22.	Do router passwords maintain the complexity required by the password policy of the organization?					
23.	Are router passwords periodically changed per the password policy of the organization?					
24.	Is SSH used for the vty lines?					
25.	Is telnet not used by applications to perform management activities such as backup configuration?					
26.	Where telnet is used, are the application, purpose, and restrictions on use authorized and documented?					
27.	Does each router administrator have a unique user ID?					
28.	Are log-in/log-out tracking and command logging for the router administrator through the TACACS+ or equivalent system enabled?					
29.	Is the https server used for router management?					
30.	Are access attempts to the routers logged?					
31.	Which version of SNMP is used? (1) Version 3, (2) Version 2, (3) Version 1.					
32.	Is there any record of SNMP community names and their members?					

	Query	Used	Y	N	Value	Score
				Response		
33.	Are default community strings used for read and read/write access changed?					
34.	Is the SNMP community string changed periodically? (in v1 or v2c)					
35.	Does router configuration restrict SNMP access to set operations, which change router variables, only to authorized IP addresses?					
36.	Has encryption for set requests from SNMP read/write community names been implemented?					
37.	Is the syslog host restricted to receive log messages from the routers only, and only administrators' systems allowed to connect to the log host?					
38.	Are the clocks of all routers synchronized?					
39.	Is there any list of services running on the routers?					
40.	Is open shortest path first (OSPF) defined on the router?					
41.	Is there any authentication mechanism employed in the implementation of OSPF?					
42.	Is directed broadcast functionality enabled on the router?					
43.	Is any protection in place to prevent a denial-of-service (DoS) attack of the network using the directed broadcast functionality?					
44.	Are dial-in connections not used to access the routers?					
45.	In case of use of routers with modems using telephone lines, is a list of such router and linked telephone numbers available?					
46.	Is the list available only to authorized person(s)?					
47.	Is there a process by which the users are authenticated on remote access of the routers?					
48.	Is authorization of changes to router configuration documented?					
49.	Are changes to router configuration documented?					
50.	Is there any procedure for changing router configuration?					
51.	Is the router configuration periodically backed up?					

(Continued)

EXHIBIT 12.11 (*Continued*)

	Query	Used	Y	N	Value	Score
				Response		
52.	Is the backup moved to a disaster recovery site/offsite?					
53.	Does the local operating system's security mechanism restrict access to the file server on which configuration files are stored?					
54.	Is there any mechanism in place for monitoring the network?					
55.	Is there a list of personnel monitoring the network?					
56.	Are the network monitoring tools secured with access control?					
57.	Is the CPU utilization/memory of the router monitored?					
58.	Is the TFTP protocol disabled?					
59.	Where the TFTP is enabled, is the process restricted to certain addresses only and disabled when not in use?					
60.	Is logging to a syslog server enabled on the router?					
61.	Is the network manager aware of the latest vulnerabilities that could affect the router?					

Applicable Score   **Total Score**

Prepared by: Reviewed by:

Date: Place:

EXHIBIT 12.12   Disaster Recovery Plan Checklist

	Query	Used	Y	N	Value	Score
				Response		
1.	Is a copy of the disaster recovery plan available?					
2.	Is the copy available with the auditee the latest plan?					
3.	Is there a process in place for developing and maintaining business continuity throughout the organization?					
4.	Is there any individual identified as owner of the plan?					
5.	Is there a disaster recovery implementation team?					

			Response			
	Query	Used	Y	N	Value	Score
6.	Have events that could cause interruptions to business processes been identified?					
7.	Is impact analysis conducted periodically to determine the impact of business interruptions?					
8.	Is a strategy plan developed based on the impact analysis results?					
9.	Is the implementation team contacts list available?					
10.	Is the auditee aware of the backup facility site/fall-back mechanism?					
11.	Are there any alternative sites?					
12.	Have plans been developed to restore business operations within the required time frame following an interruption to or failure of business process?					
13.	Is schedule for testing and training included in the plan?					
14.	Is there a single framework of business continuity plan (BCP)?					
15.	Does the BCP ensure that all plans are consistent and identify priorities for testing and maintenance?					
16.	Does the BCP identify conditions for activation of the plan and individuals responsible for executing each component?					
17.	When was the last drill performed? (1) Within 3 months, (2) From 3 to 6 months, (3) Earlier than 6 months, (4) Never					
18.	Did the drill include use of the backup facilities?					
19.	What was the outcome of the drill? (1) Satisfactory, (2) Unsatisfactory					
20.	Are inventories relating to critical systems maintained?					
21.	Does a formal reporting procedure for security incidents exist?					
22.	Do procedures address different types of incidents ranging from denial of service to breach of confidentiality, and ways to handle them?					
23.	Are audit trails and logs relating to the incidents maintained and proactive action taken to prevent recurrence?					

(Continued)

EXHIBIT 12.12 *(Continued)*

	Query	Used	Y	N	Value	Score
				Response		
24.	Is there a formal reporting procedure or guideline for users to report security weakness in, or threats to, systems and services?					
25.	Are procedures established for reporting any software malfunctions?					
26.	Are mechanisms in place to enable quantification and monitoring of the types, volumes, and costs of incidents and malfunctions?					
27.	Is there a formal disciplinary process in place for employees who have violated organizational security policies and procedures?					
28.	Backup procedures:					
a.	Are formal procedures specifying backup procedures and responsibilities available?					
b.	Is the backup procedure regularly followed?					
c.	Are the backups tested for recoverability?					
29.	Are the personnel trained to set up and use backup equipment and established procedures?					
30.	Is there a procedure for handling security of information storage?					
31.	How soon does the vendor under contract for providing support arrive? (1) Same day, (2) Next day, (3) Within 3 days, (4) Later than 3 days					
32.	Are inventories available within 24 hours?					
33.	Are consumables available within 24 hours?					
34.	Has there been no incident of business disruption arising out of failure of information system assets?					

Applicable Score   **Total Score**

Prepared by: Reviewed by:

Date: Place:

EXHIBIT 12.13 Electronic Funds Transfer Checklist

	Query	Used	Y	N	Value	Score
			Response			
1.	Is the terminal located in a secured location?					
2.	Is the terminal kept locked when not in use?					
3.	Is the terminal accessible by authorized persons only?					
4.	Is there supervision over the terminal to ensure that only authorized users access the same?					
5.	Does the system validate authorization of all users performing specific functions?					
6.	Does the system require the use of a secure key or password to validate an authorized user?					
7.	Are only authorized personnel capable of establishing a session path?					
8.	Does the system record by whom the session path/log-in is established?					
9.	On establishing a session, does the system validate terminal ID?					
10.	Does the system provide a record of attempted execution of unauthorized functions?					
11.	Does the system provide a record of all password/log-in violations?					
12.	Are violation reports reviewed?					
13.	Are passwords changed on a regular basis?					
14.	Are all sensitive functions, such as setting up new users or changing authority levels, performed under dual control?					
15.	Is there an identified administrator for setting up new users or changing authority levels?					
16.	Are all changes to user/functions authorized?					
17.	Are all accesses by administrator recorded?					
18.	Is a list of authorized users and functions available?					
19.	Is there a system that ensures that all employees leaving the EFT section have their access rights revoked or suspended immediately?					
20.	Is segregation of duties of input, verification, authorization, and collection of output in place?					
21.	Does the system prevent transmission of unauthorized messages?					
22.	Does the system validate the user as being authorized to transmit the message type in question?					

(Continued)

EXHIBIT 12.13 *(Continued)*

Query		Used	Y	N	Value	Score
				Response		
23.	Are there procedures for reporting unauthorized messages at the time of transmission?					
24.	Are all input documents checked for proper authorization by the originator?					
25.	Are there controls to ensure that extensions to the value limit (daily/individual) for messages are property authorized?					
26.	Are all messages sent in a standard format?					
27.	Is alteration to the standard format prohibited?					
28.	Does the system ensure that all validated fields are entered?					
29.	Are there controls to refuse all values beyond the authorized limits?					
30.	Are there controls to ensure that the total value of messages is within an agreed (daily) limit?					
31.	Does the system provide acknowledgement of satisfactory validation of transmitted messages?					
32.	When messages are manually entered, are they rekeyed/reconfirmed?					
33.	Are all messages checked with the corresponding originating documents by the authorizing officer?					
34.	Are originating documents appropriately endorsed at time of input and authorization?					
35.	Does the system enforce re-input to check for any differences?					
36.	Are there written procedures for handling errors?					
37.	Is an input register maintained?					
38.	Does the system generate control totals for number and value of messages input?					
39.	Are control totals checked against input records?					
40.	Does the system provide a report of all accepted and rejected messages with appropriate control totals?					
41.	Does the communications protocol use any error detection/correction techniques?					
42.	Are unbroken sequential serial numbers assigned to each message?					
43.	Are serial numbers recorded on input documents or register?					
44.	Does management scrutinize records of unbroken serial numbers for any interruptions?					

	Query	Used	Y	N	Value	Score
			Response			
45.	Is a permanent record kept of all transmitted messages?					
46.	Is this permanent record checked against a record of all accepted/rejected messages?					
47.	Is an audit trail generated of all input messages? Does it record:					
a.	A unique message reference number?					
b.	Date and time of input?					
c.	By whom the input is verified or authorized?					
d.	Who established the session path?					
e.	Date and time of transmission?					
f.	Whether the messages are accepted or rejected?					
g.	Details of the message content?					
48.	Is the audit log inaccessible to person responsible for input function?					
49.	Is the audit log scrutinized?					
50.	Is there a regular reconciliation between transmitted messages and accounting statements evidencing the funds transfer?					
51.	Are input messages notified to their originators after acceptance?					
52.	In case of interruption during transmission, does the system provide a record of accepted messages?					
53.	Are there written procedures for retransmission of nonaccepted messages?					
54.	Is an incident log kept of all interruptions to normal processing?					
55.	In case of hardware failure, is the processing terminal switched?					
56.	Is there a system preventing switching of processing terminal without prior approval?					
57.	Is duplication of messages after system recovery prevented?					
58.	Are transmissions encrypted?					
59.	Are all messages received encrypted?					
60.	Are history files encrypted?					

Applicable Score   **Total Score**

Prepared by: Reviewed by:

Date: Place:

EXHIBIT 12.14   File and Directory Protection Checklist

Query	Used	Y	N	Value	Score
			Response		
1. Is the server and directory location for significant application programs and data documented?					
2. System directories and files:					
a. Are system/security administrators aware of relevant standards regarding the configuration of security over system directories and files?					
b. Is the administrator the owner of system directories and files?					
c. Are procedures in place over configuration of security for system directories and files?					
d. Are full control (all permissions) and change permissions (read, write, execute, and delete) restricted to authorized users (i.e., the administrative account or group)?					
e. Are all share permissions duly authorized?					
f. Are access rights for system directories and files determined and assigned?					
g. Are access rights for system directories and files approved?					
h. Do auditee policies and standards exist regarding the configuration of security over system directories and files for the operating system?					
i. Are current security settings for critical system directories and files in conformance with auditee policy?					
j. Are appropriate system files encrypted?					
k. Is use of scripts, command procedures, or applications with the ability to alter directory or file security restricted?					
3. Application directories and files:					
a. Are system/security administrators aware of relevant standards regarding the configuration of security over application directories and files?					
b. Are procedures in place over the configuration of security for application directories and files?					

	Query	Used	Y	N	Value	Score
				Response		
c.	Are application program and data directories owned by the owner of the restricted user application?					
d.	Are access rights for application directories and files approved?					
e.	Do corporate policies and standards exist regarding the configuration of security over application directories and files?					
f.	Are current security settings for critical application directories and files in conformance with auditee policy?					
g.	Are accounts and groups that have been assigned access to the application directories and files been so permitted by auditee policy?					
4.	Production data directories and files:					
a.	Are administrators aware of relevant standards regarding the configuration of security over production data directories and files?					
b.	Are there formal procedures for configuration of security of production data directories and files?					
c.	Are access rights for production data directories and files approved?					
d.	Do policies and standards exist regarding the configuration of security over production data directories and files?					
e.	Are security settings for access to critical production data directories and files appropriate?					
f.	Are accounts and groups that have been assigned access to the production data directories and files in conformance with auditee policy?					
g.	Is access to the production data directories and files granted to accounts and groups adequate in view of the job profile?					
Applicable Score					**Total Score**	

Prepared by: Reviewed by:

Date: Place:

EXHIBIT 12.15 Human Resources, Job Definition, Resourcing, and Training Checklist

			Response			
	Query	Used	Y	N	Value	Score
1.	Does the job description of employees include security roles and responsibilities laid out in the information security policy?					
2.	Has a verification check on permanent staff been carried out at the time of shortlisting job applications?					
3.	Is the confidentiality or nondisclosure clause a part of the initial terms and conditions of employment?					
4.	Do terms of employment cover employee responsibility for information security?					
5.	Do all employees and select third-party users receive information security training and regular updates?					
6.	Does this training cover the following areas?:					
a.	General system security principles					
b.	Ethical conduct related to IT					
c.	Security practices to protect against harm from failure to ensure the confidentiality, integrity, and availability of information systems assets					
d.	Responsibilities associated with the use and custody of IT resources					
e.	Security of information and information assets when used off-site					
f.	Prevention of disclosure of sensitive information					
7.	Do regular campaigns exist to increase internal control, discipline, and security awareness?					
8.	Is there a backup of staff for critical job functions?					
9.	Are needs of security and control assessed and in-house or external training provided to address those needs?					
Applicable Score				**Total Score**		

Prepared by: Reviewed by:

Date: Place:

EXHIBIT 12.16 Implementation of Information Systems Security Policy Checklist

Query		Response			Value	Score
		Used	Y	N		
1.	Is there a management forum to ensure a clear direction and management support for security initiatives within the organization?					
2.	Is the forum cross-functional, having management representatives from relevant parts of the organization to coordinate the implementation of information security controls?					
3.	Is the security policy made available to all levels of users?					
4.	Is the role of information security officer vis-à-vis responsibility for implementing security policy clearly defined?					
5.	Are there detailed procedures for each policy statement?					
6.	Have proper methodologies been adopted for implementation?					
7.	Have suitable security tools been selected for implementation?					
8.	Have the roles of members of the implementation team been clearly defined?					
9.	Is the budgetary allocation for the implementation of information systems security assessed and documented?					
10.	Are periodic security audits carried out?					
11.	Are suggestions and observations, such as for updating security policies, made in information systems audit reports, security advisories, and so forth conveyed to the appropriate forum?					
12.	Are new recruits given adequate exposure to the security policy?					
13.	In case of breaches of the security policy, has the cause been analyzed and preventive and corrective actions taken?					
14.	Have incidence reporting procedures been followed?					
15.	Is the information security officer responsible for reporting noncompliance with the approved policy and incidents of security breaches to the top management?					
16.	Is the information security officer responsible for initiating corrective action for noncompliance with the approved policy and incidents of security breaches?					
Applicable Score				**Total Score**		

Prepared by:

Date:

Reviewed by:

Place:

EXHIBIT 12.17 Internet Security Checklist

	Query	Used	Y	N	Value	Score
			Response			
1.	Does the network policy specify the use of the network?					
2.	Has the auditee adhered to the requirements of the network policy?					
3.	Are all network connections routed through a firewall?					
4.	Are individual computers not allowed to use dial-up or USB modem?					
5.	Is a proxy server used to grant access to networked computers?					
6.	If proxy server is used, is browsing/downloading restricted through a centralized administration?					
7.	Is there a process/policy to request Internet access/permissions?					
8.	Is there is a process to verify whether the policy is being observed?					
9.	Are users authorized to access the Internet on a need-to-use basis only?					
10.	For computers with Internet access:					
a.	Do all computers have a firewall?					
b.	Do users understand firewall messages?					
c.	Is there an updated antivirus program?					
d.	Do users understand the antivirus messages?					
11.	Is the Internet browser updated regularly for new patches?					
12.	Internet is used for: (1) E-mail or browsing, (2) Both, (3) Don't know					
13.	Are all downloads from the Internet authorized?					
14.	Is the browser configured not to save the password/user ID?					
15.	Did the review of browser history reveal adherence to the Internet use policy?					
16.	Is the electronic commerce system well protected and controls implemented to protect against fraudulent activity, contract dispute, and disclosure or modification of information?					
17.	Have security controls such as authentication and authorization been implemented in the e-commerce environment?					

	Query	Used	Response Y	Response N	Value	Score
18.	Are electronic commerce arrangements documented and security issues specified?					
19.	Is there a policy in place for acceptable use of electronic mail and maintenance of its security?					
20.	Are controls such as antivirus checking, isolating potentially unsafe attachments, spam control, antirelaying, and so forth in place to reduce the risks created by e-mail?					
21.	Has an assessment of security risk been carried out to determine whether message authentication is required?					
22.	If applicable, have appropriate methods of authentication been implemented?					
23.	Is there a policy on use of cryptographic controls for protection of information?					
24.	Are encryption techniques used to protect the data?					
25.	Are digital signatures used to protect authenticity and integrity of electronic documents?					
26.	Is there a management system in place to support the organization's use of cryptographic techniques?					

Applicable Score   **Total Score**

Prepared by: Reviewed by:

Date: Place:

EXHIBIT 12.18 Information Systems Security Policy Checklist

	Query	Used	Response Y	Response N	Value	Score
1.	Is there a security policy?					
2.	Does the policy take into account the business strategy/plan for the next 3 to 5 years?					
3.	Is there a defined review process for the policy?					
4.	Does the security policy have an owner who is responsible for its maintenance and review?					
5.	Does the policy take into account the legal requirements?					

(Continued)

EXHIBIT 12.18 *(Continued)*

	Query	Used	Y	N	Value	Score
		Response				
6.	Does the policy take into account regulatory requirements?					
7.	Is the policy approved and adopted by the board?					
8.	Is the policy communicated to all concerned and clearly understood by them?					
9.	Are the following areas covered in the policy?:					
a.	Computer and network security					
b.	Physical security to information systems establishments					
c.	Handling of confidential information					
d.	Handling of security incidents					
e.	Privacy-related issues for outside entities					
f.	E-mail security					
g.	Application security					
h.	Interface security					
i.	Password security					
j.	Operating system security					
k.	Database security					
l.	Website security					
m.	Antivirus policy					
n.	Piracy policy					
o.	Archived and backed-up data security					
p.	Procedures for handling incidences of security breach					
q.	Disaster recovery plan					
r.	Cryptology and related security					
10.	Are persons responsible for implementing the security policy identified?					
11.	Have consequences for willful violation of the security policy been specified?					
12.	Is review of the security policy implementation done on a regular basis and on occurrence of an event?					
Applicable Score				**Total Score**		

Prepared by:
Date:

Reviewed by:
Place:

EXHIBIT 12.19 Local Area Network Checklist

	Query	Used	Y	N	Value	Score
			Response			
1.	Are standards and policies for network control established?					
2.	Have the standards and policies been updated to be in line with the current environment?					
3.	Are the standards and policies implemented and are they operating?					
4.	Are LAN installation procedures specified and documented?					
5.	Are the network layout and parameters documented?					
6.	Is a copy of the documentation available?					
7.	Is the auditee aware of the licensing conditions?					
8.	Does the installation follow the licensing conditions?					
9.	Is there a help desk for LAN-related problems?					
10.	Is the help desk number available with the auditee?					
11.	Are network restarts logged with the date, time, and reason?					
12.	Is a problem log for network-related problems maintained?					
13.	Is the problem log reviewed periodically? Does it include problem identifiers, corrective action, and signoff by the LAN supervisor or manager?					
14.	Is the LAN administrator identified?					
15.	Are procedures in place to control the following?:					
a.	Access capability of LAN administrator					
b.	Setup of new users					
c.	Change of addresses					
d.	Propagate functions					
e.	Provide access capability					
f.	Queue management					
g.	Expiry files					
h.	Restrict files					
i.	Directories and servers					
16.	Are there any empty nodes in the LAN?					

(Continued)

EXHIBIT 12.19 *(Continued)*

	Query	Used	Y	N	Value	Score
			Response			
17.	Is there a system that alerts the administrator about high connect time, high volume of data handled, usage of disk storage, and usage of printer?					
18.	Is there any documented procedure for inducting new information assets in the LAN?					
19.	Is adequate notice provided to LAN users before the system is shut down or disconnected?					
20.	Are backups taken before changing the LAN setting/installation?					
21.	Is an audit trail for log-ins and log-offs maintained in the LAN server?					
22.	Is the use of "visitor" or "guest" user ID limited, and allowed only with written authorization?					
23.	Is the LAN server(s) secured from unauthorized individuals?					
24.	Is the LAN server protected from damage resulting from electrical power surges/spikes?					
25.	Are there procedures to restrict users to valid sessions, for example, operating hours, workstation assignments, resource usage, and others?					
26.	Are user profiles reviewed and updated periodically?					
27.	Is the cabling secured to limit exposure to accidental disconnection, disturbance, or tampering?					
28.	Is other hardware, such as bridges, gateways, and routers, secured to limit exposure to tampering or other damage?					
29.	Are fire controls in place for the wiring closets?					
30.	Is there alternative routing if cabling is compromised or the primary path is unavailable?					
31.	Is there an inventory of files associated with the system?					
32.	Is a list of licensed software maintained for each LAN?					

Applicable Score **Total Score**

Prepared by: Reviewed by:

Date: Place:

EXHIBIT 12.20   Legal Compliance Checklist

			Response			
	Query	Used	Y	N	Value	Score
1.	Have users been trained on legal issues involved in using information assets?					
2.	Is there an identified individual for ensuring legal compliance?					
3.	When new information assets are introduced into the system, is there a process in place for explaining the legal issues involved in usage of the asset?					
4.	When a new information-asset-related service is installed, is there a procedure of explaining the legal issues involved?					
5.	Is there a system of recording breaches of legal compliance?					
6.	Has there been no legal dispute arising out of or augmented by failure of information assets?					
7.	Are formats and contents of automated mails and reports preapproved by an appropriate authority?					
8.	Is there any procedure to ensure compliance with legal restrictions on use of material protected under intellectual property rights?					
9.	Are users aware that an electronic mail or record is deemed to be dispatched as soon as it enters the computing resource outside their control?					
10.	Are there specific addresses authorized to which an e-mail or record is to be sent for specific purposes?					
11.	If such an address is specified, is the resource regularly checked for incoming e-mail and records?					
12.	If any electronic record is to be used as a business document, does it carry any distinguishing mark, such as a digital signature, that is (1) unique to the originator, (2) capable of identifying the originator, and (3) altered if any change is made to the record?					
13.	If a digital signature has been purchased:					
a.	Is the signature valid?					
b.	Is the process of affixing the digital signature protected from unauthorized access?					
14.	Is there no possibility or evidence of the following events occurring without authorization by the owner or person in charge of the system:					
a.	Access to computer, computer resources, system, or network?					

(Continued)

EXHIBIT 12.20 *(Continued)*

	Query	Used	Y	N	Value	Score
			Response			
b.	Downloading or copying any data, database, or information from computer, system, network, or removable storage medium?					
c.	Disrupting or causing disruption of computer, computer resource, system, or network?					
d.	Denying or causing the denial of access to any person authorized to access any computer, system, or network by any means?					
e.	Introducing or causing to introduce any computer contaminant or computer virus into computer, computer resource, system, or network?					
f.	Damaging or causing to be damaged any computer, computer resource, system, network, data, database, or programs?					
g.	Charging the services availed of by a person to the account of another person by tampering with or manipulating any computer, system, network, or using any other method?					
15.	Is the person in charge of the computers aware of the following?:					
a.	Safeguards adopted to ensure that only authorized person can enter data or perform any other operation					
b.	Safeguards adopted to prevent and detect unauthorized change of data					
c.	Safeguards available to retrieve data lost due to systemic failure or other reasons					
d.	The possible methods for transferring data for backup of the system onto removable media					
e.	Methodology of verification to ensure that data have been accurately transferred to such removable media					
f.	Process of identification of such data storage devices					
g.	Arrangements for storage and custody of storage devices					
h.	Safeguards to prevent and detect any tampering with the system					
i.	Features that vouch for integrity and accuracy of the system					
16.	Is there no possibility of the following offences occurring in the system:					
a.	Tampering of computer source documents?					
b.	Hacking of computer system?					
c.	Sending of offensive messages?					

	Query	Used	Y	N	Value	Score
d.	Identity theft?					
e.	Privacy violation?					
f.	Publishing of obscene information in electronic form?					
17.	Is there a system of checking whether any new guidelines have been enforced by any statutory or internal authorities in the area of use of information assets?					
18.	Is there a centralized database/place where all such guidelines are available?					
19.	Is there a system ensuring that such guidelines have reached all related users?					
20.	Does the audit process include the verification of adherence to legal requirements in context of information systems?					
21.	Are there no incidents involving failure to comply with any guideline, circular, and similar instructions?					
Applicable Score				**Total Score**		
Prepared by:			Reviewed by:			
Date:			Place:			

EXHIBIT 12.21 Long-term Information Technology Strategy Checklist

	Query	Used	Y	N	Value	Score
1.	Does a documented long-term IT strategy/plan exist?					
2.	Does the long-term IT strategy plan address the following?:					
a.	Existing and proposed hardware and networking architecture					
b.	Broad strategy for procurement of hardware, software solutions, vendor development, and management					
c.	Standards for hardware and software prescribed by the proposed architecture					
d.	Strategy for outsourcing, in-sourcing, procuring off-the-shelf software, and in-house development					
e.	Information security architecture					
f.	Structure of the IT department and its hierarchical place in the organizational structure					
g.	Desired level of IT expertise in organizational human resources and a plan to bridge the gap, if any					

(Continued)

EXHIBIT 12.21 *(Continued)*

	Query	Used	Y	N	Value	Score
			Response			
h.	Converting strategies into clear IT initiatives with a broad time frame					
i.	IT costs and cost management					
j.	Plan for transition, if any					
3.	Is the long-term plan approved by the Board?					
4.	Does the IT long-range plan support the achievement of the organization's overall mission and goals?					
5.	Has a structured approach to the long-range planning process been established?					
6.	Does the plan cover the *what, who, how, when,* and *why* of IT?					
7.	Does a process exist for timely and accurate modification of the long-range IT plan, taking into account changes in the organization's plan, business, and information technology?					
8.	Does the plan refer to other plans, such as the organizational business plan, growth plan, and information risk management plan?					
9.	Does the existing system support the organization's business requirements?					
10.	Has the existing system been assessed in terms of degree of business automation, functionality, stability, complexity, costs, strengths, and weaknesses before developing or changing the long-term information technology plan?					
11.	Have the following been taken into account at the time of planning and development of the long-term plan: organizational model and changes to it, geographical distribution, technological evolution, costs, legal and regulatory requirements, requirements of third-parties or the market, planning horizon, business process reengineering, staffing, in- or outsourcing, and so forth?					
12.	Has a security committee/department been formed, comprising senior functionaries from IT Department, Business Group, IT Security Department, and Legal Department, to provide appropriate direction to formulate, implement, monitor, and maintain IT security in the entire organization?					
Applicable Score				**Total Score**		

Prepared by:

Date:

Reviewed by:

Place:

EXHIBIT 12.22 Maintenance Questionnaire Checklist

	Query	Used	Y	N	Value	Score
		Response				
1.	Is identity of the maintenance person verified before granting access to the information systems?					
2.	Does a person from the auditee organization accompany the vendor during maintenance?					
3.	Is the auditee or owner of the information asset aware of the maintenance activities the maintenance person will be performing during his or her visit?					
4.	Is the vendor prevented from connecting any external storage devices to any information system asset without authorization during information system maintenance?					
5.	Is a written and signed confirmation taken from the vendor about the maintenance activities performed?					
6.	Is there a periodic schedule for maintenance?					
7.	Is the periodic maintenance schedule being followed?					
8.	Is there a process to ascertain the criticality and perform a cost-benefit analysis to identify information systems assets that need to be covered by maintenance contracts?					
9.	Have all information system assets requiring an annual maintenance contract been covered by such a contract?					
10.	Are all annual maintenance contracts currently valid?					
11.	Are all maintenance contracts renewed within the expiry date?					
12.	Are terms of the maintenance contracts being followed?					
13.	Are persons in charge of administration aware of the terms of the contract?					
14.	Is the vendor election process transparent, documented, and appropriate?					
15.	Are records maintained for all repairs and maintenance activities performed?					
16.	Are the records reviewed periodically to analyze repeated repairs and to ascertain whether the asset repair cost exceeds cost of replacement?					
17.	Is there a system for referring unsolved and recurring problems to senior persons?					

Applicable Score	**Total Score**
Prepared by:	Reviewed by:
Date:	Place:

EXHIBIT 12.23 Management Control System Checklist

Query	Used	Y	N	Value	Score
		Response			
Segregation of Duties					
1. Is the functioning of the information systems department independent of operating departments for which they handle systems and data?					
2. Are the following functions adequately segregated?:					
a. Systems development (design and programming)					
b. Technical support (maintenance of systems software)					
c. Operations					
3. In smaller installations with limited segregation of duties, do procedures provide the following controls?:					
a. Utilization of batch or other input controls					
b. Control of master file changes					
c. Balancing of master files between processing cycles					
4. Does the IT policy provide for rotation of duties?					
Procedural Controls					
5. Do system user controls include:					
a. Controls over approval of input transactions committed from outside the office?					
b. Prohibiting system department from initiating transactions?					
c. Ensuring that all approved inputs are processed correctly by the system?					
d. Controls over rejected transactions?					
e. Reconciliation of file balances?					
f. Review of reconciliation processes?					
6. Do application controls include the following:					
a. Program controls over entry of data into online systems?					

Query	Response				
	Used	Y	N	Value	Score
b. Controls over data entry, such as including up-to-date instructions, key verification of important fields, and self-checking digits?					
c. Editing and validation of input data?					
d. Data processing controls over rejected transactions?					
e. Controls for balancing transactions and master files?					
f. Control function concerning review and distribution of output?					
g. Reconciliation of output totals with input totals for all data submitted?					
7. Do general controls include:					
a. Controls over changes to system software?					
b. Controls over use and retention of records to provide backup capabilities?					
c. Controls to limit access to data processing equipment, storage media, system documentation, and application program documentation to authorized employees?					
d. Controls to ensure scheduled programs are processed, prescribed procedures are followed, and supervisory personnel are made aware if unnecessary programs are processed?					
e. Documentation of procedures for computer operators?					
f. Documentation for operation of system?					
g. Procedures to protect against a loss of important files, programs, or equipment?					
h. Insurance to cover equipment, programs, and data files?					
i. User-approved written specifications for modifications and for new systems?					
j. Procedures to test and implement modifications and new systems?					

Applicable Score				Total Score	

Prepared by: Reviewed by:

Date: Place:

EXHIBIT 12.24 Operating System Checklist

	Query	Used	Y	N	Value	Score
		Response				
1.	Is there a list of operating system(s) installed at the site?					
2.	Do the operating system(s) have valid licenses?					
3.	Are the operating system software media securely stored?					
4.	Is the latest patch available for the operating system applied?					
5.	Is there a person designated as a system administrator?					
6.	Is the system administrator trained on management of the operating system?					
7.	Is the administrator aware of the latest vulnerabilities/patches available for the operating systems?					
8.	Do procedures forbid giving users administrative privileges?					
9.	Is the administrative password changed regularly?					
10.	Is there a procedure to verify that administrative passwords have been changed regularly?					
11.	Are users locked out after a prescribed number of invalid attempts at log-in?					
12.	Do initial passwords assigned to new accounts pre-expire, requiring the user to change the password upon first log-in?					
13.	Is an audit log generated for accesses?					
14.	Are audit logs reviewed?					
15.	Are audit logs available for the past (1) 1 year, (2) 6 months, (3) 3 months, or (4) unavailable?					
16.	Is access to audit logs secured?					
17.	Is the system administrator prevented from having data access?					
18.	Is there a procedure in place to ensure that application system performance is reviewed and tested after changes have been applied to the operating system?					

Applicable Score	**Total Score**
Prepared by:	Reviewed by:
Date:	Place:

EXHIBIT 12.25   Packaged Software Implementation Checklist

			Response			
	Query	Used	Y	N	Value	Score
1.	Do application and database password controls meet password policy requirements of the auditee?					
2.	Do the application and database software have no generic user IDs?					
3.	Have the default passwords for the database and application been changed?					
4.	Does a process exist to review approved user lists for each application and database?					
5.	Are test user IDs removed/disabled before real-life use?					
6.	Does the software avoid hard-coded passwords?					
7.	Are system parameters standardized for all installations of the software?					
8.	Does the software restrict access to the database by nonadministrative users?					
9.	Is power to commit changes to the database without using the application software restricted to persons authorized for this purpose?					
10.	Does the software limit access to program code?					
11.	Does the software maintain any usage log?					
12.	If the software allows for customization, is there a procedure for approval of customization requests?					
13.	Are change requests for customization documented?					
14.	During the implementation stage, is there any methodology that prevents access to real-life data?					
15.	Is there any system in place to prevent use of an earlier version of the software?					
16.	Is the software user manual available?					
17.	Is a baseline performance level established and compared with performance levels after go-live?					
18.	Are all access attempts at the database level logged?					
19.	Is there a separate log for administrative functions?					
20.	Is security administration separated from system, database, and application administration?					
21.	Is access to sensitive system tools controlled?					

(Continued)

EXHIBIT 12.25 *(Continued)*

Query		Response				
		Used	Y	N	Value	Score
22.	Can the entire system and the production data be backed up?					
23.	Are confidential reports generated from the application maintained securely?					
24.	Is generation of confidential reports protected by an authorization procedure?					
Applicable Score				**Total Score**		

Prepared by: Reviewed by:

Date: Place:

EXHIBIT 12.26 Parameter Settings Checklist

Query		Response				
		Used	Y	N	Value	Score
1.	Are changes to parameters made only against formal authorization documents?					
2.	Is there any written record of changes made in parameters with a reason thereof?					
3.	Is the parameter change request document signed by persons making the change in parameters mentioning the date of changes?					
4.	Are any changes to user-defined system parameters automatically reported?					
5.	Are all default passwords for predefined system accounts changed?					
6.	Are all guest accounts disabled or removed?					
7.	Are records of changes to control files periodically reviewed to ensure only authorized and requested changes were made?					
8.	Is there a standardized setting for system parameters?					
9.	On checking the system parameters were they found compliant with the standardized setting?					
10.	Is there a standardized setting for application parameters?					
11.	On checking the application parameters were they found compliant with the standardized setting?					
12.	Is the administrator granted privileges prescribed by the auditee policy?					
13.	Is the password expiration time limit parameter correctly set?					
Applicable Score				**Total Score**		

Prepared by: Reviewed by:

Date: Place:

EXHIBIT 12.27   Peripheral Devices and Storage Media Checklist

			Response			
	Query	Used	Y	N	Value	Score
1.	Is the main and other critical disk storage space sufficient for the next 6 months?					
2.	Is a record of all peripheral devices and storage media received maintained?					
3.	Is a record of peripheral devices and storage media issued for use maintained?					
4.	Are storage media and other peripheral devices issued on a need-to-use basis?					
5.	Where the peripheral devices or storage media are no longer usable, is their disposal authorized and logged?					
6.	Are all data from the storage media erased permanently before disposal?					
7.	Are all storage media being introduced into the system checked for viruses before use?					
8.	Are there no extra peripheral devices lying around?					
9.	Is content of storage media brought from external environment verified for their data content on a stand-alone system before being uploaded into the main system?					
10.	Are all peripheral devices maintained periodically?					
11.	Does the problem register enlist all problems relating to peripheral devices and storage media?					
12.	Is there a record of all authorized USB ports?					
13.	Are users disallowed from altering the status of wireless connectivity, such as WLAN, Bluetooth, Infra Red, and so forth, without specific authorization?					
14.	Is use of external storage media restricted to authorized users for authorized purposes only?					
15.	Is use of external peripheral devices by vendors, auditors, and other third parties restricted?					
16.	If any external peripheral device or storage media are used by third-party personnel, are these checked for their data content before entry and departure of the personnel?					
17.	Is security of media being transported ensured?					
18.	Are the scanners protected from dust?					

(Continued)

EXHIBIT 12.27 *(Continued)*

			Response			
	Query	Used	Y	N	Value	Score
19.	Is the use of scanner restricted to authorized personnel for scanning authorized documents only?					
20.	Are printers under an annual maintenance contract?					
21.	Are the printers periodically serviced?					
22.	Is access to the printers and printout restricted to authorized personnel only?					
Applicable Score				**Total Score**		

Prepared by: Reviewed by:

Date: Place:

EXHIBIT 12.28 Physical Access Control Checklist

			Response			
	Query	Used	Y	N	Value	Score
1.	Do windows prevent forced entry?					
2.	Is lighting sufficient for a safe work environment and to deter intruders?					
3.	Are all main entry doors identified and guarded and only one kept open for entry and exit?					
4.	Does the layout of the working area ensure that unauthorized outsiders do not get physical access to computers and accessories?					
5.	Are screens of computers/terminals placed in a way that viewing of the screen and keyboard by outsiders is prevented?					
6.	Are there technology-based access control systems, for example, RFID or smart cards?					
7.	Are these technology-based access controls working properly?					
8.	Are access controls in place that allow only authorized personnel to enter into various areas within the organization?					
9.	Are the delivery area and information processing area isolated from each other to avoid any unauthorized access?					
10.	Server room:					
a.	Are server rooms/programming locations away from the main entrance?					

	Query	Used	Response Y	N	Value	Score
b.	Is the key to the server room kept with the authorized person?					
c.	Is the server room kept locked and opened on a need-to-use basis?					
d.	Is entry to server room restricted?					
e.	On access to server room by external vendors, auditors, and so forth, are they accompanied by designated personnel from the organization?					
f.	Is entry into the server room with reason thereof documented?					
11.	Cables:					
a.	To eliminate the possibility of wiretapping, are data cables/switches and other wires so located that they are not accessible from outside the premises?					
b.	Are cables in the work area not running across the floor so that people do not step on or trip over cables or wires?					
12.	Is there protective casing for all cables on the walls?					
13.	Access to documentation:					
a.	Is access to hardware and software documentation restricted and available only on a need-to-know basis?					
b.	Is access allowed only after authorization and logging?					
c.	Is access to inventory register, password maintenance register, problem log register, and other registers made by authorized persons only?					
d.	Do log files and exception report files have restricted access in possession of authorized personnel only?					
14.	Is access to peripherals and storage media restricted?					
15.	Are the backup data storage media carried out of the organization premises physically secured and kept in a way that unauthorized access is not possible?					
16.	Are there no reported events of theft of computer equipment, accessories, and documents?					

(Continued)

EXHIBIT 12.28 (*Continued*)

	Query	Used	Response Y	N	Value	Score
17.	Are only authorized persons allowed access to the printers and printouts?					
18.	Is the UPS protected from access by customers and other outsiders?					
19.	Are access violations recorded and reported to the authorized person?					

Applicable Score		Total Score	

Prepared by: Reviewed by:

Date: Place:

EXHIBIT 12.29 Physical Environment Checklist

	Query	Used	Response Y	N	Value	Score
1.	Overall environment:					
a.	Is the environment dust free?					
b.	Is there regular cleaning of all machines and equipment?					
c.	Is there sufficient light in the work area?					
2.	Protection against fire:					
a.	Are the wall and floor coverings made of non-combustible or fire-resistant material?					
b.	Is there a separation of the server room or other critical areas from combustible materials?					
c.	Has a smoking restriction been imposed and is it being followed?					
d.	Have smoke and heat-rise detectors been placed in all key areas?					
e.	Are the detectors linked to the fire alarm system?					
f.	Are the telephone numbers of the fire, police, ambulance, and other concerned persons readily available?					
g.	Does the auditee have valid fire insurance of adequate amount?					
h.	Is there an inert gas fire extinguishment system (for key IT areas)?					
i.	Are portable CO_2 extinguishers (for electrical fires) present?					
j.	Are fire extinguishers placed in a way that there is ease of access?					

	Query	Used	Y	N	Value	Score
			Response			
k.	Have a few employees been trained in the use of the fire extinguisher?					
l.	Is the fire extinguisher serviced and refilled at periodic service intervals?					
m.	Are the fire alarm switches clearly visible?					
n.	Are emergency power-off procedures displayed prominently?					
o.	Is there an evacuation plan with assigned responsibilities?					
p.	Is a periodic fire drill and training carried out?					
3.	Water damage:					
a.	Are the IT areas located above ground level?					
b.	Are there no water leaks in the IT area?					
c.	Are there no damp walls in the key IT areas?					
d.	Is there a water alarm system?					
e.	Are personnel not allowed to store water or eat and drink in the key IT areas?					
4.	Air-conditioning:					
a.	Are the temperature and the humidity of the critical IT areas monitored?					
b.	Is there an AMC for the air conditioners?					
c.	Is servicing of the air conditioners done at regular intervals?					
d.	Is the power line of the air conditioners separate from the power line of the computer system?					
5.	Power supply:					
a.	Is there reliable power supply?					
b.	Is the voltage monitored?					
c.	Is the computer power supply separate from the power supply for other purposes?					
d.	Is the power supply to the computer connected through the UPS?					
e.	Is no other equipment running on the same UPS that is supplying power to the computers?					
f.	Does the UPS have a main switch that can be switched off?					
g.	Are the personnel at the auditee organization aware of the location of the UPS main switch and how to turn off the UPS during an emergency?					
h.	Is there a maintenance contract for the UPS?					

(Continued)

EXHIBIT 12.29   *(Continued)*

	Query	Used	Response Y	N	Value	Score
i.	Is the UPS functioning properly?					
j.	Is there an alternative power supply, for example, a generator present?					
k.	Is there more than one employee who can start the generator?					
l.	Is there a system to maintain stock of generator fuel?					
m.	Is the grounding adequate for all electrical installations?					
n.	Is the grounding checked periodically, and has it been documented?					
6.	Server room layout:					
a.	Is the server located away from the main entrance?					
b.	Is the server room located away from sources of electrical or magnetic disturbances?					
c.	Are printers and plotters located in separate locations?					
d.	Is the server room free of congestion with furniture, extra machines, computer accessories, and equipment?					
e.	Is there adequate lighting in the server room?					
f.	Are the wires protected by a cover and not installed on damp walls?					
g.	Is all equipment placed on tables or on raised levels?					
h.	Is there a wide enough gap between the wall/floor and the machines to promote ventilation and access, if necessary?					
i.	Is there an emergency power switch in or near the server room?					
j.	Is there a fire extinguisher placed in or near the server room?					
k.	Is there environmental monitoring (temperature, humidity) equipment in the server room?					
l.	Is the server room free of environmental threat from neighboring premises?					
Applicable Score					**Total Score**	

Prepared by: Reviewed by:

Date: Place:

EXHIBIT 12.30 Problem Management Checklist

	Query	Used	Y	N	Value	Score
			Response			
1.	Are all faults reported and a problem register maintained that details the date of problem, date of reporting, date of attending to it, date of resolution, and how the problem was resolved?					
2.	Are corrective actions taken, along with review of the fault logs and root-cause analysis?					
3.	Are corrective measures implemented in a timely manner?					
4.	Are logs maintained for all potential or actual faults and corresponding preventive and corrective measures taken?					
5.	Are appropriate controls implemented while sending equipment off premises with fulfillment of insurance policy requirements, if any?					
6.	Does equipment usage outside the organization's premises require authorization of the management?					
7.	Is the security provided for equipment outside the premises at par with or more than the security provided inside the premises?					
8.	Are storage devices containing sensitive information physically destroyed or securely overwritten before being transported out of the premises?					
9.	Are problems not solved referred to senior management/computer department?					
10.	Are there any problems observed during processing that affect the confidentiality, integrity, and availability of data?					
11.	Are there are no recurring problems in the system?					
12.	Is the elapsed time between the problems reported and then corrected within reasonable limits?					
13.	Is there a system of regular preventive maintenance?					
14.	Are review procedures used for recording, evaluating, resolving, and escalating any operating or processing problems?					
15.	Is there a defined procedure for service quality analysis?					

(Continued)

EXHIBIT 12.30   *(Continued)*

		Response				
	Query	Used	Y	N	Value	Score
16.	Are there any patterns of recurring malfunction or repair that have resulted in frequent disruption of operations and/or excessive cost?					
17.	Is maintenance being performed as scheduled by the contract(s)?					
18.	Is there a schedule for routine and periodic hardware maintenance to reduce the frequency and impact of performance failures?					
19.	Is a summarized problem report available to the senior management?					
20.	Does all equipment, information, or software to be taken off-site require appropriate authorization?					
21.	Have spot checks or regular audits been conducted to detect unauthorized removal of information systems assets?					
22.	Is insurance coverage adequate?					

Applicable Score		Total Score	
Prepared by:		Reviewed by:	
Date:		Place:	

EXHIBIT 12.31   Security Management Checklist

		Response				
	Query	Used	Y	N	Value	Score
1.	Are responsibilities for protection of individual information systems assets defined?					
2.	Are responsibilities for carrying out specific security processes defined?					
3.	Is there a management authorization process for introducing any new information processing facility?					
4.	Has specialist information security advice been obtained where necessary?					
5.	Are appropriate contacts with law enforcement authorities, regulatory bodies, information service providers, and telecommunication operators maintained to ensure that appropriate action can be quickly taken and advice obtained in the event of a security incident?					

Query	Used	Response Y	Response N	Value	Score
6. Organizational security policies and standards:					
a. Is a person/group identified as responsible for ensuring that the processing environment complies with applicable organizational security policies and standards?					
b. Are the security maintenance team's roles and responsibilities clearly stated?					
c. Are the organizational security policies and standards defined?					
d. Are security administration personnel aware of relevant organizational security policies and standards for the operating environment under review?					
e. Are procedures in place to ensure compliance with relevant organizational security policies and standards?					
7. Security awareness and training:					
a. Are all systems and security administration personnel and users of critical systems informed of relevant organizational security policies and standards?					
b. Is there a process in place to ensure that all new employees are informed of organizational security policies and standards?					
c. Is there a security awareness program in place to ensure that end users are periodically informed of organizational security policies and standards and are aware of their individual responsibilities?					
d. Is a process in place to ensure that individuals with security administration responsibilities are kept informed of key security advisories (e.g., CERT, CIAC, and so on) and issues related to operating systems used?					
e. Are the applicable security advisories segregated and communicated to the concerned individuals in charge of the security of relevant information systems?					
Applicable Score			**Total Score**		

Prepared by:

Date:

Reviewed by:

Place:

EXHIBIT 12.32 Segregation of Duties Checklist

	Query	Used	Y	N	Value	Score
			Response			
1.	Are the following duties performed by separate persons?:					
a.	Information systems management					
b.	System design					
c.	Application programming					
d.	Production control and scheduling					
e.	Quality assurance/testing					
f.	Library management/change management					
g.	Computer operations					
h.	System programming					
i.	Data control					
j.	Data security					
k.	Data administration					
l.	Network administration					
2.	Do separate persons perform data entry and verification functions?					
3.	Do separate persons perform data entry and reconciliation to output functions?					
4.	Do separate persons perform input of transactions for incompatible processing functions?					
5.	Do separate persons perform data entry and supervisory authorization functions?					
6.	Do personnel strictly adhere to the segregation of functions?					
7.	If segregation of duties is not possible, has there been a supervisory review of all transactions and activities committed?					
8.	Do documented job descriptions state assigned duties and responsibilities and observe principles of segregation of duty?					
9.	Are employees aware of their job descriptions, duties, and responsibilities?					
10.	Have personnel been trained to establish, enforce, and institutionalize the principles of segregation of duties?					

Query	Response			Value	Score
	Used	Y	N		
11. Are usage logs reviewed periodically and any abnormalities in segregation of duties investigated?					
12. Is there a succession plan for key personnel within the IT department?					
13. Is the skill set within the organization well distributed so that in the event of absence of key personnel, availability of relevant skill is ensured?					

Applicable Score				Total Score	

Prepared by:

Date:

Reviewed by:

Place:

EXHIBIT 12.33 Short-Range Information Technology Plan Checklist

Query	Response			Value	Score
	Used	Y	N		
1. Are long-range IT plans regularly broken up into short-range IT plans for easier achievement?					
2. Does the short-range IT plan cover the following:					
a. Plan for initiatives specified in the long-range plan or that supports the long-range plan?					
b. System-wide transition strategy?					
c. Responsibility and plan for achievement of objectives?					
d. Allocation of adequate resources for achieving the short-range plan objectives?					
3. Are short-range plans amended and changed periodically as necessary in response to changing business and information technology conditions?					
4. Are continuous assessments made on implementation of short-range plans?					

Applicable Score				Total Score	

Prepared by:

Date:

Reviewed by:

Place:

EXHIBIT 12.34 Software License Checklist

	Query	Used	Y	N	Value	Score
			Response			
1.	Is there a list of the software authorized to be installed?					
2.	Is there a list of software installed in the information systems?					
3.	Is there a list of installed software for each information system asset?					
4.	Is a copy of the software license available at the site of installation?					
5.	Are the software license details, such as license number and expiry date, available?					
6.	Is a procedure defined for authorization of installation of software?					
7.	Are agencies like vendors, auditors, and so forth prevented from installing software without seeking prior approval?					
8.	Does the user name recorded in the installed software agree with the terms of its license?					
9.	Can the license number be verified from the installed software?					
10.	Does the displayed license number agree with the license?					
11.	In case of a group license, has the installation been done in terms of the license agreement?					
12.	Are there any methods to prevent downloading/installation of software from external sources?					
13.	Is access to media containing the software available only to authorized personnel?					
14.	Is the auditee aware that the use of unlicensed software or the use of software violating the terms of its license is illegal?					

Applicable Score   **Total Score**

Prepared by: Reviewed by:

Date: Place:

EXHIBIT 12.35 System Conversion and Reconciliation Checklist

			Response			
	Query	Used	Y	N	Value	Score
1.	Is a target date established?					
2.	Are the data files to be used identified?					
3.	Are differences and mismatches of data identified during conversion reconciled?					
4.	Are differences and mismatch of data identified during conversion rectified?					
5.	Are the persons responsible for certifying the conversion completion identified?					
6.	Is there a copy of the conversion completion certificate issued by the authorized individual?					
7.	Is any formal mapping procedure present to identify each data field converted?					
8.	Was any data clean-up procedure followed and the results and changes made adequately documented?					
9.	Are all system and user manuals updated with changes necessitated by system conversion?					
10.	Are the prospective users trained on the operation of the system?					
11.	Are the prospective users made aware of the security issues involved in the system?					
12.	Were control totals used to verify data integrity upon conversion?					
13.	Is use of control totals documented?					
14.	Is there any "rollback" plan to revert to erstwhile system in case the system conversion is aborted?					

Applicable Score | **Total Score**

Prepared by: | Reviewed by:
Date: | Place:

EXHIBIT 12.36 System Software Controls Checklist

			Response			
	Query	Used	Y	N	Value	Score
1.	Is access to system software limited to authorized persons?					
2.	Are all system software files housed in protected folders that are accessible only to authorized persons?					

EXHIBIT 12.36 (*Continued*)

	Query	Used	Y	N	Value	Score
		Response				
3.	Is documentation maintained of date, time, and reason for accessing or modification of system software?					
4.	Is access to the system software restricted from application users?					
5.	Is all access to system files automatically logged?					
6.	Are system access logs periodically reviewed?					
7.	Have vendor-supplied default logins and passwords been changed?					
8.	Are only authorized system utilities used?					
9.	Are unusual activities in the system reported to the specified authority?					
10.	Are system-related problems logged in the problem register along with information on who attended to it and how the problem was solved?					
11.	Are proper authorizations received for installing new versions of system software and carrying out modifications to existing systems?					
12.	Are all changes supported by a change request document?					
13.	Are all installations first implemented in the test environment and fully tested before implementation in the live environment?					
14.	Are all testing results independently reviewed before implementation?					
15.	Are installations of all system software logged and the audit trail reviewed periodically?					
16.	Is the vendor-installed system software still supported by the vendor?					
17.	Is there a version control process in place for system software?					
18.	Are all outdated versions removed from the production library?					
19.	Is a complete documentation of the system software present, including details of parameters and options defined?					
20.	Is the system software documentation updated on any change or modification?					
21.	Does file access permission restrict users to servers containing sensitive data?					

	Query	Response Used	Y	N	Value	Score
22.	Are user profiles configured to ensure that file access permissions restrict users to areas containing necessary data and programs?					
23.	Are incident reports generated for all instances of system software using more than the normal processing time?					
24.	Are operators prevented from overriding application error, system error, or equipment error messages?					
25.	Is the system startup and shut-down monitored for any error messages?					

Applicable Score	Total Score
Prepared by:	Reviewed by:
Date:	Place:

EXHIBIT 12.37 Third-Party and Vendor Services Review Checklist

	Query	Response Used	Y	N	Value	Score
1.	Are IT policies and procedures relating to third-party relationships consistent with organizational policies?					
2.	Are service providers performing services as defined by their contracts?					
3.	Are there any services provided by vendors that are not documented in the contract?					
4.	Are risks associated with the respective vendor services identified in advance and discussed with the vendor?					
5.	Are appropriate controls incorporated into the contract to protect the auditee from the associated risks?					
6.	Have necessary approvals been obtained from business and application owners?					
7.	Do contracts include provisions for continuity of services, including contingency planning by vendor, to ensure continuous service?					
8.	Do the contract contents include at least the following:					
a.	Definition of service and scope of the work?					
b.	Responsibilities and obligations of the service provider?					

EXHIBIT 12.37 *(Continued)*

	Query	Used	Y	N	Value	Score
			Response			
c.	Deliverables of service and quantifiable minimum service level?					
d.	Availability, reliability, confidentiality, secrecy, and fidelity clause?					
e.	Security requirements in alignment with the security policy?					
f.	Disaster recovery and continuity planning?					
g.	Liability and indemnity clause?					
h.	Intellectual property rights?					
i.	Cost of service, taxes, duties, other charges, and payment terms?					
j.	Effective period and terms of review/renewal/nonrenewal?					
k.	Right to have information systems audit conducted?					
l.	*Force majeure* clause?					
m.	Termination and penalty clause?					
n.	Dispute resolution/arbitration?					
o.	Nonemployment and restriction from other business relationships?					
p.	Identification of key person and notification of change thereof?					
9.	Where the organization has outsourced management and control of all or some of its information systems and networks, have the security requirements been explicitly addressed in the contract with the vendor?					
10.	Is there appropriate independence between the vendor and the organization?					
11.	At the operational level:					
a.	Are the users aware of the terms of the contract with the vendor?					
b.	Is the service being provided by the vendor per the terms of contract?					
c.	Is the support provided by the vendor satisfactory?					
d.	Does the vendor report within allowable time after a call is made?					
e.	Is identity of the vendor verified before allowing access to information systems?					
f.	Is access to information systems restricted to the area for which the vendor is contracted?					

			Response			
	Query	Used	Y	N	Value	Score
g.	Is the vendor restricted from carrying and using any external peripheral equipment or devices unless specifically authorized?					
h.	Does a person from the organization accompany the vendor during the vendor's stay and work at the organization?					

Applicable Score	Total Score
Prepared by:	Reviewed by:
Date:	Place:

EXHIBIT 12.38 Transaction Processing Checklist

			Response			
	Query	Used	Y	N	Value	Score
1.	Are startup operations free of any error messages?					
2.	Does the system prevent acceptance of a date other than the current date as valid?					
3.	Is there no self-rebooting of the system during transaction processing?					
4.	Is the real-time clock of the system showing the correct time?					
5.	Are parameters for selection of day-end/ processing/balancing reports to be backed up/printed correctly set?					
6.	Is time taken for the day-end operation or balancing operation, if any, reasonable?					
7.	In case the system remains active during the night, do security parameters restrict the activities that can be performed during the night?					
8.	Is the checksum generated automatically correct and giving no error message?					
9.	Are all batch transactions authorized?					
10.	Are there procedures to ensure that all vouchers have been processed?					
11.	Does the system ensure that day-end/balancing operations cannot be completed unless the mandatory reports are printed?					
12.	Are all transactions properly authorized before being processed?					

EXHIBIT 12.38 *(Continued)*

	Query	Used	Y	N	Value	Score
			Response			
13.	Are procedures defined to ensure that transactions or batches are not lost, duplicated, or improperly changed?					
14.	Does the system ensure that modification of a transaction is permitted only through reversal of the transaction entry and not by directly accessing and making changes to the database?					
15.	Are the person making a transaction entry and the person authorizing it different individuals?					
16.	Does the system setting for exception transactions ensure that only authorized persons can carry out these transactions?					
17.	Is an endorsement made on all physical source documents entered into the information system along with the initials of the computer operator(s) and supervisors?					
18.	Is the transaction processing free of any reported errors?					
19.	Does the software have checks to ensure that duplicate transactions are not processed?					
20.	Does the software have controls to ensure reporting of rejected transactions?					
21.	Are there procedures in place to identify and correct missing duplicate transactions?					
22.	Are there procedures in place to investigate and correct rejected items?					
23.	Does the software have controls to ensure that data have been accurately input (e.g., range checks, validity checks, control totals, and so forth)?					
24.	Does the system ensure consistency/concurrency of user inputs, if two users are accessing the same record at the same time?					
25.	Is there a formal output distribution policy?					
26.	Does the software maintain audit trails to uniquely trace any modifications, deletions, and additions?					
27.	Are hardcopy reports:					
a.	Headed?					
b.	Page-numbered?					
c.	Dated?					
d.	Identified by report/program number?					
e.	Adequately totaled/control totaled?					

Query		Used	Response Y	N	Value	Score
f.	Designed to give an "end-of-report" message, if not obvious?					
28.	Are reports distributed to authorized personnel in line with an approved distribution list?					
29.	Are there formal procedures for checking, filing, and retention of reports?					
30.	Are reports reviewed and signed by persons responsible for the same?					
31.	Does the system provide for automatic generation of serial number(s)/sequential reference number(s)?					
32.	Is there a provision for reprinting the entire transaction made during the day?					
33.	Are audit logs maintained whenever modifications of master data are done?					

Applicable Score	Total Score

Prepared by:
Date:

Reviewed by:
Place:

EXHIBIT 12.39 Utility Program Checklist

Query		Used	Response Y	N	Value	Score
1.	Is there a list of utility programs installed?					
2.	Does the list identify the information systems assets on which they are installed?					
3.	Is prior approval necessary before such software is installed?					
4.	Is there adequate protection preventing unauthorized access to information systems assets where utility programs are installed?					
5.	Is the utility software installed incapable of the following functions unless specifically authorized by the senior management for a specific purpose?:					
a.	Make data access and alter the same.					
b.	Establish connection with other network(s).					
c.	Receive or send files to other computer(s) or network(s).					
d.	Prevent access to files.					
e.	Make copy of the data.					
f.	Display content of the computer.					

Applicable Score	Total Score

Prepared by:
Date:

Reviewed by:
Place:

EXHIBIT 12.40 Wireless Network Audit Checklist

			Response			
	Query	Used	Y	N	Value	Score
1.	Is there a policy of use of wireless-enabled devices?					
2.	Have default SSIDs of the access point been changed?					
3.	Does the SSID exclude information that can identify the host organization, such as name and phone number?					
4.	Is SSID broadcasting disabled?					
5.	Is the DHCP pool disabled to enforce assignment of IP to known number of users or, alternatively, is Static IP used?					
6.	Is access point power set to minimum required to serve the target area?					
7.	If the usage area is physically long, are directional antennas used to prevent a 360-degree broadcast?					
8.	Is a system of logging available and used? (0) Used, (1) Available, (2) Not Available)					
9.	Which network encryption system is used? (0) WPA2, WPA2-PSK, AES, or later, (1) WPA, WPA-PSK, (2) WEP with 802.1x Dynamic WEP, WEP, (3) Others, (4) None					
10.	Is the encryption dependent on multiple keys?					
11.	Are encryption keys changed periodically? (0) Weekly, (1) Every 2 weeks, (2) Monthly, (3) Later than monthly, (4) Never					
12.	Is there a system of MAC address filtering?					
13.	Does the access point permit wireless client isolation?					
14.	Are wireless transmitters switched off when not in use in non-24/7 locations?					
15.	Are all unused administration interfaces disabled?					
16.	Is ability to manage the access points from the Internet side of the router restricted to specific addresses?					
17.	Have the default configurations of access points been changed?					

			Response			
	Query	Used	Y	N	Value	Score
18.	Are access points managed from a separate network?					
19.	Is the wireless interface equipped with wireless IDS/IPS?					
20.	Are session timeouts implemented?					
Applicable Score				**Total Score**		

Prepared by: Reviewed by:

Date: Place:

CHAPTER THIRTEEN

Session Quiz

I N THIS CHAPTER WE have provided a session quiz for Chapters 1 through 9. The reader is required to select the best response from the options provided. Correct responses to the quiz are available on the companion website (www.wiley.com/go/understandingisauditing).

CHAPTER 1: OVERVIEW OF SYSTEMS AUDIT

1. Directive controls:
   a. Are management actions, procedures, directives, or guidelines that cause or encourage a desirable event to occur.
   b. Are those included in an application designed per the user requirements.
   c. Detect errors, omissions, and irregularities, and identify aspects of system quality, controls, and security features.
   d. Facilitate backup, restoration, recovery, and restart of an application system after any interruption in information processing.

2. Corrective controls:
   a. Are management actions, procedures, directives, or guidelines that cause or encourage a desirable event to occur.
   b. Detect errors, omissions, and irregularities, and identify aspects of system quality, controls, and security features that need management's attention.
   c. Provide information, procedures, and instructions for correcting the errors, omissions, and irregularities that have been detected.
   d. Facilitate backup, restoration, recovery, and restart of an application system after any interruption in information processing.

3. General controls are classified into five control categories. Which of the following is *not* a general control category?
   a. Organization and operational control.
   b. System development and documentation control.
   c. Access control.
   d. Know-your-customer norms.

4. Processing controls, which are usually included in application programs, are designed to prevent or detect errors. Processing controls do not include:
   a. Failure to process all input transactions, or erroneous processing.
   b. More than one processing and updating of the wrong file or files.
   c. Unauthorized personnel receiving the transaction outputs.
   d. Loss or distortion of data during processing.

5. In a computerized system, all transactions may not have a supporting initiation document. Which of the comments is true?
   a. All transactions need to be supported by a written input document.
   b. Self-generated transactions may not have a supporting initiation document.
   c. Where supporting documents are not present, such transactions should be done using paper and pen.
   d. The chances of having no initiation documents are few and these can be manually recorded.

6. The purpose of input controls is to ensure:
   a. Authorization of access to data files.
   b. Authorization of access to program files.
   c. Completeness, accuracy, and validity of updating.
   d. Completeness, accuracy, and validity of input.

7. The three basic tenets of information systems audit are:
   a. Modularity, upgradeability, and understandability.
   b. Simplicity, integrity, and user-friendliness.
   c. Confidentiality, integrity, and availability.
   d. Confidentiality, secrecy, and fidelity.

8. Application controls include controls over:
   a. Input, output, and processing controls.
   b. File management, database management, and access management.
   c. Error detection, error identification, and error rectification.
   d. Security management, password controls, and user ID controls.

9. General controls exclude:
   a. Hardware controls.
   b. System software controls.
   c. Access controls.
   d. Processing controls.
10. Access controls exclude:
    a. Completeness control.
    b. Privilege management.
    c. User password management.
    d. Network access control.
11. Operational controls exclude:
    a. Completeness control.
    b. Complete edit checks.
    c. Sensitive system isolation.
    d. Exception reports.
12. Systems development and documentation controls do not include:
    a. Review, testing, and approval of new systems.
    b. Control over program changes.
    c. Implementation of new systems.
    d. Documentation procedures.
13. Which statement best describes the difference between a detective control and a corrective control?
    a. One control stops errors from occurring, and the other rectifies them.
    b. One control is used to prevent errors, and the other is used to warn of danger.
    c. One is used as a reasonableness check, and the other is used to make management aware of the error that occurred.
    d. One control is used to identify that an error has occurred, and the other fixes the problem before a loss occurs.
14. Access controls are designed to ensure:
    a. That only the customer can access his account.
    b. Smooth access of data from the database by the application program.
    c. That only the authorized person can access data.
    d. That the broadband connects only to your service provider.
15. Input controls do not include controls over:
    a. Transaction entry.
    b. File maintenance transactions.
    c. Inquiry transactions.
    d. Authorization to input.
16. Preventive controls are used primarily to:
    a. Stop a process and notify the operations that an error has occurred.
    b. Keep an error situation from occurring by recognizing the condition and denying its occurrence.
    c. Monitor and check error conditions that cannot be easily managed in other ways.

    d. Address complex ranges of error conditions managed by unique prevention condition statements.

17. _____ is a detective control in a computer operations area.
    a. Policy.
    b. Log.
    c. Procedure.
    d. Standard.

18. Information availability controls does not include:
    a. Backup and recovery.
    b. Storage location.
    c. Physical and logical security.
    d. Alternative computer equipment and facilities.

19. Which one of the following controls is detective rather than preventive in nature?
    a. Authorization.
    b. Batch control total.
    c. Preprinted forms.
    d. Passwords.

20. The update program for bank account balances calculates check digits for account numbers. This is an example of:
    a. An input control.
    b. A file management control.
    c. An access control.
    d. An output control.

CHAPTER 2: HARDWARE SECURITY ISSUES

1. Equipment reliability is measured in terms of:
    a. Mean time between failures (MTBF) and system redundancy.
    b. Backup equipment availability.
    c. Efficiency of annual maintenance contracts.
    d. System redundancy and mirror server availability.

2. Which of the following statements is not true?
    a. Peripheral devices should be placed into the system on a need-to-use basis.
    b. Impact printers should be placed in the server room.
    c. Separate modems should not be available on any machine connected with the banking network.
    d. Use of flash drives and floppy drives should not be permitted unless specifically authorized.

3. Which of the following areas is not considered while making a requirements analysis for hardware?
    a. Criticality.
    b. Reliability.

    c. Confidentiality.

    d. Availability.

4. Which of the following factors is not a goal of the client-server application optimization?

    a. The location of the processing.

    b. The amount of network traffic.

    c. The location and amount of data storage.

    d. The backup measures provided.

5. The business, technical, or financial criteria that will cause an organization to replace a piece of IT equipment are comprehensively termed:

    a. Equipment replacement decision.

    b. Equipment life-cycle planning.

    c. Annual maintenance contract.

    d. Business and technical mapping.

6. Communication networks are vulnerable to wiretapping, and the most effective control to secure a network is:

    a. Key management.

    b. Encryption.

    c. Network optimization.

    d. Sniffing.

7. Hardware acquisition planning does not include:

    a. The level of computer awareness of users.

    b. The identification of a demand or requirement.

    c. A specification formulation to match the requirement.

    d. An overview of the resources and the budget.

8. Preventive maintenance includes activities:

    a. To keep hardware in good operating condition.

    b. To determine why equipment is malfunctioning and then repair it.

    c. To prevent unauthorized users from accessing the systems.

    d. To ensure that the system's integrity is maintained.

9. Good practices on management of removable media do not include:

    a. "All media should be stored in a safe and secure environment."

    b. "Disposal of sensitive items should be logged."

    c. "Issue of media should be on a selective basis."

    d. "Backups should be carried to a secure off-site place."

10. What should be the preferred precautionary measure before disposal of a hard disk?

    a. Dispose of the disk by giving it to reliable people.

    b. Format the hard disk.

    c. Delete all files on the hard disk.

    d. Demagnetize the hard disk.

11. The goal of the client-server application is to optimize which four factors?

    a. The location of the processing, the amount of network traffic, the location of data storage, and the amount of data storage.

    b. The speed of delivery, the integrity of the system, and maintenance of confidentiality and privacy.

    c. Selection of the correct clients, the correct network, the location of data storage, and the integrity of the data.

    d. Availability of the system, meantime between failures, longer working hours, and database administration.

12. Uninterruptible power supplies are used in computer centers to reduce the likelihood of:

    a. Failing to control concurrent access to data.

    b. Losing data stored in the main memory.

    c. Dropping bits in data transmission.

    d. Crashing disk-drive read-write heads.

13. Which of the following do not form a part of the hardware acquisition plan?

    a. Planning.

    b. Implementation.

    c. Physical layout and design of the hardware.

    d. Operation and maintenance.

14. Network access controls include:

    a. Appropriate interfaces between the organization's network and networks owned by other organizations or public networks.

    b. Appropriate network structure.

    c. Planned layout and documentation thereof.

    d. Encryption methodology.

15. Options to achieve continuity of power supplies does not include:

    a. Multiple feeds to avoid single-point failure in the power supply.

    b. Uninterruptible power supply (UPS).

    c. Backup generator.

    d. Contract with the power company.

16. Equipment life-cycle planning (ELP) is the management practice of defining:

    a. The life for charge of depreciation.

    b. The business, technical, or financial criteria that will require an organization to replace a piece of IT equipment.

    c. The period the system can be operational before repairing requirements emerge.

    d. The period considered to compute net present value (NPV).

CHAPTER 3: SOFTWARE SECURITY ISSUES

1. While going online, the user is identified. This process is called:

    a. Initiation.

    b. Verification.

    c. Authorization.

    d. Authentication.

2. Software licenses are of different kinds. Which of the following is not a type of licence?
   a. Open general license.
   b. Per-server license.
   c. Open share license.
   d. Number of users license.
3. Authentication is a process by which:
   a. The system verifies that the user is entitled to enter the transaction requested.
   b. The system verifies the identity of the user.
   c. The system authorizes the user to perform the required functions.
   d. The user indicates to the system that the transaction was processed correctly.
4. Which of the following is not assumed by the authentication process?
   a. The validity of the message being sent.
   b. The identity of the workstations that sent the message.
   c. The integrity of the message that is being transmitted.
   d. The identity of the message originator.
5. To ensure the integrity of system software one must:
   a. Apply the most stringent access controls to system software and their handling facilities.
   b. Issue a notification on the control steps involved.
   c. Conduct a periodic information systems audit and penetration testing.
   d. Establish an authentication procedure.
6. Which of the following is not a control for implementing information access restrictions?
   a. Provision for menus to control access to application system functions.
   b. Appropriate editing of user documentation to restrict users' knowledge of information or application systems functions only to the area they are authorized to access.
   c. Control of the access rights of the users, for example, read, write, delete, and execute.
   d. Maintenance of users' log.
7. Access to sensitive information services should ideally be attainable via:
   a. A limited log-on process.
   b. A secured log-on process.
   c. A simple log-on process.
   d. A tiered log-on process.
8. Which of the following is not a component of operating systems?
   a. Process management.
   b. Memory management.
   c. Application management.
   d. System file management.
9. Which of the following is not an operating system access control feature?
   a. Restriction on connection time of users.
   b. Recording successful and failed system accesses.

    c. Recognizing and verifying the identity of users, the terminal, and the location
    d. Performing a mathematical accuracy check.

10. Programmed edit checks do not include which of the following:
    a. Dependency checks.
    b. Privilege checks.
    c. Format checks.
    d. Audit trails.

11. Which one of these types of software is involved in transmission of data from one point to another?
    a. Memory resident software.
    b. Utility software.
    c. Communication software.
    d. Application software.

CHAPTER 4: INFORMATION SYSTEMS AUDIT REQUIREMENTS

1. Methods to maintain an audit trail in a computerized environment include all the following except:
    a. Transaction logs.
    b. Unique transaction identifiers.
    c. Data encryption.
    d. Log of automatic transactions.

2. If the system does not work promptly and service is denied to the authorized user, there is a loss of:
    a. Confidentiality.
    b. Availability.
    c. Integrity.
    d. System integrity.

3. Which of the following is not an objective of an IS audit?
    a. Asset safeguarding.
    b. Financial accuracy.
    c. System effectiveness.
    d. System security.

4. Which of the following is not an IS audit procedure?
    a. Compliance testing.
    b. Analytical review.
    c. Substantive testing.
    d. Audit planning.

5. An audit trail means:
    a. A tracing of a transaction from initiation to the final output, in which the flow of events is reconstructed.

    b. The audit tools and techniques to be applied during an audit.

    c. The documents the auditor submits to the management that ensure that he or she has diligently conducted the audit.

    d. Audit reports over the years that show the opinions expressed by the auditor and the steps taken to rectify them in the following years.

6. Information systems audit objectives do not include:

    a. Adequacy and effectiveness of internal controls.

    b. Assurance that all financial transactions are accurate.

    c. An efficient and effective allocation of resources.

    d. Providing assurance that computer-related assets are safeguarded.

7. The audit trail may not include:

    a. User identification.

    b. Functions, resources, and information that have been used or changed.

    c. A backup copy of the data.

    d. A date and time stamp.

8. The concept of data integrity implies that:

    a. Access has not been given to those who do not have a need to know.

    b. Data can be accessed by processes when necessary to support the business function.

    c. Data have not been altered or modified outside of the expected and approved processing steps.

    d. Data have not been made available to processes for which the data classification has not been accredited.

9. Information system control objectives do not include:

    a. System asset safeguarding.

    b. System upgrading.

    c. System reliability.

    d. System efficiency and effectiveness.

10. System audit objectives exclude:

    a. Providing reasonable assurance that all errors, omissions, and irregularities are prevented.

    b. Ensuring compliance to policies, procedures, and standards.

    c. Ensuring the adequacy and effectiveness of internal controls.

    d. Ensuring that the MIS is optimally generated.

11. Effective information systems include:

    a. Safeguarding of information assets, using them efficiently, and having internal controls and sound management decisions.

    b. Having the best quality of hardware and software so that the system downtime is reduced.

    c. Ensuring proper attendance of the personnel of the computer department so that the support service to the information system does not fail.

    d. Having an information systems audit done regularly.

12. Which of the following are important areas of an IS audit: (i) asset safeguarding, (ii) financial integrity, (iii) system effectiveness, (iv) system efficiency?
    a. i, iii, iv.
    b. ii, iii, iv.
    c. iii, iv.
    d. i, ii, iv.
13. Effects of computers on auditing include:
    a. Extended printouts that are unmanageable.
    b. No signed documents to verify.
    c. Computerized audit trails.
    d. No persons with specific authority.

CHAPTER 5: CONDUCTING AN INFORMATION SYSTEMS AUDIT

1. The electrician has laid the power line and the communications cable together in the same conduit. He then split the conduit into two, with the power line going upward and the communications cable going downward to the server. What would be your reaction?
    a. Both wires have been laid in the same conduit. Therefore a cost-effective job was done.
    b. The power line and the communications lines are complementary and must be placed in the same conduit.
    c. The communications lines would be disturbed by magnetic interference.
    d. The layout structure enables quicker maintenance as only one conduit needs to be repaired or replaced.
2. Authentication provides identity. Which of the following statements is incorrect?
    a. The integrity of the message sent is tested.
    b. The message being transmitted is from the user transmitting the same.
    c. The user ID and passwords are authenticity controls.
    d. It verifies the identity of the individual accessing the system.
3. Which of the following is an example of a bad password management system?
    a. Enforcing use of individual passwords to maintain accountability
    b. Allowing users to select and change their own passwords, where appropriate, and including a confirmation procedure to control input errors
    c. Enforcing a choice of quality passwords
    d. Written delegation of passwords by users
4. Which of the following may not be included in the permanent file of the information systems auditor?
    a. Information system policies of the organization
    b. Historical background of the information systems in the organization
    c. The audit program
    d. Extracts of copies of important legal documents relevant to the audit

5. Which of the following needs to be considered while designing an audit program?
   a. Resource planning and consistency of tests.
   b. Audit trails and sensitivity of data.
   c. Periodicity of checking backups.
   d. Entropy of complex system.
6. Preliminary risk assessment does not include:
   a. Threats identification.
   b. Contingency plan.
   c. Controls assessment.
   d. Threats likelihood assessment.
7. Audit opinions fall in various categories. Which of the following is not a kind of audit opinion?
   a. Disclaimer opinion.
   b. Qualified opinion.
   c. Adverse opinion.
   d. Compensating opinion.
8. While reviewing background information, policies, and previous audit reports, the IS auditor may not include which one of the following in his or her review?
   a. Business strategy.
   b. Long-term and short-term IT strategy.
   c. IS security policy.
   d. Review of the financial statements.
9. What is the most important aspect of a change control system?
   a. All changes are documented and approved.
   b. Changes are managed through automated tools, preventing access by people.
   c. Copies of production are maintained in case the change fails.
   d. Changes are made offline on the pre-existing infrastructure.
10. Which of the following is not a password control?
    a. Requiring that a password have a minimum length and complexity.
    b. Encrypting passwords when in transit and when stored.
    c. Limiting the reuse of passwords through the use of a history file.
    d. Limiting the number of unique sessions an account can initiate.
11. The IS auditor primarily uses the information provided by a detailed understanding of the information systems controls and final risk assessment to determine the nature, timing, and extent of the:
    a. Substantive tests.
    b. Attribute tests.
    c. Sampling tests.
    d. Compliance tests.
12. The auditor tours the server location during the audit. Which of the following is not an objective of this audit process?
    a. To determine whether access to the console is controlled.

b. To determine whether adequate fire detection and suppressant equipment is available.

c. To determine whether the server and accessories have been purchased from the original equipment supplier.

d. To determine whether the server is connected to an uninterruptible power supply.

13. Automated monitoring and supervision does not include:
   a. Data editing.
   b. Validation routines.
   c. Voucher stamping on entry.
   d. Checks and balancing by the program itself.

14. Which of the following is the best control against unauthorized sign-on attempts?
   a. To suspend the user ID after a specified number of repeated unsuccessful log-on attempts.
   b. To ensure that every person entering the system is an employee and wears the employee badge that identifies them.
   c. To allow change in password setting only after a written authorization.
   d. To adhere to organizational password policies.

15. Of the following reports generated at the day-end, which one is most useful for the purpose of an IS audit?
   a. Users attendance record.
   b. System usage and volume of data processed.
   c. Exception transactions report.
   d. Number of batch transactions processed for the day.

16. Detailed testing of transactions is called:
   a. Compliance testing.
   b. Substantive testing.
   c. Password testing.
   d. Disaster testing.

17. Audit tools may comprise the following items except:
   a. Audit checklists.
   b. Observations.
   c. Audit policy.
   d. Application system and program flowcharts.

18. Audit documents are maintained as:
   a. Permanent file and current file.
   b. Permanent file, current file, and working file.
   c. Permanent file and points for management attention.
   d. Permanent file, current file, and dispute items.

19. General control reviews include:
   a. Application testing.
   b. Logical and physical access control review.
   c. Antivirus testing.
   d. Legal compliance review.

20. Application control reviews include:
    a. Software licensing review.
    b. Business strategy review.
    c. Short-term IT plans review.
    d. General parameter settings review.

CHAPTER 6: RISK-BASED SYSTEMS AUDIT

1. Which of the following is not a risk assessment procedure?
    a. Identification of inherent business risks in various systems and activities undertaken by the bank.
    b. Evaluation of the effectiveness of the control systems for monitoring the inherent risks of the business activities ("control risk").
    c. Conducting a compliance audit for major processes.
    d. Drawing up a risk-matrix for taking into account both the factors, that is, inherent business risks and control risks.
2. Inherent business risks indicate:
    a. The intrinsic risk in a particular area/activity of the auditee and could be grouped into low, medium, and high categories.
    b. Inadequate control systems, deficiencies/gaps, and/or likely failures in the existing control processes.
    c. The measurable and nonmeasurable aspects of risks.
    d. The changes in the industry and technological advances.
3. Audit risk (AR) is the product of:
    a. Combined risk assessment (CRA) and detection risk (DR).
    b. Control risk and business risk.
    c. Detection risk and control risk.
    d. Combined risk assessment and inherent risk.
4. Which one of the following statements is true?
    a. The audit risk remains constant irrespective of the sample size.
    b. The higher the sample size, the greater the audit risk.
    c. The lower the sample size, the lower the audit risk.
    d. The lower the sample size, the greater the audit risk.
5. An auditor anticipates assessing control risk at a low level in a computerized environment. Under these circumstances, on which one of the following procedures would the auditor initially focus?
    a. Programmed control procedures.
    b. Application control procedures.
    c. Output control procedures.
    d. General control procedures.
6. What is risk?
    a. A risk is the exposure that an organization would face if a disaster occurred.
    b. A risk is the likelihood of an organization facing a loss due to environmental attacks.

c. A risk is the likelihood that the organization would face a vulnerability being exploited or a threat becoming harmful.

d. All uncertain factors inherent in business operations comprise risk.

7. What is a risk-based IS audit?

a. A risk-based audit entails an audit in an environment where a disaster has occurred.

b. A risk-based audit requires the auditor to undergo an audit in a politically unstable environment.

c. A risk-based audit is performed at the site where the auditee is required to face a large number of important customers.

d. A risk-based IS audit entails an allocation of audit resources and monitoring according to a risk profile to minimize the impact of a crisis situation.

8. The risk assessment process would lead to:

a. Restricting the use of information assets to those authorized.

b. Creating a risk matrix.

c. Increasing the volume of processes to be audited.

d. Ensuring the involvement of senior management in IT governance.

9. Risk management consists of risk assessment and risk mitigation. Which of the following is not an element of risk mitigation?

a. Measure risk.

b. Select appropriate safeguards.

c. Implement and test safeguards.

d. Accept residual risk.

10. Which of the following best describes a "threat"?

a. A political problem in the area that causes the bank to be nonoperational.

b. Quality and ability of a potentially compromising action, event, or condition to inflict harm on the organization.

c. High rate of robbery in the area where the bank is situated.

d. Action of persons that inflict harm to the organization, its property, and its assets.

11. A risk is:

a. A circumstance or event with potential to cause harm to an information system.

b. A weakness in the system safeguards that exposes the system to threats.

c. The extent of loss the organization has to face.

d. The likelihood that the organization would face a vulnerability being exploited or a threat becoming harmful.

CHAPTER 7: BUSINESS CONTINUITY AND DISASTER RECOVERY PLAN

1. Disaster recovery plans and insurance are:

a. Controls of first resort.

b. Unreliable controls.

    c. Preventive controls.

    d. Controls of last resort.

2. A comprehensive disaster recovery plan comprises four parts:

    a. Emergency plan, backup plan, recovery plan, and test plan.

    b. Emergency plan, backup plan, operational plan, and resumption plan.

    c. Audit plan, backup plan, operational plan, and resumption plan.

    d. Audit plan, backup plan, operational plan, and test plan.

3. Vulnerability is:

    a. The areas in the system from where the hackers enter.

    b. The weakness in the system safeguards that exposes the system to threats.

    c. The cohesive strength of the threat and risks.

    d. The exposure of the system when the threat attacks.

4. System reliability control includes:

    a. Mean time to report (MTTR).

    b. Redundant computer hardware.

    c. Backup computer facilities.

    d. Mean time between failures (MTBF).

5. An organization's disaster recovery plan should address early recovery of:

    a. All information system processes.

    b. All financial processing applications.

    c. Only those applications designated by the IS manager.

    d. Processing capabilities in priority order.

6. A contingency plan does not include:

    a. Business impact analysis.

    b. Risk management plan.

    c. Incident response plan.

    d. Disaster recovery plan.

7. An IS auditor reviewing backup procedures for software needs to determine that:

    a. Object code libraries are backed up.

    b. Source code libraries are backed up.

    c. Both object and source code libraries are backed up.

    d. Program patches are maintained at the originating site.

8. The most costly disaster recovery alternative is:

    a. Mutual backup site agreement.

    b. A hot site.

    c. A cold site.

    d. Off-site archiving of data.

9. Which of the following is an inherent limitation of a disaster recovery planning exercise?

    a. Inability to possibly include all types of disasters.

    b. Assembling disaster management and recovery teams.

    c. Developing early warning monitors that will trigger alerts and responses.

    d. Conducting periodic drills.

10. A problem register should contain which of the following data?
   a. Wrong inputs made, name of person who made the wrong input, name of person who authorized the same, loss to the auditee due to the wrong transaction input.
   b. Description of the problem, name of person who created the problem, disciplinary action taken against the person.
   c. Problems encountered in the IT system, reason for the same, the date and time, the resolution, and the duration of the downtime.
   d. Problems encountered, the name of the person who reported the same, and the loss of man-days due to the same.

CHAPTER 8: AUDITING IN THE E-COMMERCE ENVIRONMENT

1. The objectives of a systems audit of e-commerce do not include:
   a. To gain an understanding of the auditee's e-commerce product line, transaction flow, and settlement processes.
   b. To ensure that adequate internal controls are in place to minimize errors, discourage fraud, and provide an adequate audit trail.
   c. To determine whether management has instituted controls that are appropriate to the type and level of risks arising from e-commerce.
   d. To ensure that the e-commerce system uses only secured communication lines provided by third-party vendors.
2. E-commerce administration activities do not include:
   a. Employee access to e-commerce forms.
   b. Generation and review of exception report.
   c. E-commerce security program.
   d. IT long-range plans.
3. The objectives of a systems audit in e-commerce do not include:
   a. Determining whether the board of directors has adopted effective policies for e-commerce and that these policies and procedures are being followed.
   b. Comments on the adequacy of legal measures available against a cybercriminal.
   c. Determining whether contingency and disaster plans are adequate.
   d. Determining whether the auditee complies with applicable regulations.
4. Electronic money does not include:
   a. Prepaid cards.
   b. Funds transfers using Internet banking.
   c. Funds transfers between two devices.
   d. Standing instructions to a bank.
5. A preliminary overview of an audit of e-commerce applications does not include:
   a. A review of flowchart of e-commerce processes.
   b. A review of the promotion of the portal through direct mailers.
   c. A review of dependence on external vendors.
   d. A review of the list of duties of employees and outside vendors.

6. Which of the following is not a purpose of document review during an e-commerce audit?
   a. Documentation for network help desk design.
   b. Documentation for security of e-commerce activities.
   c. Process documentation for monitoring of e-commerce activities.
   d. Policies and practices of e-commerce.

7. Which of the following is not a component of implementation of e-commerce systems?
   a. Approval from top management.
   b. Training of related personnel.
   c. Verification of accuracy and content of various interfaces.
   d. Service pricing mechanism.

8. Which of the following is not covered by legal consideration for an e-commerce application?
   a. Disclosure of working hours.
   b. Verification of new customers.
   c. Name of the chief executive officer.
   d. Notice stating terms of use.

9. Which of the following is not a component of Internet security administration?
   a. Review of physical and logical access security.
   b. Review of perimeter security of the premises.
   c. Review of connectivity between internal operating system and external gateway.
   d. Availability of identity verification system using multiple platforms.

10. Documentation of the auditee to be collected prior to audit of the e-commerce application does not include:
    a. Summary of strategic plan relating to e-commerce.
    b. Website program of the e-commerce application.
    c. External audit reports.
    d. Details of the nature of e-commerce activities conducted.

CHAPTER 9: SECURITY TESTING

1. Which of the following is not an objective of IS security?
   a. Safeguarding information systems from unauthorized access.
   b. Safeguarding information systems from manipulation and misuse.
   c. Safeguarding information systems from usage.
   d. Ensuring that an information system is available to the right person whenever required, for business purposes.

2. Which of the following logical access exposures involves changing of data before or as it is entered into the computer?
   a. Data diddling.
   b. Trojan horse.
   c. Social engineering.
   d. Virus attack.

3. Which of the following is the most effective control against wiretapping in communication networks?
    a. Use of identifiers.
    b. Use of passwords.
    c. Use of logical access methods.
    d. Use of encryption methods.
4. A digital signature is:
    a. A form of authentication.
    b. An actual signature stored on the computer.
    c. A checksum.
    d. A scanned image of a signature.
5. Identify the most objective and relevant evidence in a computer environment involving fraud from the following:
    a. Physical examination of hard disk.
    b. Physical observation of processes.
    c. Inquiries with people.
    d. Computer logs.
6. Information security is best characterized by:
    a. Confidentiality.
    b. Optimal resource utilization.
    c. Reporting procedures.
    d. Compliance.
7. Computer frauds increase when:
    a. Employees are not trained.
    b. Documentation is not available.
    c. Audit trails are not available.
    d. Employee performance appraisals are not done.
8. Which of the following need not be included in the encryption policy?
    a. The functionary responsible for control of encryption processes.
    b. How encryption is used.
    c. Data classification techniques used.
    d. None of the above.
9. Which of the following is achieved by the nonrepudiation feature?
    a. Preventing any communication that hurts the reputation of the originator.
    b. Preventing the ability of the receiver to deny receipt of an e-mail.
    c. Preventing an authorized recipient from reading the content of the document.
    d. Preventing the sender from denying the origin of the e-mail sent.
10. Which of the following is not a component of the Daubert Reliability Test?
    a. Appropriateness of choice of technique used.
    b. Availability of peer review supporting the technique used.
    c. Availability of vendor support for the tool used.
    d. Ability to replicate the test conducted.

About the Authors

Veena Hingarh is a professor and joint director of South Asian Management Technologies Foundation, an institution focused on research and training in the area of risk management, with a special focus on finance and information technology. She is a chartered accountant and a fellow member of the Institute of Chartered Accountants of India and earned a master's degree in science from the University of Calcutta. Hingarh is a member of the Institute of Company Secretaries of India and is an information systems auditor, certified by ISACA. Her primary area of research is financial information systems and their integration with International Financial Reporting Standards.

In addition, Hingarh has been involved with strategic consulting and training in her area of specialization and has served as a guest lecturer in various courses and professional workshops organized by the Institute of Chartered Accountants of India, George Washington University (with the Institute for International Research of Dubai), the Institute of Company Secretaries of India, and other institutions.

Arif Ahmed is a professor and director of South Asian Management Technologies Foundation. He is a chartered accountant and a fellow member of the Institute of Chartered Accountants of India and earned a master's degree in business administration from the University of Calcutta. Ahmed is a lead auditor in information security management systems, certified by the British Standards Institution. His primary area of research is risk management.

Ahmed has more than two decades of postqualification experience in the area of his specialization. He has provided strategic consulting services and knowledge workshops to his clients and has served as a guest lecturer in various courses and professional workshops organized by the Institute of Chartered Accountants of India, XLRI (Jamshedpur, India), George Washington University (with the Institute for International Research, Dubai), and other institutions. He has been an advisor in the areas of IT and finance to organizations of national importance and state-owned banks.

Both Hingarh and Ahmed have provided strategic consulting and training services to various organizations across many industries, including banking and financial services, oil and gas, electronic and print media, real estate, engineering, metals and minerals, and a host of others. They have also served as consultants on projects of the World Bank. They are coauthors of *IFRS Convergence: A Global Perspective*, and contributors to the book *Wiley International Trends in Financial Reporting under IFRS: Including Comparisons with U.S. GAAP, Chinese GAAP, and Indian GAAP*, both published by John Wiley & Sons.

About the Website

Please visit this book's companion website at www.wiley.com/go/understandingisauditing (password: ahmed123).

The website includes the following documents to supplement the information in the book:

- Printable and editable forms that are useful for setting up a business continuity and disaster recovery plan.
- ISecGrade checklists that can be printed and used to conduct information systems audits.
- Answers to the session quiz in chapter 13.

Index

Printed and bound by CPI Group (UK) Ltd, Croydon, CR0 4YY